I0092039

Race, Identity, and Privilege from the US to the Congo

Critical Africana Studies: African, African American, and Caribbean Interdisciplinary and Intersectional Studies

Series Editor: Christel N. Temple, University of Pittsburgh

Series Editorial Board: Martell Teasley, Kimberly Nichele Brown, Jerome Schiele, Marquita M. Gammage, and Bayyinah S. Jeffries

The Critical Africana Studies book series features scholarship within the emerging field of Africana studies, which encompasses such disciplines as African studies, African diasporan studies, African American studies, Afro-American studies, Afro-Asian studies, Afro-European studies, Afro-Islamic studies, Afro-Jewish studies, Afro-Latino studies, Afro-Native American studies, Caribbean studies, Pan-African studies, Black British studies and, of course, Black studies. The Critical Africana Studies book series directly responds to the heightened demand for monographs and edited volumes that innovatively explore Africa and its diaspora employing cutting-edge critical, interdisciplinary, and intersectional theory and methods.

Recent Titles in the Series

Race, Identity, and Privilege from the US to the Congo, By Brenda F. Berrian
Ama Mazama: The Ogunic Presence in Africology, By Molefi Kete Asante
The Afrocentric Pan Africanist Vision: Afrocentric Essays, By Molefi Kete Asante
Branches of Asanteism, By Abdul Karim Bangura
Transcendence and the Africana Literary Enterprise, Edited by Christel N. Temple and foreword by Molefi Kete Asante
Strategies for Success among African-Americans and Afro-Caribbeans: Overachieve, Be Cheerful, or Confront, By Chrystal Y. Grey and Thomas Janoski
Rastafari Reasoning and the RastaWoman: Gender Constructions in the Shaping of Rastafari Livity, By Jeanne Christensen
Conceptual Aphasia in Black: Displacing Racial Formation, Edited by P. Khalil Saucier and Tryon P. Woods
The Negritude Movement: W.E.B. Du Bois, Leon Damas, Aime Cesaire, Leopold Senghor, Frantz Fanon, and the Evolution of an Insurgent Idea, By Reiland Rabaka

Race, Identity, and Privilege from the US to the Congo

Brenda F. Berrian

LEXINGTON BOOKS
Lanham • Boulder • New York • London

Published by Lexington Books
An imprint of The Rowman & Littlefield Publishing Group, Inc.
4501 Forbes Boulevard, Suite 200, Lanham, Maryland 20706
www.rowman.com

6 Tinworth Street, London SE11 5AL, United Kingdom

Copyright © 2021 The Rowman & Littlefield Publishing Group, Inc.

All rights reserved. No part of this book may be reproduced in any form or by any electronic or mechanical means, including information storage and retrieval systems, without written permission from the publisher, except by a reviewer who may quote passages in a review.

British Library Cataloguing in Publication Information Available

Library of Congress Cataloging-in-Publication Data

Names: Berrian, Brenda F., author.
Title: Race, identity, and privilege from the US to the Congo / Brenda F. Berrian.
Description: Lanham : Lexington Books, [2021] | Series: Critical Africana studies: African, African American, and Caribbean interdisciplinary and intersectional studies | Includes bibliographical references and index.
Identifiers: LCCN 2020050355 (print) | LCCN 2020050356 (ebook) | ISBN 9781793642318 (cloth) | ISBN 9781793642332 (pbk) ISBN 9781793642325 (epub)
Subjects: LCSH: Berrian, Brenda F. | African American women—Biography. | African American women college teachers—Biography. | African Americans—Social conditions. | Ethnicity. | Racism. | Feminism.
Classification: LCC E185.97.B339 A3 2021 (print) | LCC E185.97.B339 (ebook) | DDC 305.48/896073—dc23
LC record available at https://lccn.loc.gov/2020050355
LC ebook record available at https://lccn.loc.gov/2020050356

*In honor of my parents, Albert and Mary,
and my siblings, Antoinette ("Toni"), Albert and Derek
—with gratefulness and love.*

Contents

Acknowledgments

I could not have written this book without Liberty "Libby" Ferda and Ervin "Erv" Dyer. For more than two years, we, the team, would meet and talk for hours about certain issues of Black identity and family, and my memories highlighted those themes. After I shared my notes and drafts of writing that I wanted in the chapters, they helped me to draw out the narrative details and the emotional core of the memories, and shaped them into connected stories.

I am forever grateful to my parents, Albert and Mary Berrian, and my siblings—Antoinette ("Toni"), Albert, and Derek. Without them, my story could not have been told. Each has taught me important lessons about being a survivor and often repeated the aphorism, "Don't put all of your eggs into one basket." In other words, if Plan A doesn't work, choose Plan B or C.

From the beginning to the end, I have been encouraged by Harriet Batson, Jacqueline Brice-Finch, Robert Carey, Shawna Davis, Fatou Diouf, Shirley Foster, Florence Gilkesson, Laurence and Ingrid Glasco, Aoife Lennon-Ritchie, Patrick and Susan Manning, Narissa Ramdhani, Reinhard Sander, Tanya Saunders, Beverly and Michael Schenz, Debra Townes, Eric Swetts of the African Studies Program, the staff, faculty, and work study students of the Department of Africana Studies at the University of Pittsburgh. I am grateful to editor Courtney Morales, Christel N. Temple, and the other readers of the Critical Africana Series of Lexington Books. Also, by my friends, who are no longer here, Delorese Ambrose, Gayleatha Brown, Editha Chlosta, Jacqueline Mullins, and Jean Closel Vilbon. And, there are so many others too numerous to list. Hence, this project has allowed me, like the Akan concept of Sankofa, to go back to reclaim my past to move forward into the present. The project has also helped me understand why and how I came to be who I am today.

Introduction

"Young lady," my father said to me. "It's time for you to find a part-time job. I've paid for your school fees and your books. You're to earn spending money for your clothes and incidentals." It was 1964, shortly after I had arrived in Hampton, Virginia, to start my sophomore year at Hampton Institute (now Hampton University), where I craved the excitement of living on an historically Black college campus as I had done as a youngster.

"Yes. Daddy," I politely and absentmindedly responded, figuring I had an entire month to land a job. Four days later, Daddy announced, "Since you haven't bothered to look for a job, I found one for you. You're to report to work next Monday morning." Emotions assailed me: surprise, embarrassment, and annoyance. But I, the obedient daughter, reported to work as a student assistant.

As usual, my father, Albert Harry Berrian, Sr., didn't like for his children to dilly-dally. Although he exuded a kind, laid-back demeanor, he was firm with a razor-sharp mind. At age thirty-nine, he lived and breathed the disciplined life of an educator and administrator. It wasn't unusual for him to devote long hours to preparing lectures and grading students' papers. He also spent quality time advising his students. Believing in hard work, he always preached the importance of a sound education. Therefore, his request for me to get a job somewhat surprised me.

Despite his insistence that I get a job, the 1964–1965 academic year was special. It was the first and only block of time I spent with my father without my mother and three siblings. We had arrived in Hampton from Jersey City, New Jersey, while Mother, my sister, and two brothers stayed behind to honor my mother's recent job promotion and to allow my sister to graduate with her high school class. Daddy lived in a guest house at the Holly Tree Inn and I settled into dormitory life. Though campus living offered a rich social

1

milieu, my enthusiasm for dormitory life and cafeteria food quickly waned after being confronted with double standards for men and women. While the female students dealt with curfews and other restrictions, the male students roamed the campus and town as they pleased. In August, when Daddy told me he was moving into a four-bedroom home on campus, I didn't hesitate to join him.

Two months later, in October, I looked forward to celebrating my eighteenth birthday.

"Don't go out to celebrate with your friends," Daddy stated. "We're going to have dinner at a seafood restaurant."

On the evening of my birthday, I ate shrimp and chitchatted about my courses, new friends, and the young man I had just met and was interested in. Daddy patiently listened, only interrupting to ask me a question for clarification. While we waited for dessert to be brought to our table, a serious look flashed suddenly on his face.

Angling his head slightly with his brow creased, he remarked, "Brenda. Although parents have children, they don't necessarily have to care for them and like them. In fact, they can mutually dislike one another."

Alarmed with this turn in our conversation, I bristled and felt the hairs on my back stand up. "Where is he going with this?" I wondered. And I stupidly uttered, "Huh?"

With a smile now on his face, Daddy looked at me and continued, "Your mother and I are proud to have a daughter like you. On this very important day, your first day of womanhood, your mother and I had something special made for you. We also want to tell you how much we love you." He pulled out a small box from the pocket of his suit jacket and handed it to me. I opened the box to see a smooth platinum ring in the shape of a leaf with a small diamond soldered on the tip.

"This diamond comes from the first engagement ring I gave your mother when she was eighteen years old," Daddy explained. "I will be giving her a new diamond ring on her birthday. Four days from now. You, your mother and sister should have expensive jewelry."

Deeply touched, I quickly put the ring on my finger and reached across the table to give my father a big hug. It was apparent my parents had given this gift a lot of thought. A diamond is an eternal promise, a permanent link between me and them. I was taking my first step into adulthood and had to stand on my own two feet.

The behavior my father displayed was typical. Not a very demonstrative man, and not one to say "I love you," he nevertheless called me and my siblings his "little chocolate drops." Or, he would address me and my sister Toni as "sweetie." Yet he spent quality time with each of his four children, having the knack to make us each think we were the "favorite" child. Most of all, whenever the entire family was together at the dinner table, he always inquired how we had spent the school day. By doing this, he demonstrated his disagreement with his own parents' belief that children were to be seen, not heard, at the dining table.

I relate these two tales to offer an insight into my father's character and mine. My father knew life was not easy. He prepared me and my siblings to experience audacity and to rise up to the challenges ahead of us. Hence, *Race, Identity, and Privilege from the US to the Congo* is about how I and my family members negotiated being insiders and outsiders and dealt with stereotypes and perceptions while learning that racism is systemic, pervasive, and poisonous. Driven by episodes in my life and those of my family within political and historical contexts with selective primary sources, I learned that all *Black* people, irrespective of their upbringings, are exposed to the danger—the difference and the oppression of being Black in a world dominated by White values and ideals. Too often for us, the message is "Black equals less valuable." I personally felt the sting of it when a White American professor dismissed my research interests and scholarship about French African and Caribbean *négritude* literature as inferior.

"You're so much like your father that the mold was thrown away," my mother would remind me. Her statement was prophetic, for I followed my father's footsteps to become a college professor who validated the Black experience in my literature courses and publications.

Proud, strong-willed people, my parents, Albert and Mary, raised their four children to walk in two worlds (one Black and one White). They gave us the gifts of positive Black cultural models to buffer us against the negative impact of White dominant values. As a result, the separate spaces of segregation, before integration, created a social kinship that provided models of success and collective empowerment for Black people. Whenever we lived in faculty housing on several Black college campuses, I met Black American writers, professors, artists, musicians, and dancers.

In 1968, as a student at Hampton Institute, my father introduced me to Léon-Gontran Damas, the dynamic French Guyanese poet of the *négritude* literary movement. That fateful meeting in my parents' living room led me to read Damas's poems that spoke directly to me about being proud of who I am. That fateful meeting helped me to decide to write about *négritude* at the Sorbonne in Paris, where I discussed the topic with Maryse Condé, the Guadeloupean writer who won the 2018 New Academy Prize in Literature.

Over the years, I have lived a nomadic life: a childhood in the Northeast and Deep South of the United States and an adulthood in Western Europe and Africa. All my life I've moved across different geographies, racial codes, and identities. Each journey has shaped the fabric of who I am, forming the tapestry of my soul. In *Race, Identity, and Privilege from the US to the Congo*,

I write about these journeys of race, identity, and privilege, noticing how my skin color (depending upon the location) can be either a reward or a danger. My life is about personal encounters and how I have dealt with painful losses such as the deaths of my parents and a beloved Jamaican friend. These losses were followed by healing and reflections on the afterlife.

My Black American identity shifted when I moved to Canada, the Congo, Gabon, and South Africa. Each time the locals perceived me to be "other" than what I am: a privileged Black American woman. In Canada and Gabon, I was seen as an African. The year my family and I spent living in the Congo, my sister Toni and I, then teenagers, puzzled over privilege, hair texture, and the racial codes the Congolese attached to our skin pigmentation. The assumption was we were Haitians, not Americans. Or perhaps we were *métisse* (mixed-race). Then, during my first visit to South Africa in 1993, I encountered something unusual: the residues of apartheid when a Coloured shoe salesman thought I was a Coloured customer who could not afford to purchase an expensive pair of shoes.

My decision to travel to South Africa was sparked initially by an invitation from a remarkable man. Two years prior, in December 1991, Nelson Mandela delivered the distinguished Heinz speech at the University of Pittsburgh for an African National Congress (ANC) fund raiser. After introducing myself and welcoming him to Pittsburgh at a dinner in his honor, he said to me, in his gentle voice, "Come to South Africa." Without missing a beat, I replied, "I'm coming." So I traveled there as a tourist in 1993 and returned three years later as a visiting professor at the University of Fort Hare, where Mandela and other ANC members had studied.

I own a black shawl that can serve as a metaphor for the richness, complexity, and beauty of the Black experience in spite of, and sometimes because of, the "slings and arrows of outrageous fortune."[1] The foundational black cloth represents the commonalities among the different people of the African diaspora. The embroidery symbolizes the intricacies across time and space that distinguishes people of the African diaspora. With their own design, the sequins represent those of us who have the privilege of education and opportunity.

I recognize resistance and renewal in my own life. In his *The Fire Next Time*, James Baldwin has written, "Know whence you came. If you know whence you came, there is really no limit to where you can go."[2] This profound statement has given me the courage to confront sexism and racism directed toward me by male colleagues in American academia. Along the way, I have rejected being stereotyped or limited no matter where I found myself.

A memoir structured mainly in chronological order, *Race, Identity, and Privilege from the US to the Congo* begins and ends with family. I was born to parents whose love and belief in me have sustained me and prompted me to journey around the African diaspora. Each journey has presented me with a challenge. Each journey has taught me something new about myself. Each journey has caused me to look deeply within my thoughts and emotions about being grateful, generous, and more compassionate. Each journey has re-enforced that I be considered beyond the narrow observations of others about me. Finally, my parents' love for music and literature—and mine—permeates these pages as I return the gift of expression by telling my story along with theirs.

NOTES

1. William Shakespeare, *Hamlet Prince of Denmark*, The Pelican Shakespeare, edited by Willard Farnham (New York: Penguin, 1970), 89.
2. James Baldwin, "My Dungeon Shook-Letter to My Nephew on the One Hundredth Anniversary of Emancipation," in *The Fire Next Time* (New York: Dial Press, 1963), 8.

Chapter 1

Expatriates in Léo

I, my parents, and three siblings crossed the Atlantic Ocean in July 1961 to reach Africa, this continent that had thrived, for me, in lore and imagination for years without counting. I, a fourteen-year-old, was so excited that I could barely stay seated in my assigned Sabena airline seat. We landed in La République du Congo (now the Democratic Republic of the Congo) at Ndjili Airport around 2 a.m. to the darkest, deepest night I had ever known. It was like my eyelids were closed as I blinked at the space around us while descending the plane's steps. In the car from the airport, my brother Albert and I waved our hands in front of our faces, but still couldn't see their shapes.

In the daylight, I and my family toured Léopoldville, the capital of the Congo and the tropical paradise our father had described: palm trees with big, loping fronds shading the wide boulevards; cleanly paved roads, tall white buildings, and the general bustle of any city in the United States. But it was naturally more exciting because it was *Africa.* As my sister Toni, Mother, my two brothers and I walked to the open-air market in Léopoldville (Léo, for short), I thought of how the scenery matched the pictures Daddy had shown us back in New Jersey months before. They were pictures he had taken himself when he had flown over to see about his new job.

"See? It is a clean, modern, wonderful city," he had said, passing the photos around so everyone could see them. A row of homes lined the banks of the Congo River and big trees had leaves which looked like they were blowing gently in the breeze. Léo looked like a resort, or a vacation spot in Florida. Daddy showed the pictures to his parents (Grandma and Papa Berrian), too, for they were living with us in our new home in Jersey City, and he knew they needed to be convinced the most.

"You are taking my grandchildren to the jungle," Grandma said, barely looking at the photos. She had said it before and she would say it again; the phrase would nearly become her mantra.

"Times are different, Mother," Daddy said to her. "Don't believe the propaganda you see on TV."

Grandma folded her arms across her chest, then pulled my youngest brother Derek onto her lap. Instinctively, he leaned his head on her shoulder and she began to rock back and forth. He knew just how to play it up. In preparation for going to the Congo, we had all trooped to Dr. Smith for vaccination after vaccination and, upon return, Albert and Derek would run into the house crying, "Oh Grandma, it hurts!" and she would hug them to her, uncharacteristically demonstrative, glancing sidelong at Mother. For her, the boys' cries were further proof that this going-to-Africa plan was a bad idea.

Grandma's reaction reminded me of Toni's friend Carol's sister. Their family had been preparing to move to Nigeria a few years before, and Toni and I relayed to Carol the stories we had heard from a Nigerian student. Although Carol was excited, her sister was not. On the school bus, she wailed like she had lost her puppy.

"I don't want to leave my friends and go to a backward African country!" she cried, loud enough to get the attention of the entire bus. Though Carol's sister was a high schooler, sitting with the high schoolers at the front of the bus, and I was still in junior high, sitting at the back, I marched right up to the front and demanded,

"Don't you want to be a queen and meet a chief?"

The girl just stared back at me.

By the time my own family was headed to the Congo, I knew my argument no longer held water. I was older now, halfway through high school. Secretly, I imagined there must be some sort of magic in a place filled with Black people. I knew the Congo was in the newspaper and on television a lot, for the Congolese were gaining independence from Belgium, and this seemed to make people excited and scared at the same time. People were fighting and people were being killed. Images of Belgians[1] racing to the airport to escape blared from the television. But Daddy said the Congo was fine; we would be safe; and if he said it was fine, I thought, that meant it was. (Also, I knew it would be different for us because we were not White. It would be safe for us because we were Black like the Congolese. We would be in the majority.) Grandma was not so easily placated.

"The African continent is not *backwards*," Daddy would say to Grandma, and here he assumed that calm, teacher voice. He continued, "Yes, there is some violence, but it isn't the norm and what can you expect? To be under colonial rule for so long and then suddenly be granted freedom? And furthermore, to be granted freedom when Belgians remain in every position of power—army officers, government officials, business leaders? It was like when the enslaved Africans were freed and many had to stay right where they were because they didn't have the money or education to support themselves or find better work. White people were still in charge of everything." After listening to his long explanation, Grandma just shook her head.

"The Congolese were not prepared," Daddy said. At the time of independence in June 1960, there were only fourteen or twenty locally educated university graduates[2] in the entire country. Different newspapers claimed different numbers of college grads, but the highest estimate was twenty, and this was among a population of nearly *fourteen million*. Before the Belgians came, the Congolese had their own sophisticated structure and system of living, of course, but much of it had been forcibly wiped away. To be a part of a changing world, the Congolese needed support, and they needed new systems of education[3] and training for leadership, which the Belgian government[4] had deliberately refrained from providing. In 1959, according to King Gordon, "9,000 Congolese were enrolled in high school. Only eight percent (742) were in the upper-classes."[4] People like Daddy could help. Daddy spoke these things to Grandma, but he was speaking really to all of us.

He reminded Grandma of the many Africans he had invited to dinner, from various countries like Senegal and Nigeria, and how Grandma had enjoyed their company and treated them like family. She got the good dishes out. She listened eagerly to the stories of their homelands.

"It's okay for them to visit *us*," Grandma said then, "but you don't need to be going over *there*."

Later, when it became clear she could not dissuade him, Grandma begged that Daddy go and leave the kids at home.

Mother took the reins.

"No. Not an option," she said. The most important thing in any situation was that we stay together. If everything fell apart in the Congo when we were there, which she thought it very well might, the one thing that would stay together would be the family.

Privately, when not with Grandma and Papa, she and Daddy discussed the move. Mother needed convincing, too, and looking at a bunch of photos wasn't going to cut it. She was justified to complain since she and Daddy had just purchased a home after moving, yet again, back to Jersey, but her reservations went far beyond a desire for rootedness.

"Aren't women being raped and Belgians fleeing in fear?" she asked.

"Aren't American missionary families going to Southern Rhodesia for safety?"

"Didn't I read that the U.S. Ambassador's life had been threatened and that a U.S. diplomat was beaten and robbed by Congolese soldiers?"

It was true. The newly freed Congo did not exactly look like a place of peace or of joyous celebration. But, if you looked only at what was going on right now—the Belgians running in fear, the violence and unrest—to form a vision of the Congo and its people, you were missing the bigger picture, and you were blind to history. I thought it would be like observing the U.S. Civil Rights marches and riots and being baffled by why Black Americans seemed so upset.

Daddy explained that though many African nations had been colonized, the Congo was unique in history as the only colony "owned" by a single man. On May 29, 1885, King Léopold II of Belgium declared himself the ruler of his new, privately owned country l'État Indépendant du Congo, the Congo Free State,[5] at the 1884–1885 Berlin Conference. In a calculated attempt to pass off his appropriation of this huge landmass, he promoted his takeover as a humanitarian act to free the Blacks from the slave trade.

Daddy told us that slave trading had been going on since the 1500s, starting with the Portuguese, who would purchase, or even steal, Congolese citizens and sell them into slavery. In chains, the people would be led onto ships heading for plantations in Brazil and later to colonized countries in the Caribbean. But by 1884, the practice of slave trading was becoming increasingly unpopular in Europe. It was, at last, seen for the barbaric human rights violation that it had always been. So King Léopold II spun a story that he wanted to save the people of the Congo from the cruelty of the Arab slave traders, knowing those motivations would be met with approval, which they were. In truth, he felt tiny Belgium was too insignificant to afford him the money and power he believed he deserved, so he stole it from the Congo.

With the Congo as his personal property (almost eighty times larger than Belgium), King Léopold II's company pillaged and profited from the country's astoundingly rich natural and mineral resources: ivory, tropical hardwood, rubber, diamonds, malachite, copper, cobalt, and uranium. (L'Union Minière du Haut–Katanga, the largest mining company, had been the principal supplier of uranium for the atomic bombs dropped on Japan in 1945 by the United States.) Worst of all, he used forced labor from the citizens. So not only was King Léopold II not "saving" the Congolese from the slave trade, he was enslaving them in their own country.[6] If workers didn't meet the daily quota of, for example, rubber, the Belgian supervisors would cut off their right hands and insist they keep working.[7] According to Daddy, this barbarity went on, nearly unchecked by the world, for twenty-three years.

A few brave journalists and missionaries spoke out about the atrocities they witnessed. But, for the most part, King Léopold II muzzled their pleas and covered up his scheme. His total profit from the Congo: roughly 1.1 billion in today's dollars.[8] The Black American journalist Howard W. French noted,

"It is worth asking how (Léopold) escaped remembrance alongside Hitler and Stalin as great criminals of the twentieth century."[9]

When Belgium took over the colony from its king in 1908, not much changed for the Congolese people. Forced-labor remained through an unfair system of taxation. People continued to die. Scholars estimated the Congo's total population loss, due to death by murder, disease, and starvation, during King Léopold II's regime and directly after, was 50 percent, or ten million. With such longstanding oppression permeating every aspect of society, it was no wonder that by the early 1960s there were only a handful of college-educated Congolese.

And now, in the months preceding Daddy's talk with Mother about moving to the Congo, the world had been watching the country carefully. It was the fourteenth African nation to gain independence, the third largest country on the continent in land size. The Congo was gaining freedom from what many agree was the cruelest colonization in history.

The ceremony to transfer power from Belgium to the Congo was held at le Palais de la Nation in Léopoldville, the grand, broad capital where I and my family would soon be living.

At 11 a.m. on Thursday, June 30, 1960, while I slept next to a clock reading 5 a.m. in New Jersey, Joseph Kasavubu, newly elected Congolese president, and Prime Minister Patrice Lumumba, King Baudouin of Belgium, and other dignitaries from around the world gathered to inaugurate freedom for the Congo. The Belgian king began with a two-page speech, describing how his country had bravely stepped in to save the Congolese from the Arab slave trade seventy-five years ago, and how the brilliant plan of his great grand-uncle had brought stability and security to the Congo. Then Patrice Émery Lumumba, the young, bright thirty-five-year-old leader of le Mouvement National Congolais (The Congolese National Movement), a political party endorsing African nationalism instead of division among ethnic loyalties, stepped up to the microphone.

He was the picture of confidence, adorned in a suit, bowtie, his character-istic half-frame dark-rimmed glasses (similar to the kind worn by Malcolm X), neatly trimmed hair parted just to the left of center.

"We have known that the law was never the same for a white as it was for a black," he said. "We have experienced contempt, insults and blows, morning, noon and night, because we were blacks."[10] His words sent silent waves of shock over the crowd and those that listened to recordings around the world. He did not read from typed notes.

Lumumba also noted, "We have seen magnificent houses in the towns for the whites and crumbling straw huts for the blacks."[11] It was almost as if he echoed Langston Hughes's "Cross," a poem published in 1926, lamenting the disparity of race and power within his subject's blood that was both Black and White, symbolized by his White father's "fine big house" and his Black mother's "shack."[12]

In his speech, Lumumba even attacked the way the French language itself had symbolized the Congolese's subjugated position. I learned that Africans were always referred to in the casual "*tu*" (you) form, while the more formal, respectful "*vous*" (you) was reserved for Whites. I'd soon discover how the Belgians used French as a weapon in more ways than one: they frequently and openly called the Congolese *les macaques* (monkeys) in everyday inter- action. It was so commonplace no one even seemed to hear it.

Words denoted power.

Lumumba's words, which articulated the anger felt by many Congolese, horrified the Belgians. Europeans had been quoted in the *New York Times* labeling Lumumba "very dangerous," and now they were afraid their strong- hold on Congolese resources would wane. Lumumba was not submissive and smiling. This would not be a quiet, superficial shift of power after all. Surely, the Belgians were thinking, if this man, who didn't even have a high school education and whose résumé included postal work and beer sales, could pose this much of a threat, how swiftly might their power be completely overthrown?

The days following independence marked what would become known as "the Congo Crisis." Anarchy arose. Congolese looted and destroyed European property. The Congolese in the army, who'd never been allowed a rank higher than sergeant major, mutinied against their Belgian superiors. And then, disunity. Two weeks after independence, the copper-rich Katanga region seceded. Rumor said Belgians were behind it. Three weeks after that, the diamond-rich Southern Kasai Province declared independence. The very groups Lumumba had succeeded in convincing to come together in pan- African nationalism were now tearing away. Everyone was scrambling for power, independence, and resources.

I watched as the scenes of Europeans fleeing to the airport splashed across the television screen. I instinctively understood that the US media loved to show negative depictions of Africa. *Look how much better we're doing than that*, the reports almost seemed to say. Meanwhile, headline stories in the United States described not only civil rights protests, but also growing strife about the US. involvement in Vietnam.

Despite the chaos, or because of it, Daddy insisted on going to the Congo. It all began on a summer day in 1960 while we were eating lunch when the sound of a ringing telephone interrupted us. Immediately, Daddy got up from the table to answer it. After speaking to the person for almost thirty minutes or more, Daddy hung up the phone and looked at us with a grin on his face.

"What's going on?" Mother asked with suspicion.

"Well, Babe," he replied. "I've just been offered a job in the Congo, and I think I'm going to accept it."

With amazement, I interrupted Daddy and Mother by exclaiming, "Wow! We're going to Africa!"

"*What?*" Mother exploded. "Have you lost your *damn* mind?" Only a week ago, Mother had complained about how many times we had moved: all because of Daddy's career.

"Babe, I'm going to do this for you and the kids," Daddy told her. "This will be my way to make more money and to get a promotion." His new job would be as director of the English Language Services (ELS) program, which he would start in January 1961 and then bring us over in the summer. Funded by the U.S. Information Agency, he was to supervise six White American teachers of English as a foreign language and a Black American laboratory technician. Daddy's connections with African students and diplomats, his membership in the American Society of African Culture (AMSAC), and his translation work for Sékou Touré, president of Guinea, had certainly paid off. The new job would pay him substantially more than his current position as a department head at North Carolina Central College, and it might put him in line for a diplomatic post or university deanship when we returned stateside.

"We will all be together," he reminded her. The family was back in Jersey City, New Jersey, and he commuted home from Durham, North Carolina, only every other weekend. Mother, Toni, and I hated it, and he knew it.

"And it's only for two years. Think what it will do for the kids' education—their knowledge of the world, the opportunities they could have in the future," he said. There it was again: the kids' education. He knew and Mother knew it was the ultimate case—one which couldn't be argued. Though he and Mother weren't inclined to demonstrate with Dr. King or sit-in or march in the streets, education was their protest, here and in the Congo. Learning was the ultimate goal for Blacks who had been disempowered. Words were power.

Those first weeks when I strolled my new, temporary neighborhood in Léo, Parc Hembise, I thought about how Daddy's pictures could not describe the way it *felt* here. Only how it looked. Surprisingly, it was cold, so cold. Since my days at the integrated school in Xenia, Ohio, I had lived in Houston, back to Jersey, and spent the previous summer in North Carolina. Houston summers were hot, like an open oven. There it was necessary at all times to have either an air conditioner or a fan, even if a handheld one, just to cut the pulsating heat. July in North Carolina was hot too, but more humid. Here in the Congo, July was not as I expected; it was not like summer at all. Because it was located beneath the Equator, the seasons were in reverse. It would only start to get hot in September, when we would spend most of our time playing at the pool.

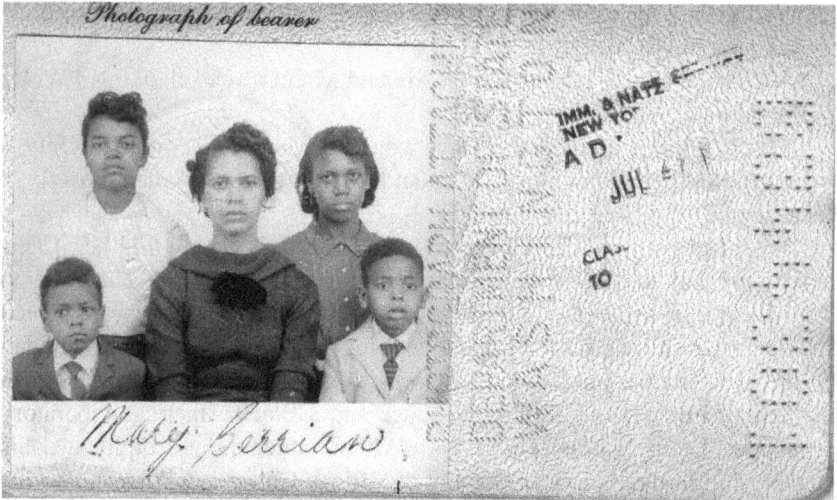

Figure 1.1 Passport of me (left back) and Toni with Mother, Derek (left front), and Albert, 1961 (author's collection).

I was bored!

Other than walking to the store for food or playing at the pool, there wasn't much to do. I was accustomed to structured cultural and educational events that filled my spare time with family—poetry readings at Daddy's university, trips to New York City for musicals, ballets, operas, and museum tours—but it wasn't that way here. That's why Toni, the boys, and I wanted to go for walks, not only to observe our surroundings, but to talk to people using French. Already I could tell I would be the translator because I had been studying French in high school. The Congolese were friendly. Women wore brightly printed two-piece outfits, layered patterns of geometric designs or flowered prints, and carried baskets on their heads and babies slung on their backs. Sometimes we would see a man facing a tree, using nature as a public toilet. Albert and Derek laughed as Mother looked away. It explained the waves of soured stench that assaulted my nose as I passed the trees.

People did indeed talk to us on the street, and that's where I realized, profoundly, that I was neither in a resort nor in a place that was just like home except for the presence of more Black people who spoke French.

"*Bonjour. Ça va?*" [*Good morning. How are you?*] someone would say while approaching me, my siblings, and Mother, either selling something or generally curious.

"*Bonjour!*" I'd reply.

"Ah. You have an accent—where are you from?"

In French, that's how it would start. Innocuous enough. But once I revealed we were from the United States...

"No, you cannot be Americans," one young man said.

"We are Americans," I repeated in French.

"No, you are not Americans," the man said. Dumbstruck, I looked at Mother, at Toni. We all stared back at him.

"Yes we are...

"You are Haitians," he said, nodding as though his pronouncement made sense.

"No, we are from America," I persisted. "We live in New Jersey, near New York?"

Certainly, he'd heard of New York City.

"No," the man shook his head forcefully as though trying to dismiss the very thought from his mind. "No. Americans are White." The only people who could call themselves American, in his view, were White.

That remark did it. Mother had enough. "We are *Black* Americans," she said, and her tone was one that translated to any language. She stormed right toward the man and he barely stepped out of the way in time as she blew past. As I quickly hurried after her, I felt stung. I had never expected to be denied my American-ness. American-ness wasn't something I thought about all that much before coming here. I had thought we would be seen as simply Americans. We were Black—didn't that count for something? Didn't that count for a lot?

In that brief exchange it was like the man uncovered something about us we hadn't meant to bring along from America. The divisions among people there, the ever-present awareness that the color Black was seen as less-than, and that we as Black people were seen as less-than. Yet here, in that moment, it felt worse somehow than living in a racist society that was not inclined to let Black people sit at the front of the city bus. Where fourteen-year-old Chicago-born Emmett Till's crushed face looked up from an open casket to remind the world who wasn't allowed to whistle at a White woman in Mississippi. Where special Black girls and boys were shuttled to all-White schools in Ohio so the schools could feel better about themselves. These were the things back home that told me that although I was in America and I was American, I was separate and distinct. And now this Congolese man had just told me the same thing: I and my family were something that was not. *You are not Americans. You are not.*

He was, I realized later, also saying I and my family were not part of everything Africans glamorized about America: Hollywood movies, flashy cars, and boxing matches. The man did not see us as America, the America he saw and probably dreamed about in the same way I had dreamed about Africa. I realized I had wanted to be part of the America everybody fantasized about.

"Brenda, there's no TV here," Daddy explained, as I described the incident to him. The only TV was in the American Cultural Center, he said. And who was shown on TV? White people. I knew that. It was a regular complaint at home, how television rarely featured Black characters in shows or commercials, as though they didn't exist. (*Amos 'n' Andy* didn't count.) I knew how TV could form imagination, too. I remembered the teasing from my Black and White classmates in Jersey.

"You're going to live in a tree in Africa!"

"Hey Jane, where's Tarzan?"

"Those cannibals are gonna put you in a pot and eat you!"

Thanks to Adeboye, one of my father's former Nigerian students who had regaled me and my sister with tall tales about his country and people, I knew there was no Tarzan or Jane.

The Congolese man who refused to believe we were Americans held equally ignorant ideas of who Americans were. When I thought about it that way, his attitude made sense.

"Remember," Daddy said. "There were only fourteen to twenty people in the entire country who had a college education when the Congo got its independence last year. They've not been *exposed*."

Daddy then explained why the man had assumed we were Haitians: many Haitians had recently arrived to work with the United Nations (U.N.) after Lumumba's sudden and mysterious death six months into freedom. His death caused an uproar, causing the Congolese government to ask for help from the U.N. Because educated Haitians spoke the French language, they were sent to the Congo. As noted by Regine O. Jackson, "By 1962, Haitians constituted the second highest contingent of UN staff experts."[13] The father of the acclaimed filmmaker Raoul Peck was a member of the group, having fled the François Duvalier dictatorship in Haiti with his wife and three sons. Many years later, Raoul Peck made two films about Lumumba: the 1992 documentary *Lumumba: La mort du prophète* (Lumumba: The Death of a Prophet) and the 2001 feature film *Lumumba*. Therefore, to the Congolese, foreign and Black meant Haitian; the educated meant White. Yet many Congolese knew about famous Black American singers such as James Brown and Ray Charles. But an educated Black? This didn't fit the paradigm. Perhaps because they were so held back from education—attaining just a high school education was a rare and commendable feat for most Congolese.

I felt better listening to Daddy. His logical explanations for why the man had called us "not" Americans and why he'd called us Haitians removed the emotion from the story. "Try to understand their point of view," he always said. And when I did, the disparaging remark made sense, and it didn't feel as personal. It still stung, but only a little. The next time someone seemed confused about us being Americans, I knew I would react better, because I understood their rationale.

It turns out I would have plenty of opportunity to set the record straight. It became a regular occurrence when I would interact with the Congolese. I would say, in French, then English, then French again, *"Nous sommes américains noirs."* [We are Black Americans]. These exchanges were exhausting, but they seemed necessary. I tried not to get angry. I tried to educate. But the telling was hard, and sometimes my explanations only prompted more questions.

If you are Americans, why do you have to say 'Black' with it?

After I had faced this question several times without knowing how to reply, I found the perfect response, *"Why do you say you're Baluba or Bakongo?"* I referred to ethnic codes I knew they would understand, and they did. A nod, a sparkle of recognition. To see this transformation—take place on the face of a questioning stranger—well, to my surprise, I found it absolutely exhilarating.

I was learning about the complexities and nuances of Blackness across the African diaspora. Most of all, I learned how American I was after moving to the Congo.

NOTES

1. Guy Vanthemsche, *Belgium and the Congo, 1885–1980* (New York: Cambridge University Press, 2012), 262. Toward the end of 1959, there were 89,000 Belgians in the Congo. During the events of July 1960, 38,000 fled, but 42,000 returned by 1964.

2. In addition to the 14 or 20 college graduates, 417 Congolese priests had received seminary training superior to the average American college education. Some sources that cited different numbers of college graduates were Ritchie Calder, *The Agony of the Congo* (London: Victor Gollancz Ltd., 1961), 37; Philippa Schuyler, *Who Killed the Congo?* (New York: The Devin-Adair Company, 1962), vii; Catherine Hoskins, *The Congo since Independence*, January 1960–December 1961 (London: Oxford University Press, 1963), 13; Thomas Kanza, *The Rise and Fall of Patrice Lumumba* (Cambridge, MA: Schenkman, 1978), 13.

3. King Gordon, *The United Nations in the Congo: A Quest for Peace* (New York: Carnegie Endowment for International Justice, 1962), 70. The United Nations Civilian Operations trained Congolese teachers and opened the Pedagogical Institute in Léopoldville in October 1961.

4. Ibid.

5. Adam Hochschild, *King Leopold's Ghost: A Story of Greed, Terror and Heroism in Colonial Africa* (Boston, MA: Houghton Mifflin, 1999), 87.

6. Ibid., iii; 129–31.

7. Ibid., 233.

8. Ibid.

9. Howard W. French, *A Continent for the Taking: The Tragedy and Hope of Africa* (New York: Alfred A. Knopf, 2004), 54.

10. Kanza, *The Rise and Fall of Patrice Lumumba*, 162.

11. Ibid.

12. Langston Hughes, "Cross," in *The Selected Poems of Langston Hughes* (New York: Vintage Books, 1994), 138.

13. Regine O. Jackson, "The Failures of Categories: Haitians in the United Nations Organization in the Congo, 1960–64," *Journal of Haitian Studies* 20, no. 1 (Spring 2014), 35.

Chapter 2

At the Roadblock

I was discovering Léopoldville (now Kinshasa) on foot by day during the week because Daddy had the car at work, and on weekends he would drive all of us around the city to see and learn about different neighborhoods, visit restaurants and shops, and go to the movies.

Early in our stay he took us to Boulevard Albert 1 (now Boulevard du 30 juin)—the wide, dual, expansive street divided by traffic islands and lined with palm and limba trees that served as the city's main thoroughfare.

"It's named after me," said Albert. "And you, Daddy!" He balanced two of Daddy's books on his head, mimicking the Congolese we would see passing by every day. The boys had taken to flagrant imitation, even pretending to unzip their pants to pee on trees, much to Mother's consternation. At seven and five years old, they were rowdy and full of energy, running circles around Toni, Mother, and me when we walked around town.

I didn't know much about Daddy's arrival in the Congo in January 1961, six months before we got there, but he gave us more details of the story as we toured Boulevard Albert 1. On February 14, 1961, Daddy, who'd been living in the country just a few weeks, stood in the company of a crowd of mourners observing the grief-stricken and moaning Pauline Opango, Lumumba's third wife and widow, marching bare-breasted down the boulevard.[1] This peaceful protest march that, with such grief visible on the faces of those marching, could have easily been a funeral procession. Since Lumumba's body had been dismembered and burned to ashes,[2] no proper funeral could take place. His widow wore no shoes and no blouse. She moaned and cried and beat her bare chest. Her two-year-old son Roland walked by her side. (Lumumba's other children were in Cairo, Egypt, under President Gamal Nasser's protection.) Her grief was public and communal. A hundred or so followers—women marching bare breasted in

19

solidarity and men marching with their heads lowered—marched behind Mrs. Lumumba for six miles from *la cité indigène* (the African section of town, or native quarter) to the United Nations headquarters at l'Hôtel Royal in the former European section. They carried white flags to signal peace. The mass moved slowly down the boulevard. Many were crying. A hero was slain. The tragic scene was not what independence was supposed to look like.

Around the world people marched in solidarity with the Congolese—in Harlem, for one. Suddenly, for Black Americans, Lumumba became like Emmett Till, and all the other Black bodies lynched by an unfair system of White privilege. Whites marched and protested, too, alongside Blacks in the United States, in London, in Moscow, even interrupting a session at the U.N. gallery. They were mourning more than one man.

Now that I was here in the place of these events, and with what Daddy was telling me about the gruesome, heartbreaking assassination of Lumumba, I knew I was supposed to feel bad, but this living history still seemed abstract and confusing.

As I walked, I thought I saw a tear in Mother's eye. Perhaps she imagined Mrs. Lumumba who had just lost her husband, walking down this street as we were, holding the hand of her son who was three years younger than Derek. While we had waited for Daddy's phone call in Jersey, the television trumpeted news of the riots, morning, noon, and night. Grandma, who knew it was best not to say anything, had had a sad look on her face, too.

Derek and Albert ran ahead to capture a lizard they had spotted. I watched them. The lizard must have slithered out of reach because the boys began to wrestle. Even when bigger Albert pushed Derek, Mother did not yell for them to stop. Daddy didn't, either. Derek yanked some grass from the ground and tossed it at Albert. They laughed, continued wrestling. They were not affected by this place we were in. I wasn't sure I was, either. It wasn't our story. It wasn't the embroidery on my black shawl. It had happened before we kids had arrived with Mother, and even though we were here now, it still wasn't our story.

Our story began the first time we encountered guns.

Sunday was the day reserved for family no matter where we lived. On Sundays, Daddy was not allowed to work. No carousing with Ted Harris, another Black American whose wife Ann and four children we all adored. Although we kept up on the news back home via the BBC and Voice of America on the radio and read the local paper, we did not read the Sunday *New York Times*, either because we simply couldn't get it or because we were *living* the international news and therefore reading about it wasn't as necessary. On Sundays, we would do other things: go for a ride; take the twenty-minute ferry across the Congo River to Brazzaville, the capital city in a nation once controlled by the French; explore other neighborhoods or the countryside; go to a restaurant, whatever.

One Sunday remains seared in my memory—the Sunday our story changed. It was late October, the expected hot summer weather we'd been hoping for in full swing. We had been out, doing something family-centric no doubt, and were driving back home.

Suddenly, the two cars in front of us begin slowing down and we lurch forward as Daddy hits the breaks. A roadblock. We have seen them before, heard about them, but hadn't yet been stopped ourselves. As we pull closer, four men wearing olive green army fatigues, black berets on their heads, come into view. One takes a breath from a tiny white cigarette, his face hidden behind the ghost-like vapor of smoke. Each holds a huge black gun that is wide at the bottom and skinny at the end. (Grandmama Josephine was the only person I had seen brandishing a gun. She had pointed her rifle at a family friend after Grandpapa's funeral and burial.) They grip the guns as though someone might steal them if they don't hold on tight. My stomach flips. Mother takes in a sharp breath.

"Stay calm, Mary," Daddy says quietly. I look ahead and see what she sees: a White man is being yanked out of his car by one of the soldiers, the skinny end of the gun pointed to his head. A woman's voice cries out, "Non!" Another soldier goes around to the other side of the car and pulls out a White woman by her blond hair. She stumbles trying to move with her head bent down but doesn't fall. He releases her hair and says something to her and she puts her hands on her head and walks forward. There are small circles of sweat on her pink shirt. She joins the man, and the two walk with their hands on their heads toward the dense forest brush a few yards off. They walk past a jeep holding four other soldiers, who laugh and jeer as they pass by.

Screaming. The same woman's voice. A gunshot. Then three more in rapid succession. Everyone in our car sits up straighter.

"Oh God, oh my God," Mother says. "What is happening, oh my God." Mother's fear unleashes her children's and I scream.

"Daddy!"

"Daddy what's going on?"

"Daddy, Daddy!" Albert looks like he's going to cry and is reaching toward the front seat for Mother who is hyperventilating.

"Children, calm down," Daddy says.

"Brenda," he turns to me. "Calm them down back there." I'm the oldest. I'm the one in charge of my siblings. I put my arms around my sister and brothers and pat their backs and say shhhhhh until we are relatively calm, shrieking silently on the inside.

The first soldier approaches the second car, just in front of ours, and leans down into the open driver's window. The other soldier has returned from the wooded area and is jumping up and down like a crazy person. If we were watching this on television, Mother would be shielding our eyes. But this is real.

The same scene plays out for the second time as a White couple ahead is pulled from their car, taken into the woods, and then rapid gunshots fill the air. Only the soldiers emerge from the trees. The men in uniform seem jumpy, almost like they are excited but may be on edge like they are nervous they will get arrested. I realize I am waiting for the police to show up, for someone in authority to step in and make it stop. To do what's right before they shoot us. But it's the weekend, and I remember Daddy and Mr. Harris talking about how the police don't work on the weekend. The police stations are completely closed from Friday evening until Monday morning, because the police are busy stealing to supplement their meager incomes.

Someone was whimpering, and I thought it was Toni or me, but it is Mother. Daddy turns to her. "Keep quiet. You look White," he says in a gruff tone that normally Mother would take offense to. *"Shut up.* Don't say one word." He never speaks to her like that. He never calls her *White*—an accusation that seems to follow her everywhere here and angers her to no end. At once I understand those times Daddy had called us from work telling Mother not to leave the house because they were killing Whites. I figured it didn't matter who they were killing; we weren't going to be around any killing anyhow. But now I realize, more distinctly than before, the cost of my Mother's fair skin. That it mattered they were killing *White* people because Mother looked, to many people, White. Whereas back home people might meet her ambiguous complexion and hair with confused looks, and sometimes she would sit right where she wanted like a day at the doctor's office in Texas, here there was danger in her appearance. Later I would find out that, when Daddy had told Mother not to go out, he had also said she could send me out instead if she needed something. She never did. Not only could I speak the language, I was Black enough to get by.

"Let me be in charge, Mary," Daddy continues. "You barely speak French." Mother closes her eyes and puts her chin to her chest as the soldier approaches the driver's window.

"Bonsoir," Daddy says. Good evening.

They ask to see his papers. Daddy hands them over. They walk around the car, circling, and suddenly—absurdly—I think of a child's game Ring around the Rosie. One of the men says we must open the trunk now. Which means we have to get out of the car. They say something I don't comprehend and Daddy tells us to get out of the car and stand. I don't utter a word. I climb out. I am petrified, trembling. *Please don't let them shoot us.*

Will they think Mother is a White and shoot her? I wonder. I wish for a moment her skin matched ours, darker. And her hair. Just for five minutes. But they don't question her. They speak only to Daddy.

I see Mother looking down at the ground on the other side of the car and I do the same. With my ears I witness Daddy conversing with the soldier. I dare not look up. This is a memory of sound, not sight. I avert my lowered eyes to Derek, who looks so small. He is the darkest in our family, maybe he's even darker than usual being out in the sun so much. Though an East Indian soldier we recently met keeps mistaking Derek (with his coffee-shaded skin) for an Indian, I wonder if he might be able to pass as a Congolese, too. But he is ours.

Two soldiers circle us, their voices are jumpy and they make sounds like "buh buh buh" and later Daddy will tell me that they were not just smoking cigarettes.

Daddy is calm and unwavering as he talks in French to the soldier who is still holding his papers. "We are from the United States. I am a teacher. We are here temporarily." He keeps his cool, but I can detect a slight quivering to his voice, so faint that only someone who knows him very well could detect it.

The soldier points to something on Daddy's papers and calls the other soldier over. They study it and suddenly,

"Monsieur l'Ambassadeur, d'accord!" He stands at attention, nods and says it again.

"Monsieur l'Ambassadeur, d'accord!" [Okay, Mr. Ambassador!]

Daddy turns to me and says we can get back in the car. I embrace my siblings and Mother, and we all climb inside and shut the doors, thankful for the glass car window and its feeble shield. The man hands the papers back and Daddy gets in. We drive off slowly. We don't want to kick up dust.

"They think I'm the U.S. Ambassador because of the embassy name on my *carte d'identité d'étranger* (foreign identity card) and they can't read well," Daddy says. No one responds. We are all sitting quietly in the backseat. No one says a word the entire ride home. Several times I am tempted to turn around to see if they are following us home so they can steal from us and then shoot us with their fat guns, but I do not.

When we arrive home safely and are finally inside with the doors locked, everyone begins to breathe again. Their battle is not with us. It is with the Whites. I saw it. I heard it. I am glad our position here is as Black Americans—which is different than it is back home and gives us some advantage here like Whites have in the United States. The construction of color is curious and even as a teenager I recognize its contradictions: the same skin can earn you privilege in one place and a bullet in another place.

The roadblocks, they are common, Daddy says. Sometimes a venue for robbery. Colonel Mobutu does not pay the soldiers; they are paid only in what they can steal. White lives become expendable. The soldiers always know they'll catch the Whites with the roadblocks, for who in their society can afford to own a car? Belgians, mostly. Some Belgians had abandoned their cars as they fled the country, so occasionally I would see a car veering wildly on the road or barreling through on the wrong side of the street and know that a Congolese who had never driven before had picked up a stray car.

Was this licentious behavior, this violence unfolding, at the core, payback? Belgium had enacted one of the most heinous forms of colonization in history. Congolese had dogs sicked on them and had their hands cut off for not meeting work quotas in the mines and fields. Held back from education and self-empowerment. Held captive to poverty that was beyond abject. The anger was visible. The anger was audible. It burst forth as gunshots.

Around the White world sympathy poured out for the Belgians who were being hurt and killed in their homes and on the streets. Where had been their sympathy for the Congolese under Belgian rule? Shock and horror bled through the reports, and it was as though everyone had forgotten the centuries of slavery and bestial mistreatment of the Congolese. Sympathy was not retroactive, and sympathy for the Congolese sounded like a whisper at best. It wasn't right what those soldiers were doing, Daddy admitted, but I could see the anger and know where it was coming from. It would be surprising for the Congolese not to be angry about seventy-five years of atrocities and terror. I realized the soldiers wanted the Belgians *to feel what they felt.*

We, as Black Americans, were outside the main narrative of the Congo-Belgian story, a very tragic tale. And yet, somehow, after the day of the roadblock, it felt more like our story, too.

NOTES

1. "Mourning March for Congo's Ex-Premier," *The Sydney Morning Herald,* February 16, 1961. http://www.google.com/newspapers?nid=1391&dot=19610216& id=E4BWAAAIBAJ&sj.

2. Ludo DeWitte, Renee Fenby and Ann Wright, *The Assassination of Patrice Lumumba* (New York: Verso, 2003), 34.

Chapter 3

Les Coiffures

Daddy's voice rang in my head, "You have to understand that people have different ways and customs; don't judge them with your own culture's eyes." I had noticed how people moved and walked very close together. It appeared no one minded such proximity. Whenever one of my parents drove into the Congolese neighborhoods, away from our own residence in the former European designated area, I saw shacks so close together they were nearly on top of each other.

Touching was inevitable. Inevitable as well as celebrated. Every day I would spot a man walking down the street holding hands with another man, or a woman with a woman. "Oooo, they are *funny*. Lots of *funny* folks here!" I said. Daddy scolded that they weren't "funny"; they were just friends, or family, or whatever. A simple show of general affection by touching—the gesture didn't mean they were gay. Still, I did not appreciate being touched, by a stranger: a girl, guy, or otherwise. I felt embarrassed, uncomfortable, like I was on display.

One day three girls, who looked to be my age, walked up to Toni and me. I had seen them several times on my way past the park. They probably assumed Toni and I were Haitian, I thought. No matter how good my French, I was never mistaken for a Congolese. Toni and I were too light skinned. Plus, Toni and I wore shorts or pants—Congolese girls always wore dresses, school uniforms, or brightly patterned getups like their mothers. That day the girls held suppressed smiles as they approached us, obviously wanting to tell us something. We found ourselves face-to face on the side of the road.

The girls greeted us, "*Ça va?*" For a moment I hoped they would invite us to be their friends until they reached out and touched our hair.

"*Tes cheuveux sont doux!*" [Your hair is soft!] they squealed.

"*Merci?*" [Thank you?] I said, confused. I wished they would let go of our hair. Toni shrugged. It was strange, having our hair admired. Toni's thin, soft hair reached the nape of her neck, and mine was thick, curly, and shoulder length. According to Mother, I had been born with good hair curls, but the texture began to shift a little bit to the kinky side when I reached age five.

Toni, I knew for a fact, disliked her hair. We both had grown up wearing our hair in braids until a few years before, when we decided to embrace our teen years with a ponytail-and-bang style, accentuated with barrettes in various colors to match the color of our outfits. Whenever we wanted to be fancy, we rolled our hair into a French twist at the back of our head or let it hang "out." However, to obtain these new looks, we both had to submit to the horror of the straightening comb because Mother didn't forget to bring it and those hot curlers that looked like scissors when opened.

One of the Congolese girls began rubbing Toni's arm, leaning in to examine the fine hair. She lifted her hand from Toni's arm, studied her fingers, and pronounced, "*Vous êtes métisses.*" Realizing she thought Toni's hair would come off in her hands, and confused about the word "*métisse,*" I asked in Congolese French, "*Métisse? C'est quoi ça?*" Métisse? [What's that?] She and the other two girls pointed to our skin. Then I reached out and touched one of the other girl's hair. Hard as a rock, her hair was, a helmet. Not the kind of hair that will brush against your shoulders like Mother's. Not even like the tight curls like mine or Toni's. As Toni and I would discuss later, her hair and the other two girls' felt very dry.

Toni and I found the Afro look to be strange. Short Afros were worn by Congolese women, and I found it hard to distinguish between men and women, so accustomed was I to seeing Black women's hair long and smooth (helped out by the hot comb or a chemical perm) or styled in braids and ponytails. I began looking first to the person's clothes to know whether to say "*Madame*" or "*Monsieur.*" I also couldn't abide seeing a Congolese girl whose hair had not been touched with a comb or a brush in days! Individual small knots sat on top of her head. Trying to comb them out, for I tried, was an exercise in patience.

I thought of how the girls' hair and our own had the same root. The hair types were cousins of a sort, perhaps from the same country of origin, but yet our hair was so different. Most likely, the girls did not use any oils or conditioners or pomades to soften their hair. Perhaps they did not braid it before going to bed, to force it to loosen some, and, as I looked closer, I wondered if they even combed it. The girls wore a short Afro, which appeared to be the common hairstyle, and the women wore them too—small, neat spheres.

It struck me we were all ooo-ing and aaah-ing and touching each other in the middle of the day, like this was just what you did. I snickered, and then Toni did, and soon the five of us fell into giggles, like old friends, and with my head cocked back, I looked through the patterned leaves of the trees and rejoiced that a heap of laughter needed no translation.

Ironically, Mother decided to get a perm to make her hair straighter. You would think she'd avoid something that might increase suspicion that she was not Black. But the politics of hair was the last thing on her mind when she did it. Her friend Yvonne Reed (the first American hired in Lumumba's government who later became Yvonne Chappelle, mother of comedian Dave Chappelle) did it, and the transformation was inarguably stunning. Previously, she had worn a puffy-like, large Afro. But, one day, Yvonne's natural hairstyle was suddenly gone. She came over to our apartment and her dark tresses hung down *stick* straight like a pageboy.

"Mary, I'm in a wedding next week," Yvonne said. When she twirled in the middle of our living room, Mother's eyes lit up.

"Did you go and get yourself a perm?" Mother asked Yvonne. "How?"

"A White man is here from Europe, Belgium or France I think, and he's doing the hair of all the government ministers' wives. I heard about it and had to go see!" She laughed. Mother was in awe. And then, she got that excited look in her eyes.

"Well let *me* go!" Mother said. "I'm tired of having to wash and curl my own hair. I miss the beauty shop."

I butted in. "Why Mother? You have *curly* hair!" She did not need a chemical perm in my opinion. She'd never had one before, always said they were harsh and unnecessary. Of course, there was a stigma attached to chemical relaxers—the accusation you were trying to be White.

Toni scrunched up her face. "Mother, your hair is fine."

"Mary, it's worth it," Yvonne added.

I wondered if it was more than the "look" Mother sought. Maybe her motivation was bolstered by knowing other Black expats as well as the Congolese government ministers' wives were going to this beauty shop seeking the same ends. I also wondered if the beauty shop Mother was going to would be like the one we had seen in *la cité indigène*, where a crowd of people would stand outside the window to witness a beautician at work.

Those beauticians were artists! One afternoon, we had watched a hairdresser divide her clientele's hair into rows of long parts. She twisted and wrapped the sections in a heavy, but shiny, black thread. Then she held a lighted match to the ends of the thread to burn them off. I watched in fear and imagined the whole section suddenly engulfed in flames and the woman running down the street screaming with her head on fire. But the beautician carefully singed just the ends and snuffed them out like a muted candle flame. The outcome was a hairstyle that resembled spokes in a Ferris wheel. In other words, the hair stood in little spikes. Stranger than an Afro. Fascinating to watch. Toni and I agreed we would never do such a thing to our own heads.

Mother was not impressed with Congolese women's hairstyles. Neither the short-short look nor the spikes worked for her. She speculated that Belgian colonialism was so brutal that most of the Congolese women didn't have the time to devote to beauty care. Much of their time was occupied with finding water, working in the fields, cooking food, and having and taking care of children. "The poor women," she would say, "worked like beasts of burden."

Mother ventured out with purpose to her step. When she had an idea in her head there was no stopping her; she was a woman who knew how to make things happen. It was the side of her I admired and emulated as an adult: the same boldness that could shock, rouse, or even offend people also empowered her to hold her head high and demand service in the Whites-only section of a shoe store.

When she returned to the apartment with a pageboy like Yvonne's, her curls gone from sight, we couldn't help but "ooooh" and "ah" and wonder whether straight hair was—despite what she had always said about Black women's hair, about mine and Toni's hair—better. With great panache, she strode through the apartment as if it were a red carpet.

But then, just a few days later, our reverential "ooooohs" and "ahs" changed to appalled exclamations of "Oh, Mother, your hair!" Her hair started thinning, handfuls of it coming out when she brushed it or even touched it. She looked with horror at the clump of dry strands in her hand.

"That damn Frenchman gave me a perm too strong for my hair texture! Now I'm about to be near bald like the Congolese women!"

She clenched her fallen hair in her fist and stormed back to the beauty parlor to "make a ruckus." Toni and I, holding back snickers, watched her leave the apartment, her gait furious. You did not want to get on that woman's bad side. Her hair, those curls, was not the texture of the Congolese women's, and the Frenchman shouldn't have treated it that way. It was softer, finer. She demanded he give her free hair treatments to restore her hair back to its normal state. It was the last time she would ever get a perm, and for the remainder of our stay in Léo, she worked to restore her hair back to its original curly texture. But it would never, for the rest of her life, be the same.

"Umm," Toni and I said. "Perhaps Congolese hairstyles *(les coiffures,* in French) are better suited for Black hair."

Chapter 4

The Proposal

Instead of going to a regular school, learning alongside other expatriates' kids or professors' kids or Congolese kids as we would have preferred, Toni and I attended the high school correspondence school of the University of Nebraska, doing all our work at home and Mother mailing it in. Daddy had considered enrolling Toni and me in the formerly European Catholic Lycée Sacre Coeur for girls (now Lycée Bosangani) and the primary Collège Albert 1er (now Collège Boboto) for Albert and Derek. Both schools offered a Belgian curriculum in French. But since I was slated to graduate at age sixteen next year, I wasn't about to get behind in my studies. A Congolese school was out of the question; the credits would not have been accepted for transfer back home.

Many of the schools[1] were run by Belgians and had shut down when they left. This explained why we would see school-age kids[2] at the marketplace or out on our walks during the day. The American School of Léopoldville (TASOL) did not open its doors for students of U.S. diplomats and missionaries and U.N. personnel until September 18, 1961, two months after Toni and I had registered for correspondence school.

Lessons and homework were done at home. Though I was challenged by the material, learning in complete isolation from peers and teachers was not, it turned out, my style. Half the time I would be gazing out the window when I was supposed to be completing lessons. I would hear the faint sounds of the national independence anthem—"Indépendance Cha Cha," a catchy tune by Le Grand Kallé[3] (né Joseph Tshamala Kabasele) who combined Latin beats with what sounded like African drums, maracas, and a high-toned guitar. On the radio, on the street, through the windows of homes, in the restaurants, the song sounded tropical and happy. It made you want to sing and sway your hips. Because the song was in Lingala, not in French or English, I sang along but I wasn't sure what I was singing. But I *did* know the lyrics had to do with freedom. *Indépendance Cha-cha to zuwi ye!*

Even Mother hummed along.

Toni and I completed all our homework in the early afternoon and had the rest of the day to explore, or, more often, simply be bored. The one respite from going to a traditional school was not attending to the social hierarchies and mercurial friend cliques. Daddy was truly "somebody" here, and Mother, too, though mostly by accessory (which annoyed her). Rarely were Toni and I around kids our own age anyway, except when we went to the pool or had get-togethers with the Harrises or visited the Haitian-American Laurent family or Julia and Roy from Panama. There were still interactions with locals on the streets as we went about our shopping, but the girls who loved to touch our hair never became more than acquaintances. We didn't see them with any regularity, and the language barrier, and maybe other barriers, was too high.

Two of our Black airmen friends, Ricky and Vaden, would come to take us to the Olympic-size, outdoor swimming pool on campus. When there was no immediate call for soldiers, they were just as bored as we were during the day. They patiently taught us how to swim in the shallow end, for we weren't courageous enough to venture into the deep end. Albert and Derek took to the water like fish, no doubt showing off for the uniformed men they so admired. Toni and I, on the other hand, were scared of the water and slow learners. Whenever I glided beneath the surface of the water, I could hear my heartbeat and my labored breath when I came up for air. Turning onto our backs, Toni and I preferred to float, enjoying the feel of the water on our bodies.

The Harrises would come to the pool some days, driving in from their suburban home in Djelo-Binza. (They enjoyed living in their sprawling home outside the city.) Pete, Karen, Lynn, and Denise swam well because they had their own pool to practice in at home. Pete, who was fourteen, had freckles sprinkled across his face and was a "Class A" trip. He liked to sashay around the pool in tight red swimming trunks.

"I wear what the *real* divers wear, folks!" he said, and we all whooped with laughter. Bold and fun-loving, Pete loved to swim, and we liked to watch his skinny body flip and twist as he dove into the pool. His three younger sisters stayed in the shallow end with us.

From time to time, a good-looking Congolese boy close to our age would come to the pool, climb up the highest diving board, jackknife into the water, and swim away like a natural. His father was Mr. Tshimbalanga (Mr. T, for short), a Congolese landscape painter and a friend of Daddy, and we had visited their home once or twice. He was cute, Mr. T's son, but that's about all I thought about him. He seemed shy, so I didn't talk to him much. The minute I pondered having a crush on a boy I routinely dismissed the thought. What was the point? I was forbidden to date until age sixteen, and anyway

I was pretty sure my glasses and tendency to prioritize studying over hairstyling or flirting made me a weak candidate for a date. Part of me was secretly looking forward to dating when we returned home, but for now it was easiest to simply not think about it.

Until Mr. T asked, on behalf of his son, for my hand in marriage.

He came over to our apartment, and Daddy called me into the living room. Mother was in the kitchen, and Toni and the boys elsewhere.

Mr. T greeted me and quickly stated his proposal: He asked if I would agree to a future marriage to his eldest son.

I could only vaguely conjure an image in my head of the boy, whom I'd seen on occasion at the pool. We'd hardly spoken! Had I missed his signals that he had a crush on me? My stomach fluttered at this thought, but, as Mr. T continued, the feeling in my stomach turned sick with dread.

Mr. T described how his son (whose name I don't recall now and probably couldn't even then) was in his final year of high school and intended to continue his studies in medicine in Belgium. After getting his medical degree, he wanted to marry me since I could speak English and passable French. Therefore, he explained, this would have to be a very long engagement. (Not unusual, I found out later, for many young Congolese couples.)

"*Monsieur T*, I've never been on a date," I said. Flabbergasted, I explained how I wanted to return to the States to date and to finish my education.

"I barely know your son," I said. "I mean," I looked again at Daddy, helpless. "I appreciate the offer but . . ."

To my relief, Daddy spoke next. "Henri, in our culture the groom's father does not arrange a marriage. The young couple decides to get married and speaks with both sets of parents."

He explained our customs for a marriage proposal, but in the face of my bewilderment, he made no mention of the crucial fact that I could not, under any circumstance, get married. Here I was in Léo, not even allowed to date, and this man wanted me to marry his son. As I watched Daddy explain away my shocked reaction, I realized a transaction had been arranged without my knowing, and that Daddy might have been in on it. A dedicated Daddy's girl who refused to leave the Congo to return home after the robbery when Mother suggested leaving, I suddenly wished for Mother by my side.

But, Mr. T said, he respected my father, and it would be good for his son to marry a girl from a respectable, educated family.

I didn't budge. I was not going to get married, even if, for some bizarre reason, Daddy would allow it. After much back and forth in which I struggled to keep from shouting or dashing away, Mr. T left.

"Daddy, did you know he was going to ask me to marry his son?" Daddy confessed he had known.

"Why didn't you prepare me for it?"

He wanted my reaction to be natural, he said. It certainly was. Shock and anger. A sharp sting of betrayal. How could he make such a decision without my consent, as though I were a princess who needed things orchestrated for her!

"I didn't want to ruin a friendship," Daddy said. He wouldn't have let me marry this foreign boy and run off to Belgium, and he surely was doing his best to respect Mr. T's customs and handle the situation in his characteristically heady, delicate way, but still I was annoyed. It was not my time to be an African princess. In fact, I no longer wanted to be anybody's princess.

Traditionally, arranged marriages between families, not individuals, were the norm in the Congo. Mr. T thought a possible union between me and his son would seal a permanent bond between his family and mine. In spite of Mr. T's assumption, Daddy handled the situation delicately enough for him and Mr. T to sustain their friendship. And I never saw or heard from Mr. T's son again.

NOTES

1. Ian Scott, *Tumbled House: The Congo of Independence* (New York: Oxford University Press, 1969), 15. The largest secondary school in Léopoldville had 1,600 pupils, but only a handful was Congolese.

2. See Maurice W. Hennessey, *The Congo: A Brief History and Appraisal* (New York: Frederick A. Praeger Publishers, 1961), 79. Fewer than 25,000 Congolese had received some kind of secondary training.

3. Le Grand Kallé et l'Africain Jazz, "Indépendence Cha-Cha," *Succès des années 50/60 Vol I*, 1984. "Indépendence Cha Cha," the first 45 rpm released in the Congo, appeared in February 1960 about four months before the declaration of independence. The lyrics celebrated the impending independence and lauded the Congolese politicians and political parties by name.

Chapter 5

The Robbery

Against our wishes, Daddy hired two male servants, a remarkable irony I recognized immediately. Several family members back home worked as maids for White people—I could picture Aunt Anna's apron hanging on the hook by the door—and here we were with our *own* male servants. Félix was tall, medium frame, brown-skinned and quiet. Joseph was short, skinny, dark, and wore clothes with so many holes in them Toni said they were about to fall off his body and pretty soon he'd be running around here buck naked. "Toni!" Mother said sternly. (Daddy bought him some decent clothes.)

This must be what it feels like to be White and have servants, I thought. It was like being an American had the currency of a kind of "Whiteness"—a privilege I could get used to. Mother had Joseph do the laundry and ironing. Félix swept the floors and cleaned the house. Mother retained cooking duty, at our own and her request. (She was as prissy about food as I was about clothes and being touched.) Once, at a dinner meeting with Congolese officials, she balked at strange, undercooked-looking meat and someone leaned over to ask Daddy, "*Votre femme, est-elle blanche?*" [Is your wife White?]

This privilege thing, though I didn't call it that then, was something to ponder. It had to do with our being American, maybe with how our skin shades differed from the Congolese, or how our hair was softer, but also it had to do with money. We could afford to employ house servants. We could afford the simplé necessities, unlike so many.

One evening this privilege thing backfired.

Our stint in the suburbs ended when we were robbed *while we were at home*. Just one month after our arrival. The men, armed with machetes, entered through the hole where the air conditioner had been in the far bedroom Toni and I shared. They were trying to be as quiet as possible but Mother was in her bedroom and heard them. By the time the six of us reached the bedroom, we were too late: even the sheets had been stripped from the beds. We were lucky. Toni and I had not been in the bedroom at the time. The men did not hack us to death with their machetes, an event which we knew happened to several others.

The robbery had been an inside job. We learned Félix had pulled the electrical plug out of the socket so the robbers could remove the air conditioner without being electrocuted. We questioned what had happened to the concept of Black brotherhood. Having a mother who cooked for a Jewish family in New Jersey, my father had hired two servants at above the medium wage rate with decent hours. Instead of working seven days a week from sunrise to sunset like most of the Congolese servants, Félix and Joseph only worked five days a week from 9 a.m. to 3 p.m., with an hour for lunch. They were free to spend the weekend with their families. Yet Félix saw us as rich Americans, not as the Black Americans who had struggled to buy a year's supply of clothes for their children. Not surprisingly, Félix was nowhere to be found after the robbery.

I was naïve, thinking I and Félix were connected by having the same skin color. More than anything, I felt a sense of betrayal. It was one thing to have a White person betray you, for you wouldn't be caught off guard as easily. In the U.S., I was accustomed to being surrounded by White schoolmates, but White strangers on the street—well, in some ways, I grew to expect encounters with discrimination. Or at least I knew how to safeguard against its shock. But from a Black person? I and my parents had higher expectations.

After the robbery, I jumped at every noise in the night, and often Derek and Albert slept with Toni and me because they were scared. When Grandma Berrian heard about the incident, she commanded us to return home as soon as possible. Mother was ready to leave. I wanted to stay near Daddy. Our family's highest priority was sticking together, and so in the end we stayed.

We moved temporarily to l'Université Lovanium's campus, where we lived in a faculty house on a hill called Mont Amba in Kimwenza, about eight miles south of the center of Léo. The campus was empty, as most faculty and their families were gone on holiday. It was also sealed in with an electric fence and one entry gate.

Many evenings, the sound of drumbeats rose from the valley below. These were not the happy, dancing rhythms of the "Indépendance Cha-Cha." Starting slow and increasing like a hurried heartbeat, the sounds were ominous, and they only came at night. I knew people in Africa communicated through drumming—a Nigerian student had told me this long ago. Toni and I imagined they were warrior-like sounds, and that the drums were telling people to come get us. At home in the United States I had watched Tarzan movies, and, though I was supposed to be more sophisticated in my thinking about Africa by now, when the drums sounded below all I could think of was danger. I knew there was violence out beyond the fence. Whenever riots and uprisings occurred in the outlying provinces, the U.N. troops would be summoned.

Once, at the airport, I had witnessed a plane debarking with Congolese and U.N. soldiers, men of many skin tones and many stories, returning from Katanga, the southern province that had proclaimed secession from the Congo. The U.N. Security Council had ordered soldiers to take "all appropriate measures to prevent civil war . . . using force in the last resort."[1] It was obvious force had been used: many of the men crossed the tarmac wounded, their arms in slings, their heads and legs wrapped in bandages with dark circles of blood seeping through. Some were carried on stretchers or limped on crutches. Mother turned her head away. We were witnessing the aftermath of violence, of what we could only imagine. Our imagination carried over into the night in our glass-paned home, and with the drumbeats' crescendo, we imagined the violence we had thus far been shielded from was finally closing in on us.

Mother assured us the U.S. airmen living in the house down the block would protect us when the drums started. But one night, I watched as the airmen ran for their home at the sound of the drums, clearly terrified, which heightened my own sense of helplessness.

With every drumbeat, I remembered the deep darkness, how close it covered me so I couldn't even see my hand. I remembered the roadblock and the sound of the gunshots. I remembered the terror of being robbed and stripped of my things while I was in the house, only a few paces away from the same machetes that were being used to murder Belgians. My nerves were raw; those drumbeats brought me to my basest fears and I succumbed to the racist stereotypes that negatively depicted Africans in Hollywood movies.

I had arrived in the Congo full of optimism, but being robbed and held at gunpoint dissolved that optimism. To my shame, I realized how the bias in the United States against Africans had seeped into my psyche. It had taken being victimized by the Congolese to bring it out. I had shared meals with many Africans in my family home. It wasn't until we moved to a third-floor apartment, surrounded by Nigerian, Indian, and Danish U.N. soldiers that I felt safe. I could not judge fourteen million Congolese people for what a few had done to us.

I thought about Langston Hughes's jazz poem "Dream Boogie" about racial inequality and a deferred dream. "Ain't you heard," went Hughes's poem, "the boogie-woogie rumble of a dream deferred?"[2]

I thought of the empty schools I passed on my walks to the market, abandoned by the Belgian teachers and administrators when they left the country. I thought of the Congolese who didn't get to imagine themselves growing up to be pediatricians or language tutors or teachers. They could barely find enough to eat. Hughes wrote about feet beating out the beat. The metaphor of the beat was a reminder of the stories unfolding behind the scenes, stories that started long before we had arrived, stories of violence and colonialism. Hughes also queried, "Ain't you heard something underneath?"[3]

Pressing our faces and hands against the sliding glass doors from inside our house, we looked out into the black night to see if the villagers were making it up the hill in our direction. We looked for the anger we knew lived out there. The "something underneath."

Many nights, as I ate dinner, I felt a creepy, crawly presence. I would look up to see faces pressed to the sliding glass doors of the dining room. All those black faces in the black night looking at me. Watching me eat. Completely silent, they would stare. There were no curtains: only a simple pane of glass separated me from them. I was frightened by their eyes staring at me from the darkness. The Congolese never spoke; they never knocked or tried to break in. When they realized I was looking at them, they placed their hands over their mouths, mimicking the act of eating.

Naturally, Mother, Toni, and I wanted to give them some food but, to our surprise, Daddy warned us not to do it.

"Never give them food," he said. "We can't feed them because they will come at dinner time in an increasing number every day."

And so I ate, avoiding the empty mouths moving and wide eyes watching as best I could. Hunger so vast and heavy, and so close. Hunger I knew existed, but I had largely been shielded from witnessing it. The Congolese from *les quartiers satellites* (settlements) had so little while my family appeared to have so much. They came often, though not every night. I felt those mouths and eyes whether they were there or not, whether I looked up or not.

When we moved for a final time to an apartment more centrally located in the Kalina district (now Gombe) of the city, my elation was manifest: I didn't need to be so scared. I also wouldn't be so isolated. I would have more to do since I would be near more people, stores, parks and city noises.

I craved, especially, the city noises, for the noises of cars honking and sirens and voices were not only familiar to me, a Jersey girl, but also far better than the sounds I heard outside the city. Better than the drumbeats, the pulsing of dreams deferred.

NOTES

1. Georges Abi-Saab, *The United Nations Operation in the Congo, 1960–64* (Oxford: Oxford University Press, 1978), 17.
2. Langston Hughes, "Dream Boogie," in *Selected Poems of Langston Hughes*, 231.
3. Ibid.

Chapter 6

Familial Connections

If my parents ever owned a welcome mat when I was growing up, by the time we moved to a new place it would be worn to tatters within a month. At least once a week, while we lived in Léo, Daddy brought home a new friend or colleague for us to meet. We made family with whomever we met. As a result, our Congo family consisted mostly of fellow globetrotters. Diplomats and teachers. The Harris family. The Laurent family. American and U.N. peacekeeping soldiers, who were also far away from their families, would jump at the offer of home-cooked food at our house and many also became our friends.

With the many people crossing our threshold, I gained more cultural currency. I met several of the Congolese college graduates. It wasn't hard to find them. There were only twenty at most and, as the most highly educated in their country, they were rising to the top with leadership positions in the new government.

The swell of freedom, of new independence, was evidenced by the increasing desire for education among the Congolese. At l'Université Lovanium, where Daddy's language laboratory was centered, there were approximately 450 students registered in October 1961: 260 African males and 140 White males (plus 55 female students, half of them White, studying to be nurses). Most of the Congolese male students came from the Léopoldville and Kasai Provinces; a few from Katanga. The remaining African students were from Ruanda-Urundi, Sudan, Cameroon, Angola, and British East Africa.

One evening, we welcomed a visit from Mario-Philippe Cardoso[1] (now Losembe Batwanyele). What my sister and I knew about him, from what Daddy said, was this: he had graduated with a bachelor's degree in psychology and education honors from l'Université Catholique de Louvain and had taught briefly in the Department of Psychology at l'Université Lovanium.

From January to February 1960, the year before we had arrived in Léo, he had led the delegation of Lumumba's MNC party to the Belgian-Congolese Roundtable Conference (La Table Ronde) in Brussels to negotiate the terms for independence and was later named the first chief of the Congolese delegation to the United Nations. A highly credentialed and smart man.

What I saw when he walked through my door was this: golden skin.

In the United States I had seen all different hues of skin. Even my own family represented several different skin tones. But I must have grown accustomed to seeing Congolese people in only a small variance of color (dark brown to ebony) because when this golden-skinned man came to my house, Toni and I looked at each other. We could communicate through facial expressions, in that silent language close siblings share, and with our eyes we said to each other:

He is handsome! Is he . . . what is he? How could he be Congolese?

Later, I cast my best guesses: Was he American? Spanish maybe, or Indian? Was he from the Caribbean? Were both his parents unusually light-skinned, like our Mother? One thing Toni and I would agree on: he was fine, and not just because of his surprising skin shade.

He greeted us with a warm smile. His curly hair trimmed short, almost like the style worn by our soldier friends. Mr. Cardoso was lean, and he wore a distinguished-looking suit. When he shook Toni's hand and my hand, we couldn't help but blush.

Then he spoke in the familiar Congolese-accented French that told me yes, indeed, he was Congolese. I realized I was gawking. Not in a mean way, but in a curious, interested way. Much like how the girls on the street regarded Toni and me. Here I beheld someone who spoke and moved like a native but looked like something else. I wasn't sure what.

As my family had come to expect of me, I pummeled Daddy with questions after Mr. Cardoso had left, trying my best to conceal any evidence that I found him handsome.

"Is Mr. Cardoso Congolese?"

"Yes, he was born in Stanleyville (now Kisangani) and grew up there," Daddy said, picking up a small journal and some papers.

"He doesn't look like it," I said. Daddy didn't reply. He wasn't grading; he was probably reading more essays on this *négritude* movement he kept talking about. In the little I'd gathered, *négritude* had to do with Black identity and education, and several of his professor friends back home and in France were writing about it. My parents were creatures of learning and curiosity, too—Daddy with anything concerning education, and Mother with family and fashion. I was generally curious about everything, and right now race particularly intrigued me. I looked to Mother because she knew what I was getting at here with Mr. Cardoso.

"His mother is Congolese and his father Portuguese," Mother said. Absently, she smoothed a hand over her hair. It was hard to tell if her hair had resumed growth; it was still thin and tired looking. Then something clicked in my head.

"Is he, then, *métis?*"

Daddy confirmed, "Mr. Cardoso is a mixed-race man. If you see a mixed-race person, chances are the father was Portuguese." Mother rolled her eyes and grumbled something about those Portuguese men, and I made a mental note to find out about that. Much later, I learned that a shortage of White women in the Portuguese colonies of Angola, Mozambique, and Cape Verde resulted in liaisons, or sometimes marriages, between Portuguese men and African women. Their children (like Mr. Cardoso) were given their father's surname and allowed to acquire an education. However, between 1959 and 1962, children from a relationship between a Belgian father and a Congolese mother were abducted and put in schools and orphanages in Belgium run by the Catholic Church. Most of the fathers refused to admit paternity.[2]

I had, I believed, made a crucial connection: *this* is what those girls had meant when they called Toni and me *métisses*. Their only reference for a person with lighter skin tone was for an immigrant Haitian or the rare Portuguese-Congolese who looked like Mr. Cardoso.

People saw in you what they wanted to see, that much was becoming clear to me. Usually that meant they saw what they thought they already knew— hence why that man had insisted we were Haitian. It fit with what he already knew, with what made sense to him.

While Toni and I were unraveling the nuances of mixed-race status and the way in which race braided with nationality and class, our brother Derek was labeled East Indian. One sunny afternoon, we met an Indian soldier named Gurmukh Singh who was immediately taken with Derek. While walking home from work, he came upon us on our front steps. He wore a green uniform and a turban on his head in the signature blue color of the United Nations, whose increasing presence in the Congo served as a reminder of how the unrest around us had global implications. It was not just the story of the Congolese. It was the story of the Belgians. Of other African countries wresting their freedom from European colonizers. Of the United States Air Force airlift and the CIA. And now, of the United Nations.

I saw more U.N. soldiers arriving every day.[3] Initially called "a temporary security force," L'Opération des Nations Unies au Congo (L'ONUC) sent in 3,500 of its peacekeeping *casques bleues* ("Blue Berets").[4] They came from countries such as Sweden, Canada, Norway, Tunisia, Morocco, and Ghana. Gradually, the number grew from 15,500 to 19,800 troops from twenty nations, becoming the U.N.'s largest operation in the world.[4] I spotted soldiers based on their uniforms. And though I was terrified of the ANC soldiers, whose big guns and wild eyes and black berets I had met at the roadblock, in general I enjoyed meeting and befriending the many other soldiers from the United States and all over the world that were staying near my home at the university campus (or later, our apartment in the city).

When Gurmukh Singh stopped walking and said hello to us in English, then bent down and patted Derek's head, I noted his friendly blue turban and was not scared. It took only a few moments to see this relationship would be mutually beneficial.

"Where are you from?" I asked.

"India!" he said, and the enthusiasm in his voice and the way his face brightened told me he would surely regale us with stories of his country, which was enough for us kids to motion him past the welcome mat and into our home.

Mother greeted him when he entered, and he bowed deeply in response, then stood at attention and stared at the floor. I looked quickly to Mother, afraid she'd get angry, misinterpreting what I saw as respect and probably shyness. She often spouted off about the patriarchal Congolese culture, especially after the day she had told one of Daddy's friends, who kept shouting and ringing the doorbell at six o'clock in the morning, to go away and the man had told Daddy, right in front of her, "Berrian, you do not have control of your wife."

"You're damn right he doesn't," she had said, and slammed the door in his face. She was not about to be treated like property as Congolese women were. Married women had to obtain their husbands' permission to open a bank account, accept a job, obtain a commercial license, or rent or sell real estate. (Women used to be treated this way in the USA.) After Mother yelled at Daddy's friend, Daddy looked at her, eyebrows etched in concern. He hated to make waves; he only wanted to make friends. Then he smiled and shook his head.

"Oh, Mary."

But Mother was no fool; she recognized Gurmukh Singh's motion of respect. Sure enough, Gurmukh Singh was eager to talk and share stories. He visited us on his way home from work so often it wasn't long before he was part of our family. We called him "Singh" like "sing." None of us called him "Gurmukh," his first name. It didn't sound right.

In halting English, he spoke to us about Indian movies, music, food, and customs. His surname, Singh, which meant "lion," was common for men of the Sikhism religion. Many Sikh women take the name "Kaur," which means "princess."

"Brenda, are you married?" he asked me, and I thought I would fall off my chair.

"No," I said quickly. At fifteen, I wasn't allowed to even date yet; the prospect itself was quite embarrassing, especially here in front of my parents and siblings. I was not looking to be an African princess anymore, nor an Indian princess.

"In India," Singh said, "Fifteen is the marriage age."

Just as I was about to pretend I needed to do homework so I could leave the room and escape a marriage proposal, Singh, who was in his mid-twenties but hadn't finished high school, told me his parents had already arranged his engagement to the daughter of a family friend who was my age. He explained brides wore red saris, widows, white ones. I exhaled.

As he spoke, Singh rubbed Derek's hair. It was cut short, and its texture was curly and smooth, probably most similar to Mother's but, like a fingerprint, all his own. Something about Derek's particular combination of hair and coffee-colored skin reminded Singh of home.

"You're Indian?" he said hopefully. Derek giggled. I did not jump in and correct Singh and begin explaining, per usual; I was simply relieved the conversation was focused again on Derek and not on marriage and me.

"I'm American!" Derek said.

"Yes, but are there any Indians in America?" Well, yes, I said, "but they are Native Americans, not East Indians." Singh looked at Derek, clearly unconvinced. Where he came from, hair was always covered in its unadulterated state; he told us the men wore turbans like his, and the women wore either small turbans or traditional scarves on their heads.

Derek wore a self-satisfied look on his face, lapping up the attention. The baby of the family, he required just a bit more attention than the rest of us. And at five years young, he was unconcerned with identity—being called Indian didn't unnerve him in the slightest. It was like pretending to be a superhero, or wearing a costume for Halloween.

One night after dinner, Singh, in his broken English, quizzed Daddy and Mother about their racial background. Looking back and forth between them and Derek, he asked Mother and Daddy about their parents, which region they were from, and whether East Indians lived there. But he struggled to articulate. We deciphered something about the way people from the Madras region of India resembled Derek's appearance. On the globe, Singh pointed us to the southeastern area of his country near the coast. He very much wanted Derek to be East Indian, it seemed. Eventually, we gave up trying to convince him otherwise.

When Singh couldn't find the right words, he would stop talking and look at me in frustration as if he thought I could interpret for him. Then one day he asked me if I would help him with his English pronunciation. At the time, I wasn't sure if it was because I was the eldest, or because I could speak a smattering of French, or because I often asked Singh to teach us words in his own language. But, for whatever reason, he chose me. I found myself flattered and eager to tutor him. Later I discovered Daddy had suggested me as the teacher when Singh had approached him asking for lessons.

"In India I will go back to school and be smarter," he said several times as though trying to convince me he would be a good student. He respected me, a fifteen-year-old girl who was still in school herself, and he wanted my approval. What a grown-up feeling!

So, at least once a week, Singh would come over after dinner and we would arrange our study session in the living room as my parents and siblings retreated into their respective bedrooms. He changed from his uniform into white pants, a white shirt, and rubber flip-flops. I helped him to read aloud, using the English Language Services textbooks from Daddy's job. I guided him to practice using English naturally, in storytelling, prompting him to describe his country, his village, his people, his reasons for joining the military, his religion, and his future life goals.

Sometimes he turned my questions back to me.

"What will you do in the future, Brenda?" he asked once. I didn't immediately answer him. Before coming to Léo, I had considered becoming a pediatrician. I liked the idea of being a doctor, and I loved kids. I was always helping to tend the cut or bruised knees and elbows of Toni, Derek, and Albert, after all. But then I went to the American Baptist missionary station in Kimpese, a town between Léo and Matadi in the Cataractes District, where I visited l'Institut Médical Evangélique (IME) Hospital. I saw mothers who had just given birth, weary and shivering, sleeping underneath beds on the cement floor because the newborn babies occupied the only available beds. Then a White American doctor, with red blood splatters on his uniform, took me to observe patients with TB of the spine. The stark images of blood, people hunched over in pain with distorted, bony spines pressing against the skin of their backs, and those mothers on the edge of pneumonia from the cold cement were enough to erase the dream from my mind. I needed a new vision for my future. If only someone would pay me to travel the world and learn. I was getting good at that.

I realized that while I was teaching Singh and he talked about his life and culture, I too was learning. It was fulfilling in the way school had always been for me, and, compared to the uninspiring correspondence schoolwork that filled my mornings, my tutoring sessions with Singh were a cool drink in the desert.

Emboldened by his trust, seeing and hearing his language improve, I felt alive.

Perhaps I might be a teacher. Like my father.

During our tutoring sessions and in conversation with the entire family, Singh was reverent about his religion, more than reverent, which intrigued all of us. We were not a particularly religious family—though I sometimes attended Baptist services and sang in the youth choir. We had gone to a Baptist church service at the American missionary station. The Congolese sat behind the American missionaries: the girls on one side, the boys on the other. There were no signs dictating the arrangement; it was both an invisible rule and a law like the one in Richmond that said Blacks were to sit in the back of the bus. In just a year, after our return to the United States in 1963, Dr. Martin Luther King, Jr. would declare Sunday morning America's most segregated hour, and I'd recall this church and the irony of the White congregants.

For Singh, everything in his life seemed to revolve around religion. Even his hair was dictated by it, as his religion forbade hair cutting of any kind. That's what tipped us off that he had a huge mound of hair under that turban.

"Singh, show us your hair!"

"Singh, do you have long hair? How long?"

"Singh, Singh, let down your hair!"

Finally, one day he let his hair down. He unwound the blue turban, slowly and carefully, building excitement as we all watched. Underneath, his dark hair was gathered into a top knot, which he loosened. And then his hair fell, and it kept falling all the way down his back past his buttocks, nearly to his knees. I wondered if this was the way every male Sikh's hair looks? Will it ever stop falling? Can I touch it? I tell you what—none of us would ever forget that long, shiny black cascade of hair. Rapunzel had nothing on him. The strong scent of mustard oil, warm and richly herbal, released in a wave.

Singh shook out his hair, and we gathered in silence around him.

Then, before I could even ask, Singh motioned for us to touch his hair. Derek went first, as was his right as the favored child who could pretend to be East Indian for Singh.

Singh's hair was soft, and so shiny you'd think it was wet. The mustard oil left a thin sheen of liquid on my fingers. Although quite different from the Royal Crown, Ultra Sheen, or Alberto V05 hair dressing I used on my own hair, it certainly kept the moisture locked in. Singh's hair was not curly like I'd guessed. There were a few waves in it, but only from being folded and twisted into the top knot; otherwise it was straight. Although it was against his religion for non-family females to touch a man's hair, Singh let us touch his hair without hesitation. In the privacy of our apartment, there were no other Sikh men to observe. And perhaps he truly thought of us as family.

Mother covered her nose with her hand and, eyes watering, discreetly inched out of the room into the kitchen. She couldn't abide the smell. The pungent fumes suggested something acidic yet edible, like onion. The rest of us remained enthralled with Singh's new look, unmoved by the scent. I couldn't believe how long his hair was.

Laughing, Singh pulled out a bottle of mustard oil from a paper sack. The thick, gold-yellow liquid could have been honey. Singh rubbed some of it onto Derek's hair.

"Oh, now I'm going to be an Indian," Derek said, and if he weren't seated at Singh's knees, he would surely have been strutting like a rooster.

We all had to admit it. Derek's hair was slick and shiny. Singh nodded with approval. For once he didn't comment that Derek looked Indian, but we all knew what he was thinking. He connected Derek to his beloved country, which he deeply missed. Derek indulged him. Maybe it wasn't such a bad idea, I thought.

The following morning, Mother had no choice but to wash the oil out of Derek's hair. He whined and begged her to leave it in, but she couldn't take him sitting next to her with the odor in his hair while she tutored him in his school lessons. She seemed reluctant as she quietly rinsed his hair in the sink, for she no doubt sensed Singh had anointed him with something more than mustard oil.

NOTES

1. Kanza, *The Rise and Fall of Patrice Lumumba*, 144–45.

2. Giulia Paravicini, "Belgium Apologizes for Colonial- Era Abduction of Mixed-Race Children," *Reuters*, April 4, 2019. http://www.reuters.com/article/us-belgium-congo/belgium-apologizes-for-colonial-era-abduction-of-mixed-race-children-idU SKCN1RG2NF.

3. Hoskins, *The Congo since Independence*, 294. Lumumba had called for the U.N.'s help in ousting the Belgian troops from Katanga. L'Armée Nationale Congolaise (ANC) had mutinied and the provinces of Katanga and Kasai had seceded, and nobody wanted a civil war.

4. Ibid., 293.

Chapter 7

A Southerner at the Front Door

We had met some American Air Force men, as they were stationed near our campus home. The White American airmen would approach us to say hello. A few of the Black American airmen paid special attention to Albert, who was delighted, as he'd grown blasé about Singh because Derek monopolized all his attention. The Black airmen knew instinctively we were Black Americans. No explanation was needed. No detangling or translating necessary. Sergeant Jackson had become a friend even quicker than Singh or anyone else we had met. He was American, for one, and he was a Black man from Wilmington, North Carolina. An instant connection. So much could go unsaid. And so much *could* be said: Mother complained to Sergeant Jackson in the same way she did to Daddy or someone else who had no choice but to listen.

"It is difficult to buy fresh meat here! I don't know how I'm supposed to cook!" she fumed one day. She told him how she'd fried what she'd thought were hamburger patties for dinner, and that meat turned so hard that none of us could cut through it. Hard as a rock, she said. We concluded that it must have been ground monkey meat, and it was the last time she tried that.

"I'll take care of it," Sergeant Jackson said, laughing. "No problem, I'll have some meat delivered tomorrow."

Mother's eyebrows shot up. He *was* a sergeant, but could he really bring her fresh meat, and do it tomorrow? How many times had she, with me translating in French, asked for meat—chicken or beef—at the store or at the outdoor markets, with no luck? For canned meats and dried goods, she and Daddy ordered a three-month supply from a company in Denmark.

The next day the doorbell rang. I rushed to answer it. A White man stood before me. I stared at him, wondering what he could want.

Mother walked up behind me.

"Yes?"

He smiled sheepishly, a gesture that smacked of deference. But this was a White man, and deference was the last thing to be expected.

"Sergeant Jackson sent me to bring you this, Ma'am," he said, and held up a cardboard box. He said "Ma'am"—I couldn't believe it! I looked around the room for Toni, but she was gone, probably playing outside with the boys. Mother took the box. Inside were several steaks and a half-gallon of American vanilla ice cream.

"Thank you," Mother said, then asked his name and rank. (The U.S. airmen were forbidden to wear their uniforms, hats, and badges.) "Pleased to meet you, Ma'am," he said. Corporal Watson was his name, or something else familiar and American.

"We appreciate it," Mother said. She did not say "sir." Corporal Watson nodded.

Perhaps Sergeant Jackson had ordered him to be extra polite to us, or maybe he somehow didn't realize we were Black Americans. Something strange was going on. It was odd enough that a White man stood on our doorstep, but even more odd that he didn't turn to go once he handed Mother the box. He seemed to be waiting for something.

"How y'all liking it here?" he asked. Mother fixed on him a steady gaze, surely trying to discern his intentions.

"Y'all" meant he was probably from the South, another shocker. A White *Southerner* was, it appeared, shooting the breeze in our doorway. Back in the States, "freedom riders" were taking the buses and railways all over the nation, suffering beatings and disgraces too brutal to print in the newspaper as they demanded the fair and equitable treatment afforded them by law, because in some places—particularly in the South—Blacks were still getting tossed off the buses onto the pavement. At age fifteen, I didn't necessarily think these weighty things or realize the significance of what was happening at the time. However, I knew enough to know the drums were beating, at home and here under my feet. It was still dangerous to be Black in a White-ruled world.

And here, thousands of miles away, a White Southerner was standing on our welcome mat. All kinds of things were getting flipped upside-down, and this interaction was much more startling—potentially threatening—than when someone from Nigeria or the Congo or India or anywhere else except home puzzled over who we were or where we came from. Corporal Watson's question, a seemingly harmless nicety, proved he wanted to linger awhile longer and talk.

After a few long seconds, Mother stepped to the side and invited him in. He crossed the threshold. Just like that. They chatted about home, what they missed, and the ease with which their conversing continued belied history.

"I will kiss the ground of America when I return," Mother said. "I will kiss President Kennedy. I cannot *wait* to get out of here!"

They discussed home, familiarity, and the conveniences that were easy to take for granted until they were gone: air conditioning; fresh, edible meat; English spoken everywhere; and a sense of safety.

Corporal Watson missed his family—he had a wife and four kids, also.

That was it. He missed home. We represented home, and suddenly it didn't matter that we were Black and he was White: all those invisible racial codes and rules in America didn't apply here. It didn't matter whether he was from the South or the North.

We were the closest thing to family contact he had.

He wasn't the only one, either. Every few weeks Sergeant Jackson sent a soldier to deliver meat or other staples Mother couldn't find at the supermarket, and often the soldier would be White. Almost every time, he showcased a deference of respect. And the real miracle was not that we could suddenly obtain meat. If Dr. Martin Luther King, Jr. could witness this recurring scene, a few grains of sand from the promised land, he'd be proud. His preaching came alive right there in our living room, because everyone was treating each other with respect.

We hadn't sought it out; it wasn't a deliberate action on our part. Communicating with people was important and necessary.

It was simply living.

Chapter 8

The Return Home

We returned home to the States in July of 1962, and I graduated from high school the next year at age sixteen. I do not remember the particulars of culture shock, only that it wasn't so much a shock as a letdown. People were not, to my surprise, anxious to hear stories of my time in the Congo. I had so many stories! What it was like to be in a place full of Black people, to be in the majority for once. Singh and my first teaching job. How I'd almost been engaged to a Congolese man. The roadblocks and the sounds of bullets firing. Nighttime drumbeats and moving mouths in the window, too.

Even my extended family seemed distanced from, uninterested in, hearing about my experiences. Grandma and Papa didn't get it, and didn't seem to want to, either. Or maybe I had described everything in my letters to them well enough. I wondered if Grandma was still holding a grudge because we had stayed after being robbed when she thought we should have come home ASAP.

The Civil Rights Movement was in full bloom, and I waited for someone to ask me what being in Africa had taught me about rights for Blacks, but nobody did. After I tried describing an episode to a friend and she interrupted to say, "So nobody tried to eat you?" I quit talking about it altogether. People might be interested in a story about the Congo if it were sensational, but otherwise they couldn't relate. It was, simply, a world apart. Among my high school friends, and among the Black community at large, the connection between independence from colonial rule in Africa and civil rights for the Black American just wasn't apparent. Not yet, anyway.

I thought, well then, I will get involved in the civil rights movement like my peers, fight for causes we all know about and believe in, within the culture we share. I became active in the NAACP Junior League in Jersey City and helped organize a bus trip to the March on Washington for Jobs and Freedom in August 1963. I was looking forward to my first big march, and this one was going to be huge and everybody knew it. Black and White Americans were coming from all over the country. Then, just a week before I was set to go, Mother and Daddy told me I was not allowed to get on the bus.

"You can watch the march on television; it will be on all day," they said. I was more than furious. Here I was about to enter college on my own, having traveled to the Congo where I witnessed the fragile, sometimes violent, steps of freedom, and I could not travel four hours south from Jersey on a bus to hear Dr. King speak about freedom and jobs for Black Americans. Not only would I miss out on a shared event with my friends, my "people," I was displaced from the heart of the action.

My parents feared for my life. They were convinced White police officers and civil rights dissenters would start shooting at the marchers. Only four months prior in Birmingham, Alabama, police dogs and fire hoses were released on adult and child protesters. Photos of the violence—bodies pressed against brick walls from the force of pressurized water, a dog biting the stomach of a young Black male who looked about my age—were printed everywhere and had become key in gaining sympathy for civil rights among Whites. Then, in June, NAACP secretary Medgar Evers was murdered outside his Mississippi home. Just eighteen days after the March on Washington, on September 15, 1963, one of the most heartbreaking incidents of the decade would happen: four little girls died in the 16th Street Baptist Church bombing in Birmingham. The girls were close to the age I'd been the day I witnessed a woman thrown from the bus and first began to understand how upside-down this world is.

My parents had much evidence for their fears.

Still, I fumed that I could not march, but I watched the historic march on television all day. I witnessed from afar the throngs of 250,000 Black Americans and activists of every color. I heard the music of the movement. The sound of Dr. King's voice, a thunderous voice rising and falling with the soul of a sermon, the rhythm of a river, echoing off the marble memorial to President Abraham Lincoln who set the enslaved free, came through the speakers loud and clear.

When I enrolled at Hampton Institute the next summer, in 1964, after a dull and tortuous freshman year at Jersey City State College, I found at last the things I'd been searching for: community, friends, men to date, women role models to emulate, career direction, and—in the awakening that surprised me most—Africa.

Daddy took a job at Hampton, and it was not a difficult decision for me to join him there to study French and speech therapy. Daddy mainly taught at Black colleges, because he often had no other choice although he later taught two semesters at SUNY/Plattsburgh. Hampton was founded in 1868 as a school meant to educate newly freed Blacks. It had also welcomed Native Americans and international students from Africa, many of whom returned home to establish schools referred to as "Hampton of Africa." The school's ideals were aligned with Daddy's lifelong pursuits and its successes spoke to the hope of his striving. One of the top-ranked historically Black colleges (called HBCUs), part of the "Black Ivy League" along with Fisk, Howard, and the Atlanta University system, Hampton had credentials. Students matriculated from Hampton and went on to top-notch graduate schools. Many students were tracked for Cornell University or another Ivy League university.

Rustic brick buildings overlooked the Chesapeake Bay, where you could see boats, white sails spread into the wind, floating by. Clusters of trees dotted the green manicured lawns where students would spread blankets and study in the sun.

The city of Norfolk, Virginia, connected to Hampton city via a tunnel-bridge, offered Norfolk State University and the Naval Station Norfolk base. Nearby were Fort Eustis in Newport News, Fort Monroe in Phoebus and Langley Air Force base. All of this meant there would be many young men who better watch out because I was ready to date.

"I am making up for lost time!" I told Mother when she worried, I was getting too crazy. I had a ball—dating was every bit the fun I'd imagined it would be in high school when I'd watched from the sidelines friends who were old enough to date while I waited to turn sixteen. (The one drawback of skipping grades and working ahead in summer school was that I was always much younger than the other students in my class.) Mother changed her tune when I told her I was in a relationship with an engineer major. She doted and she bragged, for this was every mother's dream: send her daughter to an HBCU and marry her off to a doctor, lawyer, scientist, or engineer. The pinnacle of prestige.

At Hampton I was immediately swept into a wave of Black pride. Two alumni, Flemmie Pansy Kittrell and Samella Sanders Lewis,[1] had done well career wise. Nutritionist Kittrell of class 1928 returned to work at Hampton from 1940–1944 as Dean of Women and head of the Department of Home Economics before founding the Department of Human Ecology at Howard University. From the class of 1945, Lewis became an artist, art historian, and soon-to-be editor and founder of the *International Review of African American Art*. Daddy introduced me to her when they were both teaching at SUNY/Plattsburgh.

From 1919 to 1925, Jessie Fauset was the influential literary editor of *The Crisis*, the official NAACP journal, and the mentor-promoter of Harlem Renaissance poets like Langston Hughes, Countee Cullen, and other aspiring writers. She had been a visiting professor of English at Hampton from September 12, 1949 to January 31, 1950.[2] In 1957–1958, Rosa Parks, the seamstress who had inspired the Montgomery bus boycott, worked as a hostess at the Holly Tree Inn (faculty dining). She and her husband moved to Hampton because she had been fired from her Alabama department store job.

Because of its reputation as a training academy for the Black élite, Hampton enjoyed an easy relationship with its White neighbors, many of whom would come to campus for jazz concerts, the theater, or dance programs.

While I was taking summer classes, the Civil Rights Act was passed by the U.S. Congress and Senate on July 2, 1964. It did not matter the vote was not unanimous. What mattered was that President Lyndon Johnson had met with the civil rights leaders and signed the bill to outlaw discrimination against racial, ethnic, national, and religious minorities and women. It finally allowed Black people the right to vote, fully acknowledging them as human beings and citizens. For once, July 4, the celebration of America's freedom and independence, didn't feel as ironic for Black folks as it had before. Dr. King stood directly behind President Johnson as he signed the Act into law. It was an exciting moment in history, and at first, I didn't notice who was missing.

Who impacted me the most that summer of 1964 was Mrs. Fannie Lou Hamer and her riveting speech! She proved to America at large that there was much left to be done.

A woman with only a sixth-grade education, the youngest of twenty children, a plantation sharecropper since she was a mere six years old, no stranger to poverty, who called the soil of what was considered the most racist area of the country—Mississippi Delta—home, she didn't let those hurdles deter her from the freedom fight. Her personal story bolstered her message.

The phrase she would be most known for is one that echoed the sentiments of Rosa Parks who would not give up her seat because she, like everyone else on that Alabama bus, was tired: "All my life I've been sick and tired," Mrs. Hamer said. "Now I'm sick and tired of being sick and tired."[3] You could feel it when she said it—the weight of discrimination and hardship. It was a collective tired that every Black American felt.

In an effort to focus greater national attention on voting discrimination, Mrs. Hamer co-founded the Mississippi Freedom Democratic Party (MFDP). This new party sent a delegation, including Mrs. Hamer, to the Democratic National Convention (DNC) in Atlantic City (just south of my hometown Jersey City). Mrs. Hamer spoke to the Credentials Committee of the convention about the injustices that allowed an all-White male delegation to be seated from the state of Mississippi, using her personal testimony to highlight the sufferings and discrimination against Black voters in the South.[4] Her testimony aired on national television, on all the major networks (ABC, CBS, NBC). All of America heard of the struggle in Mississippi's Delta.

Since summer school had ended at Hampton, Daddy and I had driven up to Jersey to be with the rest of the family until the fall semester started. For days the phone would ring and ring, as everybody called everybody to make sure everybody would watch Mrs. Hamer. That Saturday, on August 22, all of us—Mother, Daddy, Grandma, Papa, Toni, the boys, and I—sat impatiently in front of the television. We had rushed through dinner. Mrs. Hamer's upcoming speech was all we could talk about. White society said Mrs. Hamer was supposed to be nothing—poor, Black, and female—but to us she was everything. We said, "Go ahead, Fannie *Lou!*"

Mrs. Hamer's voice was calm, clear, and determined. In her Mississippian drawl, she recounted her vicious beating the prior June at the hands of two Black male prisoners and a White policeman in a jail in Winona, Mississippi. Simple, unadorned statements. She told of the white officers' beatings, then how the officers ordered Black prisoners to beat her.

Not once did her voice break or her eyes water. But my family and I, we felt her suffering. When Mrs. Hamer described her beatings from Black men, I recoiled as though someone had whipped me. The very idea racism can turn the oppressed into the oppressor, seemed to me, the most vicious part. Imagine the pain! Her own people doling out lashes, obeying the orders of White policemen. How did she recover from these Black men's betrayal, cowardice, self-hatred, and fear?

On a personal level, when we were robbed by those Congolese thieves in 1961, I rationalized that they had seen us as rich Americans, not as one of them. I couldn't conceive of Mrs. Hamer's capacity to forgive the men, the same ones who were suffering at the hands of Whites as she had. How ironic. She was a foot soldier for the Student Non-Violent Coordinating Committee (SNCC) to help Black women, men, and children in her home state to become first class citizens. "Hate will destroy you,"[5] Mrs. Hamer warned. During her struggle to love the Whites who had abused her, she did likewise for the Black male prisoners. Her words channeled a later poem by Maya Angelou, "Still I Rise," in which she stated, "You may trod me in the very dirt / But still, like air, I rise.[6]

We learned later Mrs. Hamer had lost an eye and suffered from permanent kidney damage from the incident. But she had risen up and continued working to register people to vote. And she was here right now, her sonorous voice reaching through a million television screens.

Sitting next to my parents, sister, and brothers, I thought of the sufferings of my own family. Both my parents knew the holes discrimination could leave in a heart. In 1928, Edward Miles, my maternal grandfather, was murdered by White policemen outside of Richmond. He hadn't committed a crime; he was just in the wrong place at the wrong time. The police said, "A mistaken identity." His violent death left a void in my mother. She, a one-year-old baby, would never know her father, feel his touch, hear his voice, or see him smile. Her mother, Josephine Miles, was left a widow with five children. Her work as a maid at menial wage did not pay the mounting bills. With reluctance, she sent her children to live with her older siblings in Virginia and New Jersey until she remarried.

My paternal grandfather, Cornelius "Neal" Berrian, was making a good living on construction sites in Miami, Florida, until some Whites in the area began to notice his and other Black men's material gain and set up Jim Crow trade unions. Like many others during the Great Migration in the 1930s, Neal packed up his wife Florence and three children. They migrated to Jersey City, New Jersey. He preferred the slow pace and greenery in Jersey to the fast paced and crowded streets of Harlem, where some of his siblings had relocated. He worked for many years for Gypsum, a large manufacturing plant, until a crane fell on his leg. Suffering from a badly broken leg that took forever to heal, Neal was cast out like a rag doll, without workman's compensation or health benefits. His life as a skilled laborer was over. Labeled a "cripple," he could only find a job as a night watchman for a cigarette factory.

When his only son, my father Harry Cornelius Berrian, joined the USMM/ Coast Guard during World War II, he was sent for training to Sheepshead Bay at the eastern tip of Brooklyn, New York. While stationed there, he found out that "Albert Harry Berrian" was listed on his Miami-issued birth certificate. From then on, he was known as "Bubba" by his family, "Harry" by his elementary and high school classmates, and "Al" by soldiers and other adults. Because he was involved in an altercation with a White officer who had called him a "nigger," my father was thrown into the brig. He too had experienced the viciousness of racism first hand.

Now my father and his family, safely in the den of our Jersey City home, watched Mrs. Hamer speak deliverance. At the end of her testimony, she asked, "Is this America, the land of the free and brave?"

It was a moment of historic witness. A woman's voice. How many times had we watched on television news coverage of a sit in, a march, a speech by a civil rights activist, and how many of those times was a woman featured?

I recognized who had been missing in the scene of President Johnson and Dr. King at the signing of the Civil Rights Act. Where were all the women?

I had always had plenty of strong Black women to emulate in my life—my own mother, my grandmothers, my godmother, and my aunts. But right then, while watching a woman give a rousing testimony on a national stage, my pride in Mrs. Hamer and Black womanhood soared.

Mrs. Hamer's work and the national attention it garnered helped to pave the way to the Voting Rights Act which was passed the next year in 1965, banning discriminatory voting practices that had blocked Blacks, particularly in the South, from voting. I wanted to pump my fist in the sky, dance in victory for Fannie Lou Hamer, Blacks, women, and for us all. Although the Act was most important in Southern states where literacy tests essentially barred uneducated Blacks from voting, I, then seventeen years old, had neither voted nor been barred by a literacy test. This legislation was a triumph. On August 6, 1965, when President Johnson officially signed the Voting Rights Act, it was not only Dr. King at his side; Mrs. Rosa Parks was there, too. Finally, a current woman activist was being recognized on the same plane as the men.

Three years later, in 1968, to standing-room applause, Mrs. Hamer triumphantly attended the DNC in Chicago as an official, seated delegate of Mississippi: the first woman since the Reconstruction period after the Civil War and the first ever Black.

Although the Civil Rights Movement was in full flux, Hampton itself was like the eye of a hurricane, a calm amid the storm. I knew what was going on out there—the civil rights leaders came to speak at Hampton. Students were involved outside the campus; for example, around lunchtime on February 11, 1960, twenty to thirty Hampton students (inspired by the four students who organized a sit-in at Woolworth in Greensboro, North Carolina, ten days prior) staged a sit-in at the F. W. Woolworth on Queen Street.[7] They were the first in Virginia to stage a lunch counter sit-in to protest the business' refusal to serve Blacks and Whites equally. The next day they visited Langley Sweet Shop, West End Pharmacy and C & L Confectionery. Next, in March, their protests in downtown Newport News[8] and Hampton led to the integration of lunch counters in the months that followed.

Almost a year later, on February 1, 1961, fifteen students refused to climb the stairs to the Lee Theatre's balcony. Instead, they sat in seats in the "Whites-only" section to watch the movie. All of them were arrested; eleven were convicted of trespassing and fined.[9] But the Virginia Supreme Court reversed their convictions in 1962 on a technicality. In 1964, a federal law was passed to integrate movie theaters and other public spaces.[10] Before the students marched downtown, President Jerome Holland of Hampton Institute called the mayor, who instructed the police to protect the students.

But the Hampton campus remained quiet. Students were glad to be there, proud to be part of this place. For some, it was a special relief to attend a Black school, when much of their prior educational experience, like mine, had been in majority-White schools. There was, of course, some division, but in general everybody got along. Those of us from the "North," meaning Philly, Jersey, New York, and D.C., were the *wow* folks, the urban radicals. We were more apt to follow Malcolm X and the Black Panthers instead of, or along with, Dr. King. There was a touch of that "country folk" stigma for those from the South, North Carolina on down, where Jim Crow segregation ruled, but still there was an underlying sense of solidarity, of striving in our various ways for a common purpose as Black folks. We also shared

Hampton with a significant number of students from Africa and from the Caribbean. The common attire spoke to the diasporic fabric that was part of us and that we were part of the tapestry: Afros and dashikis. Black pride and Africa awareness celebrated at once. This was our silent song: We believed everybody should belong.

During a gym class, Queenie, a Bahamian from Nassau, and her room-mate Florence, a Black American from Hyattsville, Maryland, introduced themselves and welcomed me to the campus. They invited me to their dorm to meet Jean, a Florida native, and the North Carolinian LaVerne. A week or so later, I befriended Lois, who had recently arrived from Sierra Leone. These women were to become my life-long friends, making moments of gladness even brighter and disappointments less grim.

My friend circle now spanned oceans of experience and cultures, and at last I didn't feel like an outsider—the forlorn high school kid who'd missed out on the experience of lasting friendship as my family moved again and again and as I enrolled in one school after another.

Sometimes the world outside Hampton beckoned us to leave campus, instead of reading in the newspapers or witnessing by means of television the racial strife, to join the fight more visibly. Many students traveled to march with Dr. King in the third and final march from Selma to Montgomery, Alabama, in 1965. Again, I was discouraged by Daddy not to go because of the threat of impending violence.

On Sunday, March 7, 1965, the ABC network interrupted its showing of the movie *Judgment at Nuremburg,* about the Nazi war crimes and the Holocaust, to show live footage of violence in Selma, Alabama. To become participants in a march to be known as "Bloody Sunday," some 600 people began a fifty-four-mile march from Selma to Montgomery. After they crossed the Edmund Pettus Bridge, they were beaten by state troopers. I had a friend and classmate from Selma who mourned for her sister, who had been hit with a billy club and choked by tear gas, along with other protesters. The force of the state trooper's billy club slammed her sister's body against a building, her head striking the brick, leaving a gash and a concussion. Troopers then hit her with a whip before she was taken to the jail. Other victims suffered fractures of ribs, heads, arms, and legs. My friend was beside herself, hysterical, wor-ried her sister would die in jail, and that her brain would begin bleeding and the police officers would ignore her cries. This was the reality down South: when you protested you risked your job, your body, and your health. Like Fannie Lou Hamer, her sister was wrongfully jailed and lashed to the brink of death.

Bloodied from a possible skull fracture, John Lewis of the Student Nonviolent Coordinating Committee, stated, "I don't see how President Johnson can send troops to Vietnam. I don't see how he can send troops to the Congo. I don't see how he can send troops to Africa and can't send troops to Selma, Alabama."[11] His words chimed like bells of truth—our country was more apt to send armed guards in the name of protection and liberty and democracy to other countries, when Americans were in need of protection from their fellow citizens at home.

When I thought again about the unabashed cruelty Mrs. Hamer experienced, the way her body was vandalized, I couldn't help but imagine the bruises and blood on her back, her legs. I had to bear witness. To see and to imagine was to honor, to acknowledge, to empathize with Fannie Lou Hamer. A pledge to keep up the fight, even when I didn't witness it first-hand.

My friend from Selma could not study while she knew her sister was in jail; she could not eat; she could not sleep.

Thankfully, her sister, though deeply injured, recovered.

I do not know if she ever marched again.

NOTES

1. Read C.A. de Gregory," Jacqueline E. Lawton's 'The Hampton Years' Features HBCU Artists," *HBCUStory*, May 15, 2013. http://www.hbcustory,word press.com/2013/05/15/ jacqueline-lawtons-the-hampton-years-features-black-artists-biggers-and-lewis. Lawton's "The Hampton Years" is a play based on the relationship of the Austrian Jewish Viktor Lowenfeld, a former professor of art and psychology at Hampton Institute, and his most-famous students John Biggers and Samella Lewis.

2. Sylvester, *Jessie Redmon Fauset*, 65.

3. Fannie Lou Hamer, "I'm Sick and Tired of Being Sick and Tired, Speech Delivered with Malcolm X at the Williams Institutional CME Church, Harlem, New York, December 20, 1964," in *The Speeches of Fannie Lou Hamer: To Tell It Like It Is*, edited by Maegen Brooks and Daris V. Houck (Jackson, MS: University Press of Mississippi, 2011), 62.

4. Fannie Lou Hamer, "Testimony Before the Credentials Committee at the Democratic National Convention, Atlantic City, New Jersey, August 22, 1964," in *The Speeches of Fannie Lou Hamer*, 42–45.

5. Fannie Lou Hamer, "We're on Our Way: Speech Delivered at a Mass Meeting in Indianola, Mississippi, September 1964," in *The Speeches of Fannie Lou Hamer*, 54.

6. Maya Angelou, "Still I Rise," in *And Still I Rise* (New York: Random House, 1978), 41.

7. Denise M. Watson, "Lunch Counter Sit-Ins: 50 Years Later," *The Virginian Pilot*, February 15, 2010. http://www.pilotonline.com/life/vp-at-lunch-counter-sitins-50-years-later-20200209-ia6qhzmpmbci3cp3b6suvosdiq-story.html.

8. Mark St. John Erickson, "With Resistance," *Daily Press*, May9, 2004. http://www.dailypress com/dailypressdp.brown09-story.html.

9. Sean Somerville, "Whites Only: Sit-Ins Yield Civil Rights Victory," *Daily Press*, January 16, 1989. http://www.dailypress.com/news/dp-xpm-19890116-on-16 -8901160049-story.html.

10. Ibid.

11. Roy Reed, "Alabama Police Use Gas and Clubs to Rout Negroes," *New York Times*, March 8, 1965, 1; 20.

Chapter 9

History and *Négritude* in the Flesh

The summer of my junior year, Hampton offered its first African history class, and I signed up, not knowing I was signing up for a class that would change everything. The professor was a man from Nigeria of Yoruba heritage whose name I do not recall. Like some of Hampton's students, he sported an Afro and dashikis. He was short in stature, but the intensity of his passion filled the room. His storytelling skills brought me back to the days when my siblings and I sat enraptured by Adeboye's tales of his homeland. The first day of class the professor asked what we, the students, knew about Africa, if we had any personal experience there.

I raised my hand.

"My family lived in the Congo when I was fourteen, in 1961, for a year," I said.

The teacher looked surprised, and instead of moving on to the next raised hand, he said, "Near the time Patrice Lumumba was assassinated, correct?"

I told him yes, that my father had arrived just after the event and witnessed a mourning parade.

The professor lingered on my story, fascinated, asking a few other questions before requesting I stay after class to talk. Though he had never been to the Congo, he had been a great admirer of Lumumba and was excited to meet someone who had lived in the Congo the year after he died. When the Congo had come *so close* to having strong leadership from a native Congolese who loved his country, who could have done so much, who could have saved the people not only from Belgian rule but also prevented the terror that befell them when Mobutu took power. So much promise, all gone.

Every class period this dynamic teacher brought history alive, describing the various African nations and how their societies functioned before European "discoverers" came in, before the slave trade began, before colonialism took hold. He showed us pictures from colonial Nigeria. Described his own village. These were people who had always had sophisticated culture and language and rich ways of life. I knew these things, but had never heard them preached in an educational setting before. That made African history more striking, more authoritative.

In one lecture the professor recounted Belgian King Léopold II's sordid deeds in the Congo. How the Congolese workers risked severe beatings, murder, or losing their right hands. To provide proof to their superiors of the number of Congolese killed or punished, Belgian officials would send to their superiors the chopped-off hands of the Congolese.

I stopped taking notes and nearly fell out of my chair. At once I had a flashback: a vision of a dusty landscape whirring by from a moving car. A Congolese village. Driving through the villages with my family, five years before, the three men I saw with their right hands missing. I had witnessed the result of this victimization my professor described. Wrists that ended in stumps. The three elderly men I had seen must have worked the rubber trees.

The reality of the whole thing hit me like a wall of hurt. I wanted to cry for the hands. I remembered seeing those men and how I hadn't thought much of their disfigurement at the time, only that it was strange and sad and I hoped the hands hadn't been removed because of a contagious disease I could catch. But now that scene came back to me with razor-edge clarity. I could see those wrists with no hands, for they had never left me. Florence reached over and asked if I was all right.

I stayed after class and told my story to the professor. He was again impressed I had actually seen people who were victimized by the Belgian regime, a story so often suppressed. He validated my experience, and once I started recounting memories—all those moments from the year in the Congo I hadn't quite unraveled or made sense of yet, the stories nobody had wanted to hear when we returned—something released inside of me. Something significant enough to affect the course of my life.

That history class sealed it, the career path I wanted to pursue. It was so good, one of those classes where you never know what time it is or how long before class was over because time itself didn't matter when you gave such focused energy and received so much in return. I felt like I had lost a friend when the semester ended. The class not only expanded my knowledge, but it nudged me to reflect on my own Black American history. Memory upon memory returned; I now saw with the clarity and context puzzling and disturbing scenes I had not understood while I was in the Congo as a young teenager.

The class was life affirming and life changing. It ignited a passion in my friend Florence, too. She went on to study for a PhD in African history at UCLA with a Nigerian advisor. The class had been much more stimulating than my speech therapy classes. I wished I could major in African history, but it wasn't an option. However, I realized my French major could allow me to study Africa more—since so much of African colonial history was tied to French literature and vice versa.

I dropped speech therapy as one of my majors and held onto French, and I was thrilled when my French classes introduced me to French Caribbean and French African literature and music. Though I didn't fully realize it yet, I craved the written words of my people, and the words of the Africana diaspora, even if they weren't necessarily American. (There were no Black American literature classes yet at Hampton, and all the reading of Black American authors I had done had happened only on occasion and always on the side.) Perhaps, in its own small way, my studies provided an avenue for me to participate in the civil rights revolution, a way to be comfortable and to excel—and where there was no threat of bodily harm.

As I continued to study French, there was no way to avoid taking classes with Daddy. I took three. We fought like dogs. He pushed me so hard in my work inside and outside the classroom that one day my classmates, unbeknownst to me, approached him to ask why he picked on me so much and to suggest he be fairer. But he knew me and knew I responded to being pushed. That kind of approach wouldn't fly with Toni or my brothers, but for me it did. He would not accept my papers if they were not footnoted adequately. For him, meticulous research of the caliber most students weren't expected to produce until graduate school was expected of me. After all, he was the dean and former chair of the Department of Foreign Languages. Although he challenged all his students, his standards were highest for me.

It was in one of Daddy's French classes where I first learned about *négritude*, other than hearing my father talk to his friends in the Congo and Richard Long at Hampton about the movement. How three Black intellectuals from French colonies—Léon-Gontran Damas from French Guyane, Aimé Césaire from Martinique, and Léopold Sédar Senghor of Senegal—came together in the mid-1930s and started a literary movement. While living in Paris on university scholarships (they were being educated to return home and work as administrators for the French), they realized the impact of their countries' colonization, the way they had assimilated and privileged French culture over their own African and Caribbean identities. They were the "talented tenth" in their own countries, and when they arrived in France, they were shocked by the way people treated them: they were seen as simply Black and, therefore, second class. They were called *nègre*—a derogatory term much like "nigger" in the United States. Called out of their skin like that, they grasped for an identity that was not tied to France, and that's when they realized that their own cultures had been erased.

They realized they knew more about what it meant to be French than what it meant to be African or Caribbean. All the trappings of social advancement for them had required assimilation. For example, in French Guyane only the educated spoke French while the uneducated spoke Creole, and yet French provided the only way to gain access to literature. French was the only language allowed at school. The French policy had been to supply only basic primary education for its colonial subjects, and only limited secondary schooling, which came with steep tuition fees for attendees. Schools offered knowledge exclusively on the history of France, the geography of France, the weather of France, the government of France, the language of France, the literature of France, the people of France, and so on. Damas lamented once that he had been more familiar with the names of plants growing in France than with those growing in his own backyard.

Undoubtedly, there were many children in French Guyane, Senegal, and Martinique, who, like myself at age ten, wrote and illustrated stories of people without the faces colored in. White people. They too drew White people: the only people they associated with printed stories, with school; the only people they ever learned about. Even in a society, unlike the United States, where the majority of people were Black and looked like them. That was the power of colonial rule. It had so permeated their psyche that they hadn't even realized it.

The three Black friends in France launched a crusade to uncover the cultures that had been hidden from them—their own cultures. They created a new literary expression, words radiant with a new life and a new language. Césaire came up with a name for their quest: *la négritude*, the study of Blackness.

In class, we read Damas's poetry collection *Pigments*, and I swooned with the cadence of his words. Repetition. Simple but direct, to the point, and piercingly beautiful. Poems that expressed anguish and urgency, a subjugated voice seeking to be heard. The poem "Hocquet" (Hiccups) conjures the voice of Damas' mother, who was of mixed ancestry and fully assimilated into French culture, the mark of "élite society" in French Guyane. Her voice, ironically, merges with the oppressor's when she dismisses her son's preference for a banjo or a guitar instead of a violin, ending with "They are not for *colored people* / Leave them to the *black* folks!"[1]

The rhythm of *négritude* verse was inspired by the jazz-like quality of Harlem Renaissance poetry—all three *négritude* intellectuals felt connected to the experience of Black Americans. When they read aloud the original English and French translations of Langston Hughes's "The Weary Blues" and Sterling Brown's "Strong Men," they loved the sounds, the modulation, and the themes. (Césaire even obtained a Diplôme d'Étude Supérieure with a thesis on the South in Black American poetry at L'École Normale

Supérieure.) It felt like hearing music when I read Damas's poetry, music like the kind Mother would blast through the house while she cleaned, or when she and Daddy would dance together spontaneously in the kitchen or living room. Ella Fitzgerald, Sarah Vaughan, Sam Cooke, or Arthur Prysock. Damas's words syncopated across the page, like words marching down a staircase. Poems that begged to be read to a beat. "Ils sont venus ce soir" [They Came That Night] evokes the tom-tom beats of an African storytelling ceremony that gets interrupted when a slave trader suddenly appears on the path. His presence escalates the drum rhythm to "the frenzy of hands/ the frenzy of statue feet,"[2] resulting in the storyteller's death and that of many others.

I thought of the beats I'd heard in Léo, rising from the valley in the night. Sounds were coming back to me. My African history class cultivated understanding and my own experience provided context. *Négritude* poetry, in a way, fused the two.

I learned Damas's poetry sparked a revolution, like a freedom march. Translated into several African languages, other colonized people read it and felt propelled to action. Provoked by his volume *Pigments,* the Baoulé people of la Côte d'Ivoire refused to serve in the French army against Germany in 1939. In turn, French authorities banned *Pigments.*[3] They seized and destroyed printed copies, and police broke into Damas' apartment to search for more. I could picture those police hunting down poetry, the same kind of police who hosed down marchers in the street.

Léopold Senghor was the first president of Senegal elected after independence from France in 1960, the same year of Patrice Lumumba's brief incumbency as prime minister of the newly freed Congo.

I was fascinated by how Black expression of the 1920s and 1930s—Harlem Renaissance music and literature in the States—influenced these African and African Caribbean scholars across the globe, and how their creative work, in turn, spoke to civil rights happening three decades later in the United States. The *négritude* poets were determined to find an influence that was *not* a European colonizer, and they chose the voices of Black Americans. They could have sought literature from Africa itself, yet they felt a special connection to the Black experience in America. A place where Blacks had been enslaved and were mightily outnumbered by their oppressors.

Some part of me recognized how this Black expressionism touched the larger world, even people who might not have read poetry by Léon Damas or Langston Hughes or Black artists from this time period. The art cracked open society in a way that allowed Fannie Lou Hamer in the South to speak. The Harlem Renaissance first opened up new ideas about identity and new possibilities for how Black people could have a role and fit into society, and that ushered in the Zeitgeist of protest. Here I was in the midst of this protest movement, the 1960s, and had come upon *négritude*. Words and art moved mountains.

What really clenched it for me, I believe, was my experience living in the Congo. I knew—we all knew—how momentous the Civil Rights Movement was, even as we were living it, but because I could clearly see my recent past knit within both an historical movement and a current movement, I could feel those waves of influence converge in my bones.

One day I encountered the poetry in the flesh. I returned home from class to the house I was sharing with my parents and siblings, to see a man sitting on the couch in the living room being served coffee by Mother. Daddy and he rose as I entered. The man, wearing an expensive-looking suit and tie, was very slight next to Daddy, and he was smoking a cigarette. Since Mother normally forbid smoking, the visitor had to be *very important* to be allowed to pollute her living room.

"Brenda, *fais la connaissance de Monsieur Damas*," [Brenda, Meet Mr. Damas] Daddy said..

I responded in French, automatically, before the words had set in and I realized who was before me. Léon-Gontran Damas! In person, here in my own house. I couldn't believe it. Damas was so short—maybe an inch or so taller than me. "We are doing a book," he said in French, motioning to Daddy. It was the book Daddy had been working on, along with his colleague Richard Long for a year now, a collection of essays from various authors on *négritude*.

Damas then told me he was a poet. I smiled at his humility. I told him I knew all about his poetry. In fact, I had recently decided I wanted to do a project on *Pigments*. He nodded and spoke approvals, obviously pleased. How pleasant he is in person, I thought. His skin was brown, not a deep dark brown like some of my friends from Africa or the Caribbean, and I remembered he was considered a "mulatto" in French Guyane with his Amerindian, White, and Black heritages.

I did not know Daddy was friends with Damas, but then again Daddy knew a lot of movers and shakers. It was like he had a backstage pass to any event involving Black intellectuals, here and in Africa. (Shortly after that, I discovered he was friends with Mercer Cook, the first Black American U.S. ambassador to Senegal.) Daddy and Richard Long were completing the book on *négritude* and bringing Damas to campus as part of Hampton's centennial celebration. I took French language classes with Professor Long. He and Damas were going to attend the First World Festival of Negro Arts in Senegal, that year, in 1966.

Daddy said Damas would be giving a speech about *négritude* and his poetry on campus that week.

Damas' presentation repudiated the French assimilation policy. Afterward, I re-read sections of Césaire's book-length poem *Cahier d'un retour au pays natal* (*Notes on the Return to the Native Land*) in which he calls upon Blacks to take pride in their race. He writes about his island (Martinique) and the sufferings of his people; recalls Toussaint Louverture's imprisonment during his fight for Haiti's independence; imagines a nostalgic African past; expresses his anger about the lies and crimes that the West had perpetuated against the Black race; proclaims his *négritude*; and voices his refusal to hate.

One section that spoke to me, in particular, reminded me of my negative thinking about the drumbeats in the Congo. Césaire had observed a weary "Negro as big as an ape,"[4] who tried to be very small on a trolley seat in Paris. When Césaire, the *élite* student-poet, noted how the French were shifting away from the Black man and felt his own inclination to move away too, he suddenly realized that the French saw him and the working-class man across from him through the same lens. Disgusted with his own attitude, Césaire called upon *négritude* to deliver him from being a man of hate to one of love, for no race has the monopoly on beauty, strength, or intelligence.

At last, I found words that spoke to the story I knew. And I found a field of study I knew I'd be truly vested in long term. I would become a scholar of French African and French Caribbean culture, music, and literature. I wanted to do more than witness now—I wanted to *participate* in the intellectual discourse, produce work of my own that would speak to the art, and experience that felt so rich to me. I would go to graduate school to get a master's degree and, maybe, even a PhD, too.

Meanwhile, as I was soaking in history and verse, I was falling in love with a man named David from Sierra Leone. Lois, my Sierra Leonean friend, introduced me to David at a function that was held in a Catholic church near Hampton's campus. Chocolate brown, lean, and nearly six feet tall, David flashed me a smile that reached his eyes.

We were a match knit in the ocean of our souls, and we wanted to get married. We inspired each other, made each other laugh, and taught each other. He shared my interest in the *négritude* movement; he too knew what it was to live under colonial rule; and he could feel those poems in his bones. He appreciated my stories of living in the Congo; Sierra Leone had gained independence from Britain in 1961, just a year after the Congo had wrested power from Belgium.

He finished his education before me and wanted to take me home to Sierra Leone with him. He was an engineer and wanted to build roads and bridges and improve the overall infrastructure of his country. I wanted to go, too, and after completing my French degree I was ready to say "I do" and jump the next plane to Africa. Hampton had reignited and bolstered my love for the continent, and what better circumstances to return to it than with a heart brimming with love? To marry David and live with him in Sierra Leone would feel like being an African princess. I laughed at the thought of my childhood fantasy.

I remembered the clean, modern city of Léopoldville, where I'd lived with my family six years prior and could easily envision myself in Sierra Leone. But when David and I approached my parents to discuss the details of our impending future, they reined us back to reality.

Daddy told me it would *not* be like our time in Léopoldville. He had recently visited Freetown, the capital of Sierra Leone, on a fact-finding mission because Hampton supported some secondary schools there. He found the living conditions sub-par. Like most West African nations and cities, the city of Freetown was not modernized. Léo had been an exception. I would likely be living in isolated areas as David would be working on building access to those areas.

I neither spoke Mende (David's birth language) nor Krio (the language of Freetown). Plus, I was only twenty-one years old and wanted to continue my education.

With a heavy heart, I told David I could not go to Sierra Leone with him. He said we should break up, then, as it didn't make sense to continue seeing each other if we wouldn't get married. I begged him to stay in the United States so we could be together. He replied that skilled Africans ought to go home. (Today I agree with him.) Neither one of us really wanted to say goodbye. We parted ways but not before making a pact: If one of us married someone else, we would call or write the other to meet the bride or groom.

My heart dipped to its deepest valley when, two years later, he called me from New York to meet him and his wife-to-be.

I completed a master's degree in French at Hampton while working full-time as a French Resource Teacher for the Newport News Public School System. During the 1967–1969 school years I traveled by car to four schools a day: two Black elementary schools in the morning and two White middle schools in the afternoon. The job involved teaching seventh grade French and supervising the fourth to sixth-grade teachers, who had attended workshops to teach French. The desegregation of schools in the Hampton Roads area did not occur without some bumps in the road. In September 1961, fifteen-year-old Robert Rice, son of a Hampton Institute professor arrived at the all-White Hampton High School. After a few heckles, he was permitted to enroll by the placement board.[5] The desegregation of the Hampton schools occurred in 1966. A full five years later, the Newport News schools were integrated in 1971.

Teaching in the schools kept me busy, and I didn't mind being so busy. I was happy to be making some real money at last, and the job kept me from thinking about David and the what-if of our future that did not exist anymore. I knew I'd be continuing my education at some point after the master's, for now that I'd turned down marriage and a life in Sierra Leone, I was even more motivated to go on.

Then, just before I graduated from Hampton with my master's, Martin Luther King, Jr. was assassinated. The country mourned. All the progress of the last decade felt suspended in the balance.

Former president of Morehouse College, another historically Black college, Dr. Benjamin E. Mays delivered the benediction for the program at the 1963 March on Washington and the eulogy at Dr. King's 1968 funeral. Mays had known King since he was a student at Morehouse. At the annual fall convocation, in September 1968, Dr. Mays gave the keynote address for the dedication of the newly constructed Social Sciences building of Hampton Institute as the Martin Luther King Hall.

Dr. King had been selected as Hampton's graduation commencement speaker that year, and I had looked forward to seeing him in person at last. Instead, U.S. Senator Edward W. Brooke III of Massachusetts gave the commencement speech. Senator Brooke was the first elected Black American Attorney General of any state in American history and the first Black American elected to the Senate by popular vote. He advocated against discrimination in housing and co-authored the 1968 Fair Housing Act. His words invoked the spirit and memory of Dr. King and urged us to go out and make change.

My father, the Dean, handed me my diploma.

There was work left to be done in the world, for all of us.

NOTES

1. Léon-Gontran Damas, "Hocquet" (Hiccups), in *The Negritude Poets: An Anthology of Translations from the French*, edited by Ellen Conroy Kennedy (New York: Thunder's Mouth Press, 1975), 50.

2. Léon-Gontran Damas, "Ils sont venus ce soir" (They Came That Night), in *Negritude: Black Poets from Africa and the Caribbean*, edited by Norman Shapiro (New York: October House, 1970), 35.

3. Ellen Conroy Kennedy, "Léon Damas," *The Negritude Poets*, 43.

4. Aimé Césaire, "*Cahier d'un retour au pays natal*" (Notes on a Return to the Native Land)," *The Negritude Poets*, 74.

5. Erickson, "With Resistance."

Chapter 10

A Canadian Fixation

The summer of 1968, I attended classes at l'Université Laval in Québec, Canada, where I befriended three Canadians. Together we watched Neil Armstrong walk on the moon, planting the American flag into the rock and pronouncing "one small step for man, one giant leap for mankind." We naively agreed it shouldn't be long before a woman walked on the moon.

Lucie invited me twice to spend the weekend with her and her family at their summer home on the outskirts of Montréal. Upon meeting me, her aunts found it difficult to accept I was born in the United States, not in an African country. Caribbean people and former slaves from the United States by way of the Underground Railroad had settled in Novia Scotia and Upper Canada during the nineteenth century. It wasn't until the 1960s, after the change to the Immigration Act removing a bias against non-White immigrants, that Jamaicans and Haitians began to settle in the urban centers of the Québec and Ontario provinces. People with dark skin were rare still in the late 1960s, especially in rural areas. The topic of my American identity came up again when my friend Nancy and I were invited to spend the weekend with a friend, I'll call her Olga, on her father's farm near Sherbrooke.

At dusk on a Saturday, Olga, a Polish Canadian, drove the narrow, country roads to a dance hall so the three of us could square dance.

I have always disliked the isolated countryside and will never entertain the idea of living outside a city for a long time. I can enjoy the landscape and think of it as an adventure only as long as I know I'll only be out in the country briefly and can return home within twenty-four hours to the civilization found only in a city. Well, this weekend excursion was my welcome to backwoods Canada.

While Olga parked the car on the grass, we saw light spilling from the wide-open front door and could hear strains of a recognizable country music tune. The three of us got out of the car and walked toward the simply constructed wooden building. I mounted the wooden steps onto the porch while humming along. I peeped inside. Several dozen people were stomping and twirling across the hardwood floor, while the fiddle player, eyes half closed, gyrated his own instrument and tapped his foot.

I walked on in, friends behind me, ready to do-si-do. The music tempo increased, like it does when the dance really gets going. Suddenly, the party stopped: like an E. F. Hutton moment, when the seemingly preoccupied clusters of people immediately quiet at the words "E. F. Hutton says . . ." The dancers and musicians came to a standstill. Every person, one by one, turned toward us while the music slowed and finally stopped. It was so quiet that I could have heard a rat piss on cotton.

I whispered to my friends over my shoulder, "Why has everyone stopped dancing?" They didn't say anything, didn't even look at me, which is when I recognized this frozen moment had suddenly divided us. The room had hushed not because the three of us had entered, but because of me and me alone. I turned back to the crowd.

All those faces were turning pink, the way faces of fair complexion do, and many looked down at the ground. It was a shame I recognized immediately. They were in shock at the sight of my skin, and embarrassed by it. At that moment, I was the only Black spot in an isolated area of Canada, maybe even the only Black person any of them had ever seen. Perhaps this is why I dislike the wide-open countryside so much—all that barren land, ripe for unawareness. But today it was just too funny. I held back laughter as I shouted, in English and French, "Please, do-si-do. I haven't square danced since *the seventh grade!*" I smiled, a confidence in the face of a room of strangers that must have been cultivated through my teaching. Several people returned my smile, and you could feel the relief fill the room. I was no threat to their party, and I was no stranger to their dance.

Some of the dancers began to stomp and dance as the fiddler struck a new tune. Just before I could get to the dance floor, a few people approached me and immediately wanted to know who I was and where I was from. Their astonished, undisguised curiosity reminded me of being in the Congo. I braced myself for the touch of someone's hands in my hair. When I told them that I was from the States, several of them shook their heads and said, "No, where are you *originally* from?" I said again that I was from the States. "But," one woman said carefully, "Where were you originally from before going to the States?" They figured if I was in the Québec province, I had to be from either a French-speaking African nation or a Caribbean island. They didn't want to accept that I was born and raised in the States. It was an encounter outside the national boundary of the States, and once again, like that man on the street in

Léo almost a decade ago, I confused their understanding of who was Black, who was American and, here in Québec, who could speak French.

That night reminded me of prior encounters about my American nationality, but I was not embarrassed or flustered about this negation. I was not tired although I puzzled over why people were so fixated on their own imaginings of culture, appearance, and citizenship that they could not accept a Black woman as American-born. This time *I had changed*, and I didn't mind square dancing in a sea of Whiteness, way out there in the countryside.

Not one bit.

Chapter 11

A Bump in the Road

I was moving right along, making my way as a young professional, master's degree in hand, now teaching children French in Newport News, Virginia. But I wanted more. Literature beckoned me: the *négritude* poets. I missed them like old friends.

I quit my teaching job and began a PhD in French literature, enrolling at Pennsylvania State University (Penn State) and hoping to study the *négritude* poets.

Three years in, I encountered a profound, fundamental resistance to Black art.

One morning at 8 o'clock, my advisor, Professor L (a White American who had modified his name so it was more French-sounding), woke me with an urgent phone call and brusque demand that I come to his office right away.

I got out of bed, showered, brushed my teeth, and arrived at his office wondering what could possibly motivate him to rouse me out of bed that early and speak in such a scolding tone. Was there something I was supposed to do, some form I needed to sign, but had forgotten? Did I somehow miss a deadline?

I tapped on his office door.

"Come in."

He held a paper in his hand, and as I took a seat across from his desk, I saw that the paper, along with red slash marks all over it, had my name on it. It was the one I had just handed in last week on *négritude*.

"You think you're going to get one over on me?" he said. All I could think was that he must think I'd plagiarized! But I would never do such a thing. I knew how to cite sources correctly.

"Professor L, what do you mean?" I tensed, knowing that whatever came next was not good.

"You," he pointed an accusing finger, "come to this prestigious school . . ." He shook his head and his chest heaved. He was clearly outraged—I'd never seen or heard a professor act so unprofessional. "Get one over on me"—not even my own brothers talked to me like that.

"How inconsiderate of you," he continued, "to write about some Black people. There's no such thing as 'notable' Black writers."

I could not respond. I was in shock. How dare he! This meeting was going to get ugly. If he were going to disrespect me and disrespect the literature that way, well, I was ready to de-glove. I dropped the respectful "Professor L" and said,

"Excuse me, but there are *Black* writers, these poets in the 1930s . . ."

"No, I am talking about *real* literature. This is an upstanding institution of higher learning. You can't come in here and think you can get away with writing about some Black people," he said.

"Are you unaware," I said, knowing that right then I had crossed into the boxing ring, "that one of the writers of the constitution for the Fifth Republic of France was *Léopold Senghor!*"

We stared each other down. A thin line of smoke from a dying cigarette in the ashtray on his desk twirled and danced in the air. The cigarette reminded me of Léon Damas smoking in my very own living room, bantering with my father and drinking my mother's coffee. A brilliant, humble musician of words. Unlike this disrespectful fool in front of me.

I was understandingly perplexed because the department recently had hired a young assistant professor who had conducted extensive research in Senegal for his dissertation, which I felt was a boon for the study of African work and thought it evidence that the department valued such academic study.

I could not keep the anger out of my voice as I announced to Professor L that I was leaving. Leaving but not quitting. I would go somewhere else.

"It's going to take me awhile to get out of here but you're not stopping me," I said, and I was probably close to baring my teeth right then. "I am *not* going to write about White writers."

I called Daddy, who did not try to talk me down or scold me for being hot headed. Immediately he began calling on his connections. And connected he was; that was the thing with Black academic circles—everybody knew everybody, and everybody was, for the most part, willing to help everybody. We were part of a community. An unspoken advantage of segregation none of us would fully understand until it suddenly vanished. Within days Daddy had found a solution: I should apply to the Sorbonne in France, where there were several professors in my area who could and would probably be delighted to work with me. Would I be willing to go to France to study? Would I? Yes. If I had to leave my own country to study poets from my own country and the arts movements those poets inspired around the world, so be it. Now I had something to prove. Study abroad would be difficult; and the Sorbonne was known for its rigor. Daddy said it was the "Harvard and Yale of France." After all, Angela Davis had gone there. Famed scholars and authors taught there. But I could hear him smiling. He knew I could and would excel over there.

Chapter 12

Crossing the Ocean à Paris

On July 7, 1971, my plane landed in Paris. It was my first international trip on my own, and I was just visiting the city before going to live in southern France (le Midi) for several weeks. I enrolled in summer school at l'Université d'Aix-Marseille ("Aix" for short) in Aix-en-Provence, a town nineteen miles from Marseille. Before taking the train to Aix, I spent a few days in Paris. I had been dreaming of brick boulevards, *baguettes*, and the sounds of spoken French coming from all directions. It was like a scholar of Egyptian history finally visiting the pyramids of Giza. Moving to France, I was entering the epicenter of my language study and the site where *négritude* was founded. I was going to experience *real* living in Paris.

In the cab on the way from Orly airport to my hotel, I ignored the sounds of news coming from the radio in favor of catching my first sights of Paris at dusk. Lights on the Eiffel Tower were just beginning to glow, illuminating the magnificent spire reaching to the sky. No limits. Then the car lurched and the driver gasped and began to cry. His hands gripped the steering wheel as the car swerved and my first thought was that he was drunk. He started rocking back and forth in his seat, wailing and crying and carrying on like somebody in his family had just died. I was about to get car sick for the first time in my life, jolting around unbuckled in the back.

"*Monsieur! Qu'est-ce qu'il y a?*" [Mister! What is the matter?]

"*Loooeee! Loooeee! Loooeee!*" he said, gasping between sobs. I shouldn't have asked, because he kept saying it, louder and louder. "*Looooeeee!*"

I tried to get him to breathe, to tell me what was going on. He spoke quickly and with his thick accent it sounded like he said, "*Armstoom!*" He pointed to the radio. After several repetitions, my own eyes watching the road more than he was, I finally made out what he was crying over. The newscaster

had just announced the passing of Black American jazz trumpeter and singer
Louis "Satchmo" Armstrong.

Apparently, as would be confirmed later in my experience, the French were
prone to emotional outbursts and a lot of them adored Armstrong. Just about
every French person I was to meet owned a Louis Armstrong record.

Well, I didn't.

The cabbie's blubbering slowed and he seemed to regain control over the
car. Remembering that I was American, he said,

"*Ah, Looeee! Mademoiselle, n'êtes-vous pas triste?*" [Louis. Miss, aren't
you sad?]

"*Non*," I said, and I looked out the window to avoid his shocked expression
in the rearview mirror.

Armstrong's music was hard not to love, sure. That low, gravely expressive voice with a tremulous vibrato that matched those sweet trumpet strains.
Frequent pops of effervescent improvisation made every song a surprise. The
feel-good tunes were effused with warmth.

But Louis Armstrong pandered to Whites in my view. He was wildly
popular among them, gaining notoriety and privilege that most Blacks never
attained. For years he and his All Star band performed before segregated
audiences. In large part, I thought, because he never said anything to upset
his White audiences. He was the wide-eyed, smiling Black with a white
handkerchief that gave credence to the antebellum "happy enslaved man"
propaganda. And people listened to him.

Once, in September 1957, he publicly criticized President Dwight
Eisenhower for not intervening in the Little Rock Nine situation,[1] and within
days those Little Rock students had federal troops' protection when they
entered to desegregate Central High School. But, on the whole, he refused
to use his fame for civil rights, even though we knew, and he knew, how
much difference he could make. He preferred to play his trumpet and sell his
albums. Whenever he appeared on TV, I saw how he acted, his groveling and
buffoonery, and I and my family were quick to change the channel.

So, no, I was not upset that *Loooeee* had passed away, I told the cabbie as
he delivered me, finally, in one piece, to my hotel. I did not elaborate. I was
too tired to puzzle over how to translate "buffoonery" in French. Let him love
his *Loooeee*.

Perhaps my attitude at the time was too sharp and unforgiving as I was still
reeling from Professor L's remarks. He had struck something deep within me
in his denial of Black art, a representative of the liberal educational establish-
ment that, once moved to the underbelly, was as prone to seeking the privilege of studying Black *belles lettres* as quickly as White bus riders tossing off
Black people who sat at the front of the bus. He had made me feel powerless
and small. In the immediate aftermath, I had activated my survival mode

and focused on getting out of there, away from Penn State. Now that I was gone, the layers of realization could settle in. Though Louis Armstrong had bothered me, right now the thought of him struck me in a newly pained way.

So it was that with my first encounter with a French connection to American culture (a Black artist, even) in Paris, I did not react in the way others expected of me.

I was enamored with Paris, the City of Light, and knew I wanted to stay. I returned home after summer school and went right back in October 1972. Transferring my credits from Penn State, I enrolled in the Sorbonne, moved into student housing, and quickly settled into a scene of vigorous learning and fun.

La Cité Internationale Universitaire, the neighborhood of forty student residencies constructed along national boundaries where I lived and walked through, was an oasis of urban life. It was like a preened gated community within the city, beautifully landscaped with benches, well-kept gardens, and pavements so clean you might think someone spent a whole week cleaning them.

After a day of class and homework, my friends, especially Jackie from California and Maryvonne from Martinique, and I would have *un pot*—a drink of tea or coffee—while enjoying the sunset on a café terrace in the Latin Quarter. Then we would stroll the busy rue des Écoles to the *Présence Africaine*[2] (meaning "African presence") bookstore for a reading. Dedicated to the art and literature of the African diaspora, the bookstore hosted readings by published and aspiring artists. It also housed a notable literary press that published books on culture and identity, and was supported in part by the French and various African governments.

In the cramped space overflowing with books and young intellectuals in dark leather jackets, we would hear poets recite their work. The 1970s were a time for poetry. Some who attended fancied themselves poets, too. Going to hear poetry was the thing to do. I was surprised how often Black writers from the United States performed in France. There weren't many Black residents in the country at all! Yet Black poets were valued and their work celebrated just as much as others. In contrast to the sentiments from Professor L with which I had left my country, this embrace of the Black aesthetic repaired my soul. The audience was always multi-colored; art mattered more than skin color. The acceptance bolstered a sense of pride and hope in me that I hadn't known was there. I knew there was no way France was racism-free, of course, but, by all accounts in the space of art and creation no race existed.

Music added to the poetry performance, prompting the listener to nod to the rhythm, to feel it body and soul. Ted Joans read his poetry to jazz be-bop. I remember drum beats punctuating the lines of so many poets like a pulse. I could recite from memory Mari Evans' "I'm a Black Woman" to any clap or shoe tap. A poem about a tall woman as strong as a cypress tree who is "still defying place / and time."[3]

At most readings the Guadeloupean Maryse Condé would be there, dark-skinned, beautiful, fiercely independent, and smart. Maryse and I quickly bonded. She, too, was taking classes at the Sorbonne where she and I would meet at the bookstore. There at the *Présence Africaine* readings, I would glance her way to check her reaction. She would lament not being able to see her three daughters, who were living with her estranged Guinean husband's friends in Abidjan, Côte d'Ivoire. Maryse worked at *Présence Africaine*, shelving books and writing book reviews for the journal. She would tell me she was "scratching out" a little novel or play on the side. (In October 2018, she became the most famous French Caribbean woman writer of her generation to win the New Academy prize in literature, an alternative to the Nobel Prize.)

Maryse was working on her doctorate in comparative literature about Black stereotypes in Caribbean literature. She alternated teaching at the Jussieu and Nanterre campuses of l'Université de Paris. Sometimes she gave a guest lecture for the Dahomean Stanislas Adotevi's Afro-American World class at Jussieu. Both Michel Fabre and I were in the class.

When I was taking Michel Fabre's course on Afro-American literature, I learned "America" included *all* of North America which meant the United States, Canada, Mexico, and the Caribbean. I had never before thought of "America" as "the Americas," which was bigger than just my country. Fabre had recently agreed to be my advisor, only after I had enrolled in Adotevi's class (with him as an unexpected classmate) and proven my mettle first.

A young-looking, slightly built man with thick glasses and a beard, Fabre had a quiet, thoughtful presence. He was famous for his biography of the Black American writer Richard Wright and was probably the first White person I had known to have such encyclopedic knowledge of Black American culture and literature.

Embarrassed, I told him his class was my first ever Black American literature class. I had not formally studied Black American history or literature in my home country, not even at the historically Black university where I had earned my bachelor's and master's degrees. Majoring in Black Studies just had not been an option. My learning had come through attending readings and lectures by writers, historians, critics, and politicians who came to Hampton, and through meeting the many artists and scholars my father had brought home for dinner over the years.

Fabre was surprised. He took off his glasses, rubbed his eyes, and motioned for me to take a seat.

We read Ralph Ellison's *Invisible Man*, and poetry by Dudley Randall, James Emmanuel, and Langston Hughes. Fabre invited the famed James Baldwin to class, to all of our surprise. There Baldwin was, looking just like he did in photos, and just like he did when I had come upon him weeks before. I had seen the familiar face materialize on the street as I was walking back to my dorm. I noticed when there was a Black person around, of course. We were a rare sight indeed. (The only Blacks I'd seen around Paris with any regularity other than students in my classes and at *la cité* were the West African men who swept the streets at dawn.) He strutted along, be-bopping like there was music playing in his head, cigarette dangling, that expressive face with its deep grooves forming parentheses around his eyes and mouth.

"Are you James Baldwin?" I said in full-on American English.

"Yes, I am," he said simply.

"Well, hello! I am Brenda Berrian," I said, as confident as can be. He just laughed. Asked me what I was doing in Paris. I told him I was studying at the Sorbonne, and that I'd registered as a local so I could get cheaper tuition since I was nearly fluent in the language.

"Good for you," he said. "We need more like you."

The day he came to class, Baldwin stood in front of the room, grey-blue scarf swept around his neck, very French and celebrity like, I thought. He took deep, dramatic drags from his cigarette, releasing the smoke slowly upward.

He talked about Malcolm X and his ideas about African nationalism and Black power in the United States. He discussed his work on "Sonny's Blues," and shared stories of writing *Giovanni's Room* and *Go Tell it on the Mountain.* His reading was just like something you would see in *Présence Africaine*, full of heart and drama. Measured silences, tapping on the desk, the rise and fall of his vibrant voice and rolling enunciation all served to transport listeners away from their own lives and into the life of James Baldwin's illustrious, colorful imagination.

Our class was fairly diverse, but no matter what color you were or where you called home, you couldn't help but get caught in the rapture of Baldwin.

Another aspect of Paris I noticed immediately was the aura of protest permeating the air. It was like I had stepped off the plane right back into the American Civil Rights Movement. Here people weren't protesting racial inequality, but everything else, it seemed: The post office went on strike for almost two months. The pharmacies went on strike. Then the grocery stores. The French loved to strike, and the work stoppages had started before I got there.

The first major student-led strike in Paris happened in May 1968, just a few weeks after Dr. King was assassinated in Memphis, and it shook the entire country of France to its feet. Students on the Nanterre campus complained about not being able to circulate freely between the residencies of male and female students. In addition, they protested being taught in hastily built classrooms, where teachers would simply read from their lecture and leave. After 150 of them occupied a building at Nanterre, they took their protest to the Sorbonne in the middle of the Latin Quarter. The strike quickly escalated with the closing of the university campuses and culminating in a battle between

6,000 students and 1,500 *gendarmes.* Then about one million factory workers joined the students.

When I arrived in the 1970s, the change in education as a result of the strikes had started, for the government had passed new bills that changed the structure of the university system. For example, Fabre's classes were small—only thirty or so students—and engaging so organically that I had the impression the interaction had always been that way, that the strike hadn't made a difference. In Fabre's classes, we students could have discussions, even about vexing issues like racism.

Though my graduate-level classes were more diverse ethnically than I had experienced in either my predominantly White primary and secondary schooling and my predominantly Black university experience, they were still mostly White. Maybe 20 percent of the students hailed from the French Caribbean or from former French African colonies. I was the only Black American in the classes I took.

The students were interested and engaged with Harlem poetry, as was I. But I took a more sit-back-and-observe position in the class, fascinated with the way people interpreted the words of my people.

Sometimes students would turn to me to verify the truth of the words. I was suddenly seen as an expert on black feelings, as if there were but one monolithic voice of the Black experience.

"I am not the authority on all things Black in America," I would remind them. "And not all Blacks feel the same way!" In honesty, I was learning right alongside them, too. But also, I would get impatient when the other Black students would ask me details about segregation and discrimination. It baffled me.

Maryvonne, a Martinican friend, and I would laugh about it sometimes, the way our classmates acted like they didn't know what racism was.

Students would ask me what it was like to live with such terrible discrimination. I could understand the question coming from the White students, but when someone from the Caribbean or Africa said it, I was caught off-guard.

"How difficult it must have been—*pauvre Brenda!*" (poor Brenda) said someone whose face was just as dark as mine, in an accent just as non-Parisian as mine.

"They're in denial!" I told Maryvonne, and she agreed.

They would say they had no idea what segregation was like. Just because in their countries they were in the majority, as Blacks outnumbered Whites. That was when I spoke up, to remind folks their lives were also defined by White rule. Racism wasn't just in the United States. It was a strange sort of defense I was holding up to my classmates, though not as a means to say U.S. segregation wasn't the mess that it was, but to remind them they knew it and had probably experienced racism in their countries, too.

When you are sheltered and surrounded by people like yourself, you can avoid the effects of racism for a few years maybe, when you are a child. It had been this way for me, in fact. My family cocooned me. Sheltered me. But I still had to live in this world, and it wasn't long before I saw a woman get thrown from a bus and realized that the world had its own ideas of value and hierarchy that put Blacks at the bottom and Whites at the top.

"But our own teachers are Black," my Caribbean classmates would say, denying the fact their education was ruled by the French. I pointed out how they spoke French at school and Creole at home. Creole was officially outlawed at school. *That* practice was racist.

I reminded them of things I had learned during my research on the *négritude* poets, that until 1964 there was only one university in French West Africa, in Senegal. The French had done it deliberately, made sure there was only a small number of educated Senegalese (39%) and the rest from former French West African colonies.

Maryvonne had told me teachers from mainland France were paid more than teachers in Martinique. And that in order to become a teacher you had to take your final exams on French time, even if that meant you were taking a test at 2 a.m. in the morning in Martinique. I pointed these things out—probably too argumentatively sometimes. (Already I was seen as outgoing and aggressive, especially by the women from Africa.)

"They refuse to acknowledge their suffering!" I complained to Maryse. She agreed. Maryse had no trouble delineating the racism of her home. She described the internal racial prejudice in the Caribbean, how color struck the people were there. This accomplished woman had been ostracized, even in her own family for her dark color.[4] Relatives had told her she wouldn't amount to anything.

She knew the biases within the university system here in Paris. She taught at l'Université de Paris X-Nanterre ("Nanterre" for short) that had been constructed in a bleak shanty town. It was where the administration liked to push the Black students, she said, seven miles on the northwestern edge away from the city center, causing some unspoken, but intentional, segregation. Though there were people from all over the world, including Africa and the Caribbean, in every section of the university, there was an overwhelming Black majority in Nanterre.

Fabre's response to our cut and thrust during class was always very gentle. He would listen intently to whoever was speaking, looking into the students' eyes, no matter if the speaker's comment was, in my view, plain stupid.

"It's funny how we can see things in other countries, but not our own," he would say diplomatically.

Yet, when the French Caribbean students and I began reading *négritude* literature, suddenly they would remember *that* French Caribbean. When

Damas wrote of learning about French geography and history in class but none of French Guyane and Africa, they knew it had been the same for them. Suddenly they had taken a seat on the bus.

To be fair, my classmates, although they were my age, had been in school their whole lives. I had been on my own, teaching, for two years, and it seemed I slipped into "teacher mode" when I felt someone needed some learning about racism, even though I was not the teacher.

I observed the vestiges of living in a racist world in the lives of my friends Jackie and Maryvonne, but I was filled with affection for those women and we were not in class together and so I kept my mouth shut. It was not a generalized racism against Blacks they were dealing with. It was more personal, more hurtful. It had to do with being a Black *woman* and getting her heart broken.

Maryvonne was very pretty and very dark. Smart as a whip: we would help each other with language, speaking and writing in French and English. When she talked about her boyfriends, it was clear to me they treated her poorly. Hardly called. Wouldn't show up for dates. When she showed me photos of her former boyfriends, I noted she preferred to date fair-skinned men. Once she was in a long-term, serious relationship with a man who broke it off with her and within months married a fair-skinned woman. Maryvonne was crushed. They had talked about getting married, and she was hoping he would propose. Instead he had said to her, "You didn't expect me to marry *your* shade, did you?" Some African guys were interested in her, but many others shied away.

During the colonial period, French Caribbeans had worked on behalf of the French government as *administrateurs de colonies* (overseas colonial administrators) and after independence as *coopérants* (technical advisors) for le Ministère de Coopération.[5] Some Africans viewed them as traitors because the French considered the Caribbeans to be more civilized. However, René Maran,[6] the poet and novelist born in Martinique of French Guyanese parents, disproved this myth in writing when he was assigned to Oubangi-Chari, French Equatorial Africa. In his first novel *Batouala* (1921), he exposed the exploitation of Africans by French colonials in Central Africa and became the first Caribbean to win the prestigious Prix Goncourt.

Colorism, intraracial prejudice, affected Jackie, too. Jackie was my Paris "little sister." She was younger than me and had an older sister back in California. Since I missed Toni, and Jackie missed her sister, there was no doubt we filled those holes for each other. We would cook our families' "soul" food together and reminisce. She would press my hair, until finally I decided I didn't want to fuss with it anymore and let it grow into an Afro. Jackie's hair, by contrast, was long, full, and wavy. Jackie was also a stunning painter and excelled at the prestigious l'École des Beaux-Arts (School of Fine Arts) in Paris. And she loved to dance! We would dance all night until the sky took on that soft pink hue of dawn from one of Jackie's paintings. Sometimes we even told people we were sisters, though we looked nothing alike, and they always believed us.

Jackie had come to Paris not only to study art but to reunite with a Congolese guy she had met while studying abroad as an undergrad in Bordeaux of southwestern France. He now lived three hours northwest of Paris in Rennes. She always went to him because he rarely traveled to her. I think I saw him only once the whole year. He hesitated about her meeting his family in Congo-Brazza although he had visited her and her family in California. And of course, he rarely called. She was always knitting him scarves and hats. At least one weekend a month she would bound out of the dorm, all smiles, a newly knitted *foulard* (scarf) wrapped in tissue paper, ready to board the train and visit her man. She would return at the end of the weekend all smiles still, but with hands empty and a sad sort of gloom about her countenance.

I said nothing about what I observed, and how I suspected racial residue played into these relationships and how Jackie and Maryvonne deserved better. I just enjoyed my friends, who had plenty of time for having fun in Paris with their girlfriends because their love interests were not that interested in spending more time with them.

Maryse and I talked about the dating scene. How discrimination and race and womanhood intersected, both outside and within communities.

When we discussed my studies, for example, how I was in deep with the *négritude* poets, Maryse shook her head. She was not impressed with the movement.

"Sexist," she said. *Négritude* was all about the men.

"Césaire's wife Suzanne did all that work getting his poetry out there, but do you ever hear about her? No. Or about the Nardal sisters in Martinique, those literary salons they held in their apartment, making sure Langston Hughes and all those Black American poets met the *négritude* guys."

French Caribbean women and a Black American woman were keys to the emergence of *négritude*, but their role had been obscured by what scholar T. Denean Sharpley-Whiting calls a "masculine genealogy of critical consciousness."[7] The Martinican sisters, Paulette, Jane and Andrée Nardal, held a weekly Sunday gathering, called *un cercle d'amis* (a circle of friends) in their apartment in Clamart, a southwestern suburb of Paris. Their ethnically diverse and gender-inclusive gatherings were frequented by Harlem Renaissance writers and artists and African and Caribbean politicians and students from Claude McKay, Hale Woodruff, and Langston Hughes to Léopold S. Senghor, Aimé Césaire and Léon G. Damas.

Fluent in English, Paulette became one of the most important cultural intermediaries and connections between the Harlem Renaissance writers and the

African and Caribbean university students. In the summer of 1931, Paulette, a Haitian dentist; Léo Sajous, a Black American teacher of French at Tuskegee Institute; Clara Shephard; and a French Negrophile Louis-Jean Finot founded *La Revue du monde noir* (Review of the Black World), a bilingual (English and French) journal with six issues.[8] *La Revue du monde noir* conceived Black culture as a transnational tradition rather than a subset of French colonial history.

In a November 17, 1963, letter about her and her two sisters' Sunday gatherings to Jacques L. Hymans, the historian and author of *Léopold Sédar Senghor: An Intellectual Biography*, Paulette wrote that the men (Césaire and Senghor) "took up the ideas tossed out by us and expressed them with more flash and brio . . . we were but women, real pioneers—let's say we blazed the trail for them."[9]

Suzanne Roussi Césaire, wife of Aimé Césaire, wrote seven essays between 1941 and 1945 about the construction of a new Martinican cultural identity with a focus on flora, folklore, politics, history, and cultural diversity for *Tropiques* (a cultural and literary journal founded by her, her husband Aimé, René Ménil, and Aristide Maugée in Fort-de-France, Martinique).[10] Major scholarship about these women's contributions to *négritude* didn't start being published until the late 1990s.

Maryse said, *"C'est dommage."* [It's unfortunate.] She had a point, for I was beginning to see in sharp relief how women around the world were affected by discrimination. "Women hold up half the sky, and you know it," Maryse said. Regardless, I still remained enchanted and inspired by the male poets. Already I imagined making a copy of my *doctorat du 3e cycle* diploma and mailing it to Penn State, addressed *attention Professor L*, along with a typewritten note with four words, "I told you so." There wasn't time to turn back now.

During the summer of 1973 in Paris, I witnessed another Black woman's hurting heart, but in this case both the man and the woman were devoted wholly to each other and wanted nothing more than to let love live. A love story not unlike Romeo and Juliet unfolded before my eyes.

I shared an apartment with Florence, the Black American friend from Hampton Institute, and Anta, a Senegalese student of economics from Saint-Louis, a town 152 miles north from Dakar. She had fallen in love with Aziz, a very handsome Senegalese engineer.

She was a Wolof, and he, a Toucouleur. Because of complex social structures and ingrained caste distinctions, Anta's family considered Aziz to be a persona non grata. Her family was of free, noble lineage; Aziz's wasn't. Because ancestry is a major concern in marriage, Anta's family put a lot of pressure on her to end the relationship. It wasn't easy for her because Aziz was genuine, kind hearted, and very loving toward her. He urged her to marry him and for them to stay in France to avoid family pressure.

Tall, slim, and regal, Aziz would appear in the doorway, dressed Western- or Muslim- style. One day he arrived in a white damask *boubou*. Florence and I swooned with the sight of the white *boubou* against his chocolate skin and his thick, luscious mustache.

The summer of 1973 couldn't have been more perfect weather-wise. Gloriously sunny, warm days were spent in the manicured parks or in the open-air cafés. Florence and I had a ball, hanging out with African, Caribbean, and Black American students. We held impromptu dinner parties and pancake breakfasts. Anta gave us lessons on how to cook Senegalese dishes such as *maffe*, *yassa* and *riz au graz*.

Florence and I went out on dates with African guys, dining at inexpensive restaurants and exchanging kisses along the Seine. There was nothing like breathing the scent of expensive, musky cologne on a man while dancing closely in a dark, over-crowded nightclub. Meanwhile, we listened to Anta crying as she struggled over her decision to end her romance with Aziz. She could not stand up against her family. Finally, the day came when she told Aziz she couldn't marry him. Aziz was crushed. He left a note, asking me to meet him in a café.

He asked, "Will you please intervene on my behalf?"

I said, "No."

I made it a practice not to get into the middle of a couple's disagreement. I didn't want him or Anta to shift their pain or anger onto my shoulders. Dejected, slumped in a chair, Aziz asked me what else he could do to change Anta's mind. I advised him to wait. Perhaps she might call him.

Back at the apartment, I found Anta laid up in bed with swollen, red eyes.

After I recounted my conversation with Aziz, she looked at me and Florence.

"I won't call him. It's best to make a clean break," she said. As though she were completely and utterly powerless, her whole body seemed to shrink against the pillows in surrender. "Nothing is going to change." Sadly, her words were to ring true for they never married.

Back home, Daddy left teaching forever for a job in university administration, something that surprised us all. He had been dedicated to teaching for so long. However, he was getting tired of it, and it paid much better to be a dean or provost, or even the associate commissioner of education for the state of New York, which he did for four years.

His career move was a synecdoche of a larger movement. Though we didn't recognize the full scope of it yet, the effects of integration were blooming: employment opportunities that Black scholars had been shut away from were now opening up. Therefore, and perhaps unsurprisingly, top Black scholars were leaving the HBCUs for higher-paying positions at traditional White universities. They were in effect migrating away from the tight-knit community of Black scholars. A slow disintegration that none of us saw coming.

NOTES

1. Terry Teachout, *Pops: A Life of Louis Armstrong* (Boston, MA and New York: Houghton, Mifflin Harcourt, 2009), 332–34.

2. The Senegalese Alioune Diop founded *Présence Africaine* in 1947 in Paris.

3. Mari Evans, "I Am a Black Woman," in *I Am a Black Woman* (New York: William Morrow, 1970), 12.

4. Read Maryse Condé, *Le Coeur à rire et à pleurer: contes vrais de mon enfance* (Paris: Robert Laffont, 1999); rpt. *Tales of the Heart: The Stories from My Childhood*, trans. Richard Philcox (New York: Soho, 2001).

5. Véronique Hélénon, *French Caribbeans in Africa: Diaspora, Connections and Colonial Administration, 1880–1937* (New York: Palgrave MacMillan, 2011), 35; 121–22.

6. Chidi Ikonné, "René Maran, 1887–1960: A Black Francophone Writer between Two Worlds," *Research in African Literatures* 5, no. 1 (Spring 1974), 15. Maran wrote *Batouala* in atonement because he had been fired, tried, found guilty, and fined fifty francs for striking an African man with his fists in 1919. Unfortunately, his victim died of the mistreatment.

7. T. Denean Sharpley-Whiting, *Negritude Women* (Minneapolis: University of Minnesota Press, 2002), 12.

8. Jennifer Anne Boittin, "In Black and White: Gender, Race Relations and the Nardal Sisters in Postwar Paris," *French Colonial Studies* 6 (2005), 124.

9. Paulette Nardal's November 17, 1963 letter, quoted in Jacques Louis Hymans, *Léopold Sédar Senghor: An Intellectual Biography* (Edinburgh: Edinburgh University Press, 1971), 36.

10. Kara M. Rabbitt, "The Geography of Identity in Suzanne Césaire's 'Le grand camouflage,'" *Research in African Literatures* 39, no. 3 (Fall 2008), 121.

Chapter 13

The Street Sweepers

In the early Paris mornings, when I would return home from a night out dancing, or when I would rise early to teach English lessons, I noticed African men sweeping the streets. The city was still sleeping, but I could hear and taste the beginnings of things. The smell of warm buttery croissants and *chaussons aux pommes* (apple turnovers) from the bakeries. The fragrant purple *muguet* (lily) flowers. It was quiet, and you could hear the birds chirping and the swish-swish of those tattered straw brooms. Such tranquility before the bad smells—open-air urinals, sweat, and the unfiltered Gauloises Caporals and Gitanes Brunes ("brown gypsies") cigarettes everyone smoked—emerged along with the maddening crowds.

No matter how distracted I was or how hurried, I would stop when I saw one of the men in his blue one-piece uniform or heard his broom. I always took note of where the Black people were wherever I went (most Black people probably do this, on some level, by instinct), and especially when I was traveling abroad. Those men signaled a Black community out there in Paris beyond the art and academic circles. I wanted to know who they were. *What is their story*, I wondered.

I gave a polite hello as I walked by and listened to their accent as they returned the greeting, trying to place it, as if I could. I never tried to start a conversation and ask them where they were from there on the street. The query felt rude. I wasn't sure how to ask it. I knew they were poor, and here I would be a privileged American in Paris trying to pry into their lives like some nagging anthropologist.

Then, by accident, I discovered their stories.

I decided it was time to get some African clothes. I was tired of being broke. Even with my part-time teaching job and scholarship money, it was still tight, but I had been careful with my cash and felt it was time to splurge. There had to be a store in *la Goutte d'or* (the working-class 18th arrondissement populated by North and West African immigrants) where I could buy some authentic African wear, but I could not decide on which one. I asked everyone in my orbit until finally someone suggested I go to a certain building in another immigrant section of town, where there were several tailors who made African clothes. I grabbed my street guide, told Jackie she was coming with me, hit the Métro, and debarked in a run-down neighborhood similar to what I had seen in the States. Boarded up storefronts. Litter in the streets. Dark. Even in the middle of the afternoon it was dark over there, as though the sunlight just couldn't reach that far.

Luckily, my handwritten directions were very precise. The crumbling brick building I was looking for was so far off the beaten path I wouldn't have even seen it otherwise. It was the kind of place your eyes skim over, because you either assume no one lives there or it's too sad to imagine that people do.

"Brenda, are you crazy? We shouldn't be here," Jackie said as she grabbed my arm.

"What are you talking about? Girl, come on!" I said, pushing the buzzer at the heavy wooden door.

"Did you tell anyone where we were going?" she said. It never occurred to me. It never occurred to me to take extra precautions or treat this adventure differently from any other adventure in the city. It never occurred to me to be scared. The door was unlocked, and when no one answered the buzzer I walked in, with Jackie following behind.

It turned out to be *un foyer de travailleurs africains* (a dormitory for migrant men from West Africa). Bunk beds lining the walls of each room, every inch of space accounted for. I came upon a tall man and told him I was looking for a tailor to make me some clothes. He nodded and walked with me and Jackie down the hall.

"Where are you from?" I asked him, in French.

"Mali," he said, smiling wide.

"Very nice!" I had never met anyone from there.

Jackie tapped my shoulder nervously as we walked into the room the man had directed us to. Everything seemed to be concrete, gray, and damp. A single naked light bulb hung from the ceiling. We could see a tiny room adjacent to this one where a hole in the floor served as the bathroom, the Turkish toilet at its most rudimentary.

Stacked on a table were bolts of brightly colored fabric—dashiki style, floral pattern, geometric shapes, and solid-colored cotton cloths.

Ousmane. That was the name of the man who became my tailor, or something like it. He hailed from la Côte d'Ivoire. He worked during the day and sewed on the side. Several of the men could make clothes, I soon discovered, but because I had met Ousmane first, they respectfully allowed him to make the sale. Within minutes of introducing ourselves to Ousmane, we had attracted a small circle of men who had been lounging on their beds. Someone offered us a rice dish. There was a small two-burner electric *réchaud de table* (hot plate) in the corner, obviously a communal one.

"Okay!" I said, and Jackie sighed. I looked around the bare-but-cramped room. The tiny beds, made neatly with thin, frayed blankets tucked atop. What a gesture, I thought, to offer us food.

Someone rushed over to the hot plate, and several men crowded around while Ousmane showed us his many bolts of fabric. They nodded approvals as I chose a bright blue Guinean print fabric. Tickled that we had garnered a little audience, I looked to Jackie. She smiled and shook her head in a way I knew meant she still thought I was crazy, but I could see she was relaxing some. Ousmane took my measurements, modestly aligning his measuring tape along my arm, around my waist and bust, his fingers never touching my skin. His bashfulness reminded me of Singh, our Indian soldier friend who was too shy to show Mother how to wrap a new sari he had given her around her body. What a difference from those lewd remarks I would hear on the street from men who had watched American Blaxploitation movies like *Super Fly* and thought "Hey baby!" was a perfectly acceptable catcall for a Black American woman walking by.

The men here at *le foyer*, immigrants from West Africa, were eager to engage in conversation. They brought over two small wooden chairs for us and put steaming bowls of rice with sauce in our hands, and we asked what brought them to Paris.

In broken French they described how they had come here to work. Many had two or three menial jobs. Without an education, a language fluency or a structured avenue for entering society such as school, their options were limited. One man, Pierre, in describing his job, stood up and made a motion with his hands sweeping back and forth. *Un balayeur* (a street sweeper)! I had finally met one. I wondered which section of the city he worked in.

One man said he was feeding his wife and five kids back in Guinea with his modest income.

Another chimed in to say he was feeding eight in the Central African Republic.

Another: six.

Every month when they got paid, they went straight to the postal service and sent most of their modest salary home, keeping only the very minimal for themselves.

I thought about how once a month, after we got paid, a group of us would treat ourselves to ice cream, which was rare and trendy for Paris because prior to the 1970s ice cream was unheard of. For us to spend six dollars to get that sundae? Whoa! Big treat. Fresh vanilla, smothered in hot fudge syrup with shaved almonds on top. Or *pêche melba*, raspberry-peach sauce poured over vanilla ice cream with whipped cream. It was the kind of extravagance that made being a young, single student in Paris fun. It was the kind of Paris these men never got to see.

Pierre slipped away quietly while the others were describing their families and returned with pictures which he handed to Jackie and me. He had two daughters and a son at home, whom he hadn't seen for nearly two years.

To say the men were friendly wouldn't capture the way they welcomed us in. They didn't need to say why they were so eager to visit with us. In their genial laughs, I detected that twinge of longing and homesickness. At once I wanted to give them all my money so they could go home to their families and live life fully. But there were ten of them and one of me. Though I had been feeling broke the past year as a student, I was wealthy, enormously wealthy, in comparison. A comparison so sharp that the thought of it nearly brought me to tears.

It was almost dark when Jackie and I emerged and headed back to the Métro. We hadn't been aware of time's passing from inside the shadowy building.

Jackie was touched by the generosity of the men, too. She would not, however, be accompanying me back to pick up my clothes. I don't know why. Perhaps she was too busy with her art classes and two part-time jobs. Instead, Florence went with me, and Janis, a Black American graduate student at Brown University, accompanied me one time.

It would be a lie to write that I never experienced racism in France. Paris had its own breed of hate, and sometimes it was difficult to distinguish specific hate like racism from general rudeness of the French people. Much of the racial strife in France was directed at Arabs, particularly Algerians. Many French people died during the long Algerian War for independence; most French families had lost someone. But there were moments of disdain toward people of color in general, particularly foreigners.

France consistently maintains a color-blind model of public policy. The government refuses to collect data on the race or ethnicity of its citizens. Instead, it has constructed policies aimed at geographical areas or social classes that disproportionately contain large number of minorities. In May 2013, the National Assembly voted almost unanimously to drop the word "race" from the Constitution. Regardless, France is a multi-cultural and multi-ethnic society since the end of World War II when a large number of immigrants began arriving from its former colonies in search of employment.

Jackie and I would go to the open-air markets on rue Mouffetard, rue du Dragon, or at Métro Maubert-Mutualité to get fresh fruits and vegetables. Shoppers were not to touch the produce. You pointed at what you wanted. That was true for everybody. But, if you were Black or a foreigner (especially a *Black foreigner*), the merchants would deliberately sneak a bruised or rotten fruit into your bag so the whole thing would go bad. One bad fruit turns them all, as they say, and symbolically that's what they were saying about people like us.

After returning home with a putrefying fruit too many times, Jackie and I decided to play a game with those merchants, turning our backs while each merchant was preparing our order, pretending to look ahead to another stand while he dropped a rotten tomato in our bag. Then Jackie would start to pay while I grabbed the bag, pulled out the rotten piece and threw it at the vendor's head. (I don't think Jackie thought I would actually do it.) Once it was a tangerine, and I can still see the man's expression of surprise and horror as he ducked out of the fruit's path, terrified and cowering. A fool's prank thrown right back in his face.

At that instant I felt I had suddenly become my mother. What I just did was *exactly* what she would have done, and this realization hit me with surprise. I had always thought of myself as more like Daddy, the calm educator, than Mother, the hot-tempered one. Mother never tolerated injustice of any kind waged against her. She was the one who would demand service at the doctor's office when they tried to deny her. She was the one who would march into the school and petition for justice when her son was wrongly accused of touching a White girl. She was the one whom people sometimes described as abrasive, but was always first on their list for social gatherings of any kind. She would have thrown the fruit in the man's face and kept on walking, and as I walked away from that market, I was reminded of how much Mother's courage had influenced my sense of self confidence in being a Black woman.

I began to wonder if there were women immigrants in Paris, and if so, where they were. We received maid service in the student housing buildings, and I learned these maids were French, mostly poor. Or female immigrants—not from West Africa like the street sweepers—but from Spain, Italy, and Portugal. White immigrants.

Relocating somewhere new to work a menial job that paid hardly anything was not a life I could relate to. By age twenty-five, I had moved dozens of times already, at first with my parents and now on my own. In Paris, I was on top of the world, learning and growing toward a future that grew brighter and more exciting every day and who knew where I would end up moving next. I knew racism and sexism were forces against me in the world, but thanks to the fierce confidence of my mother and the determined encouragement of my father and the many economic and educational privileges granted to me throughout my life, never did I doubt I would succeed.

Occasionally, in Paris, I would see an African woman with a White child and learned African *nounous* (nannies) were being seen more frequently in

Paris, arriving with French families who had lived in Africa and brought their nannies back home with them.

I returned regularly to *le foyer* to visit my friends and buy African clothes, bringing along friends living in Paris who were willing to venture to that part of town and friends from the U.S. who came to visit me. (Florence bought some dresses too!) Eventually, I went alone. There was never any reason to be afraid. I decided I never wanted to be afraid of impoverishment. The men brought such richness to my experience in Paris; I learned what could never be learned by watching a film, attending a lecture, or researching in the library.

The men always offered me rice and fish or rice and chicken or a drink of African tea. They would ask me about my studies. They would ask about the United States and try to speak English. On one visit I asked Pierre if his daughter had passed her school exam, and he clapped his hands and said yes, obviously touched that I had remembered.

They treated me like a cherished friend. All I was doing was getting something I wanted—tailor-made clothes—and engaging in conversation, but they treasured my visits.

I bought some *boubous* (long dresses) and two blouse-and-skirt sets. The clothes were beautiful, the prices cheap, and I always gave a little more than what Ousmane charged, thinking of the pictures of women and children, their families, in Africa. When I tried on the clothes, two men would hold up sheets, turning their heads away, eyes closed.

I was certain they treated their wives well. The sacrifices they were making to make sure their families could get by was evidence enough. They had left home and moved far away so that their wives did not have to seek indentured servitude. I wanted to ask Jackie if she thought her boyfriend would ever do such a thing for her, but I didn't.

Early Paris mornings thereafter, amid the fog and slowly swelling sunlight, above the sounds of chirping birds and the smell of fresh baked goods, the swishing of the broom would call my attention and I would look to see if the dark-skinned man sweeping the street was one of the men whose name I knew and who were so special to me now.

He never was. Not once did I see any of my friends sweeping the neighborhoods I lived and studied in.

But at that moment, watching *le balayeur* working along the pathways I walked, I felt, at least, that I knew a small part of his story. I would stop and wave as if to say, "*Merci*" [Thank you].

Today the hum of green street cleaning machines has replaced the swish of the brooms.

Chapter 14

I Am Not My Hair

Hair and its connection to political statements and identity framed several of my own encounters. Fifteen years later, well after I had gone back to the United States, I returned to the African continent unrecognizable as a Black American precisely because of my hair.

Like many of my peers and colleagues in Jersey and D.C. in 1975, I sported a big, elegant Afro. Four inches high. For Black Americans, of course, the Afro had become a visible, political statement of pride. Post-civil rights, still fighting for change and equality. Also, it indicated, I thought, a hint of feminism, and I know Angela Davis would agree. Women could wear short hair, too. They didn't have to keep it long. Women could wear an Afro just like a man. Women could discard chemical relaxers because their natural-born hair was beautiful as is. For me, I simply rocked the hairstyle. It was an extension of my personality, Toni said. Independent, unencumbered, and not shy. Perhaps "unencumbered" also referred to the fact that although I had boyfriends, I often preferred to stay single and on-the-go.

I had finished my doctoral dissertation by December 1975, and after living in Paris to study North American studies at the Sorbonne with the famed Michel Fabre, I returned to the United States. Mother and Daddy were living in Silver Spring, Maryland (a suburb of Washington, D.C.). Toni, now married with a son, was in East Orange, New Jersey, and she wore her hair permed. My brothers both lived in Petersburg, Virginia, and attended Virginia State College.

I wasn't scheduled to defend my dissertation and subsequently go on the academic job market until June 1976, so I spent time reconnecting with old friends from Hampton Institute, working odd jobs and immersing myself in the cultural events and party scenes in D.C. One day I received a telegram, confirming I was hired as an assistant professor of English language and literature by l'Université Nationale du Gabon (National University of Gabon). There must be a mistake, I thought, for I hadn't applied for a job.

I quickly wrote the one friend I had in the country. Victor, the youngest brother of my ex-boyfriend in Paris, had given my CV to Professor Joseph Ambouroue-Avaro, the dean of la Faculté des Arts et Sciences Sociales (Faculty of the Humanities and Social Sciences) at the university, who had said to him he needed a professor who could teach English composition, English African literature, and Black American literature. Victor said he thought of me because not only was I a good fit academically, but he knew I had wanted to teach in Africa.

I felt drawn to the African continent and had wanted to go back and live there ever since my stay in the Congo. The previous summer, I had traveled to Dahomey (now Benin), Togo, Ghana, and Nigeria, expanding my experience of West Africa. I did not go back to the Congo, which was now called Zaire. Lumumba's assassination in 1961, the immediate aftermath of which my family had witnessed, had only been the start of a long period of oppression. The dictatorial regime that followed and lasted more than thirty years proceeded to strip the country of its natural resources and oppress its people almost worse than colonial Belgium had done. Violence and war killed thousands and tore the spirit of the place apart. The world's reaction to the Congo's extended heartbreak amounted to closed eyes and an indifferent shrug. I did not want to close my eyes and shrug, but I did not want to endanger my life by going back to live in the Congo, either.

The dean in Gabon had obtained his degree in France, too, and was impressed by my qualifications and experience. With trust in his friend's

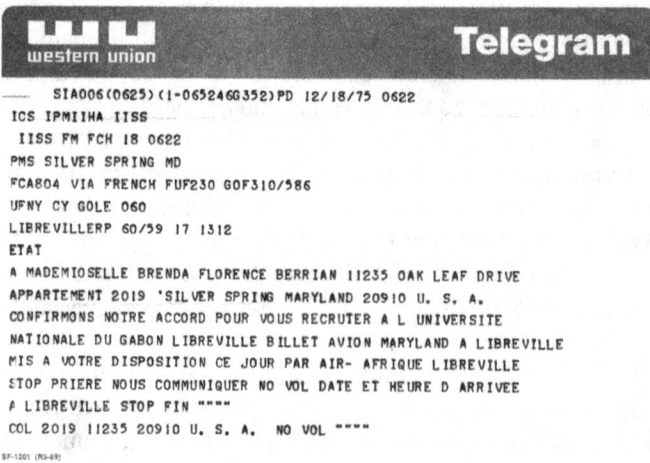

```
██ ██ ██                               Telegram
western union

———    SIA006(0625)(1-0652460352)PD 12/18/75 0622
ICS IPMIIHA IISS
 IISS FM FCH 18 0622
PMS SILVER SPRING MD
FCA804 VIA FRENCH FUF230 GOF310/586
UFNY CY GOLE 060
LIBREVILLERP 60/59 17 1312
ETAT
A MADEMIOSELLE BRENDA FLORENCE BERRIAN 11235 OAK LEAF DRIVE
APPARTEMENT 2019 'SILVER SPRING MARYLAND 20910 U. S. A.
CONFIRMONS NOTRE ACCORD POUR VOUS RECRUTER A L UNIVERSITE
NATIONALE DU GABON LIBREVILLE BILLET AVION MARYLAND A LIBREVILLE
MIS A VOTRE DISPOSITION CE JOUR PAR AIR- AFRIQUE LIBREVILLE
STOP PRIERE NOUS COMMUNIQUER NO VOL DATE ET HEURE D ARRIVEE
A LIBREVILLE STOP FIN """"
COL 2019 11235 20910 U. S. A.   NO VOL """"

SF-1201 (R3-69)
```

Figure 14.1   The December 18, 1975, telegram from l'Université Nationale du Gabon (author's collection).

recommendation, he hired me without even meeting me. He assumed I was a Black American, and with that image came his idea that I wore my hair in an Afro. He was right, at least initially. I received the letter in October, and on New Year's Eve 1975, I boarded an Air France plane to Paris with my big hair, my books, and some African dresses. Though my final destination was Gabon, it was easier to fly through Europe to get to Africa, an obvious residue of colonialism. I arrived on New Year's Day 1976, and met up with my best friend Jackie, her dance instructor Jeff, and three more friends at a Cameroonian restaurant. Jeff was also a bongo player from Trinidad, and his ocean-blue eyes were startling against his deep ebony skin. In Trinidad, where he was a Shango priest, he told us, blue eyes signaled magical powers.

At the restaurant I am enjoying the start of dinner before going out on the town. Tall tapered candles decorate the table. My seat faces the heavy French doors at the entrance of the restaurant. The doors keep opening as people spill in for dinner, and the cold air hits me in the chest. After ten minutes I say I'm going to do something about it, and I lean over to scoot my chair back and get up, when suddenly Jackie cries out, "Don't move."

"Oh *no!*" someone yells. "Put it out!"

Jeff begins beating my head with his thickly calloused hands like it's a bongo. He is banging hard, on the verge of hurting me, and I'm about to smack him, when Jackie and our other friends start hitting my head, too.

I scream, "What are you doing?"

My eyes are closed and it's happening so fast, and there's a hand on my back to keep me from standing up fully or breaking away. People at the table next to ours start screaming. The hands keep beating, and then they stop. That's when I notice the harsh stench of burned hair.

"Your hair was on fire," Jackie says breathlessly.

The maître d' is gasping, dashing around in a flurry. "Free champagne!" he yells to our table as he whizzes by. "Free champagne!"

Jackie leads me to the bathroom and I look in the mirror and scream. My scream echoes off the walls, for it is an animal-like wail from deep within. My hair is literally seared off, leaving mounds of gruesome, charred ash from the front to the very back of the crown. It looks categorically violent, and I see how quickly the fire had consumed my hair, for in those few seconds it had burned almost down to the scalp. I see how close the fire had been to my head and my face. How I could have nearly died or suffered permanent scarring.

Jackie and I are silent while I stare in shock at my reflection.

My huge Angela Davis Afro is gone.

Then I touch the top of my head, and the hair just slips right off like a wet wig. Jackie and I pull mounds of warm, burnt black hair off my head and toss it into the garbage can. Only the very back of my hair above my neck remains.

Figure 14.2   Me sporting my large Afro in Paris, 1973 (author's collection).

"I guess you want to go home now," Jackie says. She looks at me as though she suspects I might cry. But suddenly I'm about to laugh, for my face is not ruined. It's only hair; it will grow back.

"Go home?" I say. "Why should I? It's New Year's Day, I'm not going home!"

I didn't mind looking a little crazy with a short, patchy fuzz in the front and a puff out back; I was happy to be alive and not needing plastic surgery. That itself was cause enough for a celebration. "*Je veux faire la fête!*" I said.

[I want to party.] "I'm gonna be stinking, but I'm going out to have a good time!"

In the morning, Jeff evened out my hair into a "baldie" style. It had burned nearly all the way down to the scalp, so he cut it very short, less than a quarter inch high, all over.

Two days later, on January 4, I boarded the Air Afrique flight to live in an African country once again. I arrived in Libreville, Gabon, and was quickly shuttled to a luncheon with university administrators, other faculty, and the students who had enrolled for classes that semester. The luncheon's purpose, I was told, was to give everyone a chance to meet the new faculty.

The festivities were about to begin, but something was holding it up. The president of the university, whom I recognized from his photo, was pacing back and forth on the stage. "One of the newly arrived professors is a Black American," he says into the microphone, "but where is she?"

"Here I am," I say, but he doesn't hear me. Perhaps, I think, it's because I am wearing a blue-and-white outfit, similar to what local women in Gabon wear.

"Where is the Black American?" He's walking back and forth, right in front of me. I stand up.

"I am the Black American."

"No, you're African, you've got a bald head," he says and resumes pacing. Apparently, it matters that I'm wearing African clothes. It's my hair he's reading more than anything.

Then, incredulous, he turns back to me. "*Where is your hair?*"

In his mind, Black American women had an Angela Davis Afro. The image was ubiquitous in the media. The first time I had seen an Afro was in the Congo, fifteen years prior, a time when it was a rarity back home. How ironic was that. Now an Afro was what distinguished Black Americans, a hairstyle I had just *lost* a scant forty-eight hours before. The Gabonese should have seen me in the Montmartre restaurant! But it seemed no matter what you were or who you were, you were marked with something—skin, hair or accent—in the imagination of people everywhere. Imagination led to an assumption and, when you dismantled the expectations of the imagination, the result led to bafflement. The hair-searing incident had erased my Afro and thus a piece of my "American-ness," even to this highly educated man who should have known better. I knew that being a headstrong professional woman in a staunchly patriarchal society would likely challenge many people.

I had no idea my hair, or lack thereof, would, too.

Chapter 15

A Future Decision

Paris was an adventure that had to end sometime, and my signal it was time to go was when the money ran out. My scholarship and part-time teaching job ended in June 1974, forcing me to return to the States to work a series of odd jobs in the Washington, D.C. area. I had finished all my coursework; spent a summer traveling to London and West Africa; and conducted research for my dissertation on *négritude* and its roots in Harlem Renaissance poetry. I finished writing the dissertation three times before Monsieur Fabre accepted it by December 1975. I planned to defend my dissertation the following June.

When I discovered Fabre was coming to New York, and I could take him a final draft of my dissertation, I invited Daddy along since he had read Fabre's *The Unfinished Quest of Richard Wright*. Having read my father's *Négritude: Essays and Studies*, Fabre was also pleased to meet him.

At home, the Civil Rights Movement had ended. People sported big Afros and bell-bottom jeans. The politically correct term for Black people in America had changed from "Black American" to "African American." The Vietnam War was over. Times were hopeful.

I was hopeful, too. Ready for my next adventure, wherever it would be. I knew that I was ready to be a professor, and that I wanted to return to Africa again someday, but I didn't know the two would coincide so quickly. Then, as I stated earlier, I received a telegram from l'Université Nationale du Gabon offering me a one-year lectureship, and I hopped on a plane in Paris on January 4 with the new teenie-weenie Afro on my head that did not look like an "American Afro" according to the university president.

With a population of just under one million, Gabon's economy was booming from oil, magnesium, uranium, gold, and okoume wood. There were more jobs than people, thus many expatriates were recruited to fill teaching jobs and other positions. Created in 1970, l'Université Nationale du Gabon (now l'Université Nationale Omar Bongo, UNOB) had two faculties: Arts and Social Sciences and Law and Economics. Only three Gabonese professors among the large expatriate faculty taught at the university in 1976. Others came from France, Senegal, Haiti, Martinique, Guadeloupe, Guinea, and Morocco. There was one other American, Sarah Milbury-Steen, a White American Fulbrighter, but I was the only Black American.

When I met Andrew L. Steigman, the U.S. ambassador to Gabon, he asked, "Are you Al Berrian's daughter?"

Surprised, I said, "Yes."

"Your father and I worked together in Léopoldville," he said. Once again, Daddy's connections were connecting with me, and he wasn't even in the country!

Teaching in Gabon I learned as much as I taught my students. I had to earn the respect of the male students, who were deeply entrenched in patriarchal societies where women were not respected as highly as men and rarely held positions of power. One male student even refused to look at me or stop talking with a fellow classmate when I lectured. I had to teach him a thing or two.

I was surprised when the students, who were in general eager and grateful to learn, did not buy the books on my course reading list as required. They were accustomed to second-rate education where they either shared books or only read photocopied excerpts. I used a portion of my salary to photocopy sections of the books and other readings for each of them, and for some of those students my class was the first time they had owned or read an entire novel.

Although you might not have a television or a telephone in Gabon, and in many places in Africa, you were more connected to people than ever. It was the "Do Drop In" welcome mat that invisibly lay before every door. You always cooked more food than you needed in case someone dropped by. Invited guests were expected to bring along friends, too. And if someone in the neighborhood *did* have a TV or phone, everyone shared. It reminded me of when we got a color TV at Hampton, and everybody came over to watch it. The neighborly sense of communion was more pronounced in the South than in the North back home, and in many ways, Africa reminded me of that.

When June came, I returned to Paris for my dissertation defense, the final step before I completed the doctorat du 3e cycle, the culmination of all that work. I had concentrated on getting myself educated for the past twenty-nine years, and I had gone as far as I could go. Daddy was proud. It was time to continue the intellectual work of teaching the next generation, for there was much more uplifting to be done. I remembered how little I had known of African writers even as a student at Hampton. I saw how badly schools needed professors to teach Black American literature, even in Africa itself. I wanted to be part of the change.

Jackie was still living in Paris, so I stayed with her and studied hard the days leading up to my defense, where I would sit before a stage and answer questions and critiques from three professors. Of course, we planned to go out on the town after I was done, to kick back and celebrate. We sang Diana Ross's "Love Hangover" and danced around the apartment, in short bursts, when I took a break from studying. Jackie had left her former boyfriend for a Cameroonian filmmaker who seemed to treat her better, and I was proud of her as we sang the lyrics, "I've got the sweetest hangover/ I don't wanna get over . . ."[1]

Then Jackie flipped the TV on while she prepared dinner and that's when we heard news reports of continuous riots happening in Soweto, South Africa,[2] in the wake of what had started on June 16. In Gabon I had no access to television, so although I had heard briefly about riots happening in South Africa, I did not yet know details and had no images in my mind. I had to leave the continent of Africa to fully understand what was going on there. Jackie and I both stopped what we were doing and turned up the volume as the screen replayed aerial views of masses of people moving chaotically across the countryside, military jeeps, billowing smoke from buildings set afire. White men in army fatigues chasing Blacks with German shepherd dogs, each on a leash.

They were kids in school uniforms running and the officials were shooting them. Kids! Unarmed. Falling. Falling bodies. The sound of gunfire and children running would forever stay imprinted in my memory. Jackie and I immediately ran out to get *Newsweek* and the *International Herald Tribune* newspaper. We read the reports about what was happening, we turned up the TV, but I could not get the images out of my mind.

It looked familiar, too familiar.

It looked like war.

It looked like the Congo in the wake of Lumumba's death.

It looked like Birmingham in 1963.

Decade-old memories rose up before me: the fire hoses, the dogs, the riots, the assassinations of Medgar Evers, Martin Luther King, Jr., and Malcolm X. The woman thrown from a bus in the middle of Richmond, Virginia. I thought about the fight for desegregation of public schools, hospitals, restaurants, and trains.

We read how the colonial government in South Africa passed legislation forcing Black schools to teach in Afrikaans. No indigenous languages, and no more than half of the curriculum in English. More Africans had been attending school since the early 1970s, and students, already faced with the lack of equipment and materials and with paltry employment prospects after graduation, protested the government's decree. Afrikaans was the language of the oppressor.[3] Their language was now being forced upon students and teachers throughout all of South Africa. The Afrikaans language represented to Black South Africans not only the oppressor but apartheid as a whole, the systematic, legislated racial discrimination that had ruled the country officially since the 1950s and unofficially a hundred years before that: pass laws; poverty; no worker rights.

Afrikaners had shot school children. Once again, the image of the four girls from Birmingham, Alabama, who had been killed in the bombing of the 16th Street Baptist Church, flashed across my mind.

I bent over and hugged my body, as hurt and sorrow engulfed me inside out.

Jackie and I learned that 15,000 students and teachers marched in what started as a peaceful protest, and that once the first shot rang out, mayhem ensued. At the end of that burning day, casualties were reported at 200, but later estimates put the number much higher, closer to 600. Thousands were wounded. We watched the events unfold in shock.

Then came the Sam Nzima photo which would gain instant international attention and sympathy for South Africans: a dead twelve-year-old child, bloodied, in the arms of another child, a boy, with a young girl in a school uniform crying and running alongside, their faces twisted in such anguish as though they wished they could die, too. The young boy's name: Hector Pieterson. The girl beside him: his sister, Antoinette. The one carrying him: an eighteen-year-old fellow student. Physical torture against a *child* was the sight of something so horribly wrong that no one, no matter his or her politics, could deny.

They were children, marching peacefully, motivated by the Black Consciousness Movement which was all about gaining knowledge about their own people's history and identity and realizing their own potential and worth, while resisting forms of oppression. Like *négritude*. Like the voices of the Harlem Renaissance. White-dominated rule had so subjugated the mind that, as student leader Steve Biko said, Black consciousness had to reverse that mind-colonization and produce Blacks who "[did] not regard themselves as appendages to white society."[4]

On June 24, 1976, at my doctoral defense, I thought of how the essence of uprising and the violent response to it by those in power was playing out painfully in South Africa. Then, while I sat at a small desk in the middle of a large lecture hall and looked up at the three committee members, my thoughts raced backward to a day in March 1925. On that day, the sixty-seven-year-old Anna Julia Cooper defended her dissertation, *"L'Attitude de la France à l'égard de l'esclavage pendant la Révolution"* (France's Attitude toward Slavery during the Revolution), at the Sorbonne.[5] The first Black American woman to do so. A community activist, scholar, high school principal, and author of *A Voice from the South*,[6] Cooper devoted her life to the education and empowerment of Black American youth and adults.

In attendance at Cooper's oral defense was the Martinican Jane Nardal. In a letter to Alain Locke, a philosophy professor at Howard University, she recounted how she had been transformed by Cooper's words: *"Pourtant, ma curiosité, mon intérêt, déjà sollicité par d'autres faits nègres, commencaient à s'éveiller"* [My curiosity, my interest, already captured by other things Nègre, began to awaken.][7]

Fifty-one years later, at age twenty-nine, I followed in Cooper's footsteps by earning my *doctorat du 3e cycle* from the Sorbonne. My defense only lasted ninety minutes during which I championed my reading of how the *négritude* poets reclaimed words of the Harlem poets. I also answered questions and critiques before an audience of friends, curious students, and strangers. Afterward, the professors left the lecture hall to deliberate for forty-five minutes about whether I had passed and at which *mention (*rank). When they returned, Monsieur Fabre announced I had passed with the high-ranking *mention très bien* (cum laude).

Although our hearts still hurt for those students in South Africa, Jackie and I celebrated that night, because you still have to dance even when the world is on fire.

June 16 in Soweto unleashed a string of uprisings throughout South Africa in the following months. Students, mineworkers, sympathetic Whites. I wanted to know more about South Africa and its people. It seemed so distanced from the progress happening everywhere else. I wanted to see Black South Africans triumph in a land ruled by Blacks and live to see a better day. For now, it seemed a terrifying place, and I didn't know if I wanted to go there.

But go there I did, to see for myself, a full seventeen years later.

NOTES

1. "Love Hangover" was released on *Diana Ross* in March 1976.

2. Soweto is the acronym for South West Townships outside of Johannesburg.

3. Afrikaners had settled in South Africa in the 1600s, well before the British came and took over. The Afrikaners felt they were entitled to rightful ownership, never mind the Black South Africans who were there before them. Although the Afrikaners felt oppressed in their own way, they still had privileges over the Black South Africans with representatives in the apartheid government.

4. Stephen Biko, "The Definition of Black Consciousness," in *Steve Biko I Write What I Like*, edited by C. R. Aelred Stubbs (San Francisco: Harper & Row Publishers, 1978), 51.

5. Anna Julia Cooper, "The Third Step: Cooper's Memoir of the Sorbonne Doctorate (1945–1950?)," in *The Voice of Anna Julia Cooper and A Voice from the*

South and Other Important Essays, Papers and Letters, edited by Charles Lemert and Esme Bhan (Lanham, MD: Rowman and Littlefield, 1998), 328–29.

6. On June 11, 2009, the U.S. Postal Service issued a 4-cent Anna Julia Cooper commemorative stamp in the *Black Heritage* series.

7. Jane Nardal's December 27, 1927 letter to Alain Locke, quoted in Brent Hayes Edwards, *The Practice of Diaspora: Literature, Translation and the Rise of Black Internationalism* (Cambridge, MA: Harvard University Press, 2003), 126–27.

Chapter 16

In Search of Sister-Brotherhood

"We need to maybe start hiring more minorities, but the question is: Can we find them?" Hearing this, my throat tightened. In an air-conditioned auditorium, university deans and department heads, tenured and non-tenured faculty filled the seats. Secretaries took notes to bring back to their staff. No one flinched. Though I can't recall who said this, the phrase remains sharp in my memory. I remember the White man shook his head. Someone else piped up, "But we have *standards*. What do you mean we have to hire people of color?"

I wanted to scream aloud. How dare these White men say such a thing, as though the few people of color in the room, including me, were invisible? At this university-wide open-faculty meeting, one of the agenda items was how to address the pressing issue of "diversity" in our institution's faculty. In the silence of the unanswered question of minority scholars' existence and legitimacy, I waited for my blood to calm. It didn't.

"Excuse me," I said, rising from my seat in the middle row. People in the rows in front of me turned around. I detected a few groans. They knew my face. I was one of only six women of color with tenure (three in Africana Studies) in the Faculty of Arts and Sciences in the entire university system of more than 3,000 professors, and I was very involved in committees. "I find it interesting you say that to hire people like me your standards have to go down. Take note. I went to your White schools, I had your White teachers, got your White degree." I looked at him directly now. "So how can the standards go down?"

Silence continued, but now it was an uncomfortable silence. Good. I had made them as uncomfortable as they had made me (and the few other minorities in the room) feel.

"Now Dr. Berrian," came a familiar patronizing White male voice. "Don't be so angry."

"I am not angry," I said. "I am stating facts. Please explain to me how the standards are going to decline when we've been exposed to the same people you've been exposed to. Why are you insinuating that I'm angry?"

I knew what he meant by "angry." White faculty members love to say, "the angry Black woman." And what's the other one? "Belligerent." A man speaking his mind is so expected that it rarely merits any sort of surprise. A woman speaking her mind is bold, dangerously daring, and audacious. A Black American woman speaking her mind, particularly in response to offense, is labeled "belligerent," meaning unprofessional, emotive, stirring up dust over nothing. You can't call it righteous anger over injustice because the person in power does not see his actions as offensive.

It was not supposed to be like this, not when I signed on.

Back in 1976, nearly ten years prior to that awful meeting, fresh from teaching in the city of freedom, Libreville, in Gabon, I landed a job at the University of Pittsburgh. Not a visiting position—it was tenure track at a traditional White institution (TWI). A symbol of commitment, of settling down. A 401K and a mortgage. I had to seriously consider: could this place—a small Northern city of perpetual gray skies—become my home?

Daddy pointed out I couldn't just roam Africa, going from temporary contract to temporary contract, forever. (He never implied I needed to "get married and settle down" like many of my friends' families would say, just the "settling down" part.)

The Black Studies Department that hired me thrummed with vibrant energy. The carpet still smelled new. A feeling of shared purpose and commitment permeated the place, from students and faculty: because ten years ago, there was no such thing as a Black Studies Department on any American campus.

The nascent department had, like others of its kind, arisen out of protest.[1] On a chilly January night in 1969, forty-eight members of the university's Black Action Society locked themselves inside the Cathedral of Learning computer room for a seven-hour sit-in. Fed up with the status quo and with being taught a one-sided, distorted view of American historical and cultural development, they handed a list of demands to the president. They joined a chorus of others around the nation who, in the aftermath of the Civil Rights Movement and Dr. King's assassination, pushed for more inclusion in higher learning and the chance to study topics related to Black culture and history. They took cues from a movement that started on the West Coast, where the first Bachelor of Arts degree granting Department of Black Studies in the College of Ethnic Studies took root at San Francisco State College (SFSC, now San Francisco State University).[2]

The movement to create Black Studies programs, centers, and departments went on while I was at Penn State, and then in Paris, drinking in the thrill of student life and literature, shoulder-to-shoulder with other artists and academics, listening to poets read their work in the cramped *Présence Africaine* bookstore. I heard about what was going on at American universities, through Daddy, who still had his hand in academia.

In Pittsburgh, the computer lab takeover worked. The students' requests were answered, and a Department of Black Community, Education, Research, and Development (DBCERD), or Black Studies, was born. It became one of the largest departments of its kind in the United States. In 1991, its name was changed to the Department of Africana Studies.

Jack Daniel, the first co-director, had a reputation for running the department like a family, getting to know students and their parents and encouraging camaraderie among faculty. Women were among the first hires, too. The poets Sonia Sanchez and Etheridge Knight, Black American literati whose rhythms encouraged political and social activism, were recruited. Vernell Lillie forged the Kuntu Repertory Theater with Rob Penny, for which they held playwriting workshops open to the community.

A young, chain-smoking August Wilson taught some of them.

The Department had a mission that extended beyond the ivory tower: service in the community. Barbara A. Sizemore, who became the first Black American superintendent of a major school district (Washington, D.C.), had joined the faculty. She garnered a grant to work closely with the Pittsburgh Public Schools to understand the achievement gap between Black and White students on standardized tests. I conducted workshops in the public schools for English and French teachers. Dennis Brutus, the South African activist poet, joined too.

Here I was back in the same state of that terrible university where the professor insisted, to my face, that there existed no Black Francophone literature of merit, that I couldn't possibly earn a PhD studying *négritude* poets. Now, with a doctorate in hand and two years of teaching experiences across the globe, I was promised the freedom to teach whatever related literature I wanted. With the multi-disciplinary thrust of the department—Africana-centered courses on subjects such as economics, literature, history, health, and more—I could use film, music, and other subjects to enrich my courses. I could help build the emerging discipline.

The best part? The department touted a Pan-African focus, with a roster of four African men, four Black American women, one Caribbean man, and five Black American men. The goal would be to become as representative of the Africana diaspora as possible with one-third Black American faculty, one-third Black Caribbean, and one-third African. After roving around newly independent Africa, I couldn't wait to be part of a Pan-African group, even though I wasn't happy about the insufficient number of female faculty.

Black American students naturally viewed the departments of Black Studies within major universities around the country as safe havens. They were like mini-historically Black colleges and universities (HBCUs), as the 1970s proved a time for more Black Americans to gain entry into traditional White institutions (TWIs). It changed the landscape of HBCUs, too. Black American faculty was drawn away from teaching at HBCUs with sudden opportunities for higher-paying jobs, reduced teaching loads, and the perceived prestige at TWIs. I felt, in a way, that my teaching in this new field would continue my father's legacy.

I thought, I could handle gray skies and cold winters, a too-small city, and people who didn't visit their neighbors or even say "hello" to you in the elevator, in exchange for academic enterprise, curricular freedom, and a community like this. Exciting scholarship. A sisterhood-brotherhood kind of place. That's what I expected, but things don't always work out.

Because Black Studies units sprang out of protest across the nation, a large number of them were founded in hostile and skeptical environments. Such departments would debunk the long-standing, but false, myth that Black Americans had nothing of value to contribute to American history and culture. University administrators set them up hastily, hoping they would not last. In some cases, graduate students, not traditional tenured faculty, were hired to chair the new departments, deliberately pushed into positions well beyond their ability. For example, Curtiss Porter and Jack Daniel, the first co-directors of DBCERD at the University of Pittsburgh (often referred to as "Pitt"), were graduate students. Although they were set up for failure, the two men exhibited strong organizational skills to formulate a bachelor degree-granting, inter-disciplinary department with a focus in the humanities and social sciences.

As happens, when you join a family, over time you start to see the imperfections, foibles, and weaknesses.

After a few years, a split between the traditionalist and the non-traditionalist stances took place between Porter and Daniel. While Daniel supported the traditional route of tenure and scholarship, Porter pushed for tenure based upon his engagement of the academic curriculum in the life of the Black American community. Porter strongly believed his work in developing the department ought to count in lieu of publications. His stance and the struggle about the direction in which Black Studies should go as a discipline fragmented the faculty and led to Porter's resignation.

Meanwhile, the wider university "family" in Pittsburgh transformed into a bullfighting arena at times. I was often the squeaky wheel at meetings. When White professors looked at me with surprise whenever I said I had gone to the Sorbonne, I turned the conversation into a lesson, reminding them how they shouldn't be surprised that a person who looked like me had studied abroad. I fought for tenure for the Black American scholars in my department, when White administrators looked questioningly at their publications. Scholars in Black Studies had to publish in the top journals that were run by Black Americans, but also in journals run by Whites, because the Black American journals were often not recognized or seen as legitimate by the usually all-White tenure review committees convened by the dean.

I realized the road, past and present, was even more winding and troublesome for Black American women. When I complained, I backed it up with research to subvert being dismissed as either the "strong Black woman" (SBW) or the "angry Black woman."[3] In 2010, women of all races accounted for only 31 percent of tenured faculty in U.S. colleges and universities. Among all women faculty, a mere 7 percent were Black Americans, and they continue to be blocked from climbing the professoriate ranks.[4] In 2017, the National Center for Education Statistics listed a total of 60,408 full professors, among which were 2,806 Black American women.[5]

I, a retiree, had been a member of that small minority.

The number shrank even more when I chaired Africana Studies for six years. Among the thirty departments in Arts and Sciences, I was the only Black American chair and one of three women chairs. The work was time consuming, sometimes thankless, and other times rewarding. I, like the other twenty-nine chairs, followed the dean's agenda for all the important decisions were made in his office. I ran a department on a ridiculously small operating budget. Whenever the department ran a search for a new faculty member, I invited the seniors to participate in the process. Soon-to-be graduate students or full-time members of the work force, they needed to learn how to handle being interviewed for a job.

My six years were very fruitful because the faculty was awarded government, university and private grants and published more than usual. Whenever I encouraged a faculty member to publish to improve the content of her or his course, I was obligated to do likewise, being awarded with external and university grants. Marta Effinger, one of the department's outstanding majors, won the 1991 Lorraine Hansberry National Playwriting Award, and her play "Union Station" was performed at the Kennedy Center and by Professor Lillie's Kuntu Repertory Theater at Pitt. By upholding high standards, I noticed others followed suit. The reward was a much happier and more productive department for students, faculty, and staff.

The negative aspect was my having to expend energy on gender-based personnel matters. Not only did I encounter racism at Pitt, but sexism as a Black American woman in Africana Studies. Figuring out how to handle the Black American and African men required me to step out of the traditional, socialized role of "protecting the brothers" and being loyal to them. I questioned: What about their loyalty to me and their protection of me? As Nellie Y. McKay eloquently stated about Anita Hill's October 1991 allegations of sexual harassment against Clarence Thomas during the confirmation hearing for the U.S. Supreme Court, "in all of their lives in America . . . black women have felt torn between the loyalties that bind them to race on the one hand, and sex on the other . . . yet they have almost always chosen race over the other: a sacrifice of selfhood as women and of full humanity, in favor of the race."[6] Knowing this pattern of silence, I initially hesitated about airing out the department's dirty linen, but, as a chair who was concerned about my dignity and integrity, I made some difficult decisions. Like Anita Hill, I was vilified by men whose professionalism disappeared somewhere in the wind.

An untenured Black American male lecturer refused to abide by the three-course contract per semester that he had previously signed with my predecessor. The former, South African male chair had allowed the lecturer to teach the same two courses during both the fall and spring terms to the detriment of the majors. Students were complaining that they couldn't graduate without taking the other courses. After I relayed the students' complaints to him, the lecturer childishly stated, "I'm not teaching the other courses because I don't like you."

Irritated at his brazen childishness, I replied something to the effect of, "I don't like you either so we're even. This isn't an 'I like you' contest. Simply teach the courses you had signed to do or face the consequences."

The man was fired by the dean for not fulfilling his contractual obligations. In retaliation, he filed a lawsuit against Pitt and publicly accused me of abusing my authority. Over a year later, he succumbed to a fatal heart attack in the street in front of the administration building.

The lawsuit was closed.

When I was an assistant professor, I found a love letter on my desk after my evening class. Decorated with a hand-drawn heart and arrow, the kind carved onto tree trunks by teenage boys.

Brenda, you have pierced my heart, it read, and when I recognized the signature it gave me a sinking feeling. Once I knew who it was from, I realized the term "love letter" was too generous. It was an indecent proposal. The hairs on the back of my neck pricked up. This man was dangerous. His office was just around the corner from mine, and I knew he was in there, waiting for my response.

I was working late again and the office area was, of course, empty. No question he'd planned it that way. I wished I could dash out of there and get to my car in the parking garage, but I couldn't walk by without him noticing. The elevator took too long. Even if I did escape and make it down the hall, he would surely catch me before the doors of rescue opened.

I took a deep breath.

In my opinion, the man, who was from Kenya, was a hasty hire and an example of tenure gone wrong. A decent scholar, but a sub-par teacher, I hated to think he was one of those only working in Africana Studies because it allowed him to stay in the U.S. And on top of that he was completely nuts and disruptive. He had been engaged to a Black American woman and stalked her so fiercely that she called the cops, filed charges against him, and had to leave the college where she was teaching because she was so scared. My colleagues and I all knew what was going on, because once again that's how family works. Almost immediately after his fiancée became his ex-fiancée, he zeroed in on the secretary. She feared staying after 5 p.m. because he taught a night class and she did not want to be alone when he was near.

Now, with this letter, he had turned his attention to me. Probably thought that because I was the youngest in the department, I made an easy target. Didn't he know I'd been living in African countries and knew all about this nonsense? The culturally acceptable way for men to treat women, the aggressive come-ons, the multiple wives, and the rampant cheating. I needed to nip this behavior in the bud, immediately.

I had been proposed to several times in Africa, though every time I knew it was, in large part, because I was Black American and these African men wanted me as a token, for the thrill of having a Black American woman on their arm for a while, not for who I was. Often their first desire was for a White woman, the taboo, so long the forbidden fruit; second in line was the Black American woman. Sometimes a man simply wanted to add me to his roster of wives, but I will never be a co-wife—it's just not in me. I grew a thick skin about saying "no," and saying it forcefully—even to the high-ranking diplomats and professors, with whom I enjoyed fancy dinners on their dime—and not worrying about whether I broke a heart. Of course, I did not assume they were all stalker crazy. I had many African male friends who treated their wives well, but I also possessed a finely tuned radar for spotting that streak of lowdown, no-good foolishness.

My pulse quickened at the thought of confronting the man who had the audacity to write me a note like this, at work! I reminded myself I had two brothers, a father, a boyfriend, and five uncles. If he threatened me physically and needed someone to show him a thing or two, I had options.

I quickly dialed my father's direct office number in Maryland. When he answered, I explained the content of the letter to which he responded,

"Brenda, you must take the offensive because the man is a coward. I can drive to Pittsburgh, threaten him and kick his butt, but I can't stay. When I leave the city, he can still act ugly. Show him you're in charge."

With my mind whirling with possible scenarios, and before disconnecting the phone, I said, "Okay, Daddy."

Letter in hand, I walked around the corner where his office door stood open. I gasped when I saw him in the chair with his feet up on the lowest, opened desk drawer, legs flanked wide, tongue slowly grazing his lips. Hand resting on his thigh. He held the phone to his ear but wasn't talking. He looked at me like he had been waiting for me, and the air was thick. Then I realized he was propositioning me, not for marriage but for sex. Completely vulgar and beyond disrespectful. Adrenaline intensified under my skin. Anger inflamed my courage.

"Perfect!" I yelled, in a voice louder than I knew possible. "Perfect!" I pointed at his crotch and stooped into a running stance. "I'm coming to get you!" and I charged forward making motions to kick my foot between his legs. Just before I hit the target, he jumped up and dropped the phone, shielding himself.

No other words were exchanged. I crumpled the note and dropped it at his feet.

I shifted the defense from me to him, proving I was not afraid. I drew a line in the carpet he couldn't cross. Call me bullheaded, call me mean, call me "the angry Black woman," but I did what I had to do.

After that, the man was putty in my hands. Putty.

"Hello, Dr. Berrian," he would say sweetly as he walked by my office to his. I returned his greeting with a smile. We shared books on occasion, exchanged brief words about classes and the state of politics in Kenya.

Unfortunately, he continued to stalk women from time to time, but never again did he make inappropriate advances toward me or any other female staff or faculty member in the department.

During the academic year of 2009–2010, I chaired the department for a second time after spending an enjoyable, stimulating month in Bellagio, Italy, as a Rockefeller Foundation scholar. I sent a warning to a Nigerian part-time teacher who had been using his shared office space for storing books to ship back to Senegal and the Gambia, by permission of the former Sierra Leonean male chair. Piles of books towered to the ceiling and stayed there for over a year, causing a fire hazard, and his Black American office mate complained several times over the lack of work space. After I warned the teacher and calmly requested that he move the books, then made arrangements to have the books removed when he didn't respond, the man stormed into my office screaming.

"You're a mean, spiteful woman!"

Upon hearing the shouting, the female administrative assistant and male work study student rushed into my office. I told them I was fine. The instructor needed to lower his voice and speak to me in a professional manner, and if he didn't comply, I would call the campus police. His behavior was not only a breach of professionalism, but a cultural faux pas. I was the man's elder, and in Africa you respect your elders above all else. Yet, to him, I was a woman above all else. He did not appreciate having a woman to tell him what to do.

The part-time instructor finally, with great agitation, removed the books. I wrote him a letter explaining his services were no longer needed by the department. Because his job was not tenure-stream, I had the authority to dismiss him.

Barbara A. Sizemore, one of the other female faculty members who had become my mentor, lamented with me about the condescension we had to confront from some of the African male scholars. "I tell them, I'm not your wife. Go talk to your wife like a dog, not me," she said. I had witnessed the way men in Africa treated their wives, like property. I even knew American women who ended up trapped in unhappy marriages because once the dating and engagement were over and the marriage began, their men suddenly seemed to turn on them. Order them around. Speak harshly, even call them names. But the husbands weren't *turning* on their American wives. They were enacting the treatment commonly reserved for wives in their own culture.

I wondered if there was more to it with the occasional African faculty members who acted crazed though, something about being in an American institution that made them feel threatened. I was reminded of Ann Petry's short story, "Like a Winding Sheet,"[7] in which a working-class Black American man is disrespected by his White female boss, and out of his frustration, because he is powerless to retaliate against his boss, he returns home and beats his wife.

Though a lot of what used to be blatant expressions of racism and sexism had retreated into hushed, covert offenses in American society by the 1980s, there was nothing sly or hidden about what these African men were doing. The things they said aloud! Barbara and I talked about how hurtful it was to hear things like, "Know your place" or "You behave like Sapphire." What I often said to the man was that *he* didn't know *his* place, he was only here by the graces of *my* people—those courageous students who risked humiliation and dismissal from college for staging sit-ins and protests for the creation of these degree-granting departments!

The sister-brotherhood I expected didn't exactly happen. Where was the I-help-you-you-help-me kind of alliance among minority faculty within a White university? I and other Black American colleagues particularly expected it from the Africans. In the early stages after independence, when I taught in Gabon and met Black American colleagues who worked in other African nations, we agreed the camaraderie between us and the Africans was wonderful.

In the department, the Africans enforced their own kind of alliance. I actually heard two of them bickering outside 107 my office door, and one said, "I know I'm better because I'm Igbo and you're Yoruba." I hate to use this word, but because Africans use the word. I'll do it: "tribal." Fighting like rats over the turf. And I'm thinking this is crazy; I've been on enough conflict committees to know that there's competition and unfitting interactions among people throughout the academy at large, but what is wrong here?

Colleagues at other universities confirmed it was happening across the United States. When you hire one African, he (or she) tried "to bogart" and pushed to bring in others from their country, regardless of qualification. Case in point, the part-time Nigerian instructor had been allowed to abuse his privileges only because, in my opinion, the Sierra Leonean chairperson had been treated like a chief by the Nigerian's family during his short visit to Nigeria. A Ghanaian colleague announced that for the department's open position, he didn't care if he had to ram it down our throats, but he would make sure we hired a West African candidate who was not qualified for the advertised position. My vote was no, and the Ghanaian was in the corner at the next department meeting saying, "There goes *that* woman." Outvoting me, my colleagues succumbed to the Ghanaian's bullying and brought the candidate in, and he was difficult.

Would the dean have hired an unqualified candidate for a position in one of the traditional departments? I seriously doubt it even though he suggested he would have done something like that when I made an appointment to lodge a complaint about the departmental vote. His disregard for Africana Studies couldn't have been clearer. He had the option and had exercised it in other cases, to overrule the department's bad decision. I'm more than certain that he wouldn't have approved the hire of a French language professor for a science department.

The Dean's actions made me question: Was the university suddenly a microcosm of what I saw happening in African countries? In the newly formed governments, post-independence leaders would push into power others within their clan and ethnic group, no matter their ability or qualifications. In the words of James Baldwin, "The only thing white people have that black people need, or should want is power—and no one holds power forever."[8]

Constance M. Carroll, a Pitt graduate and the current Black American chancellor of the San Diego Community College District, wrote, "Black women in higher education are isolated, underutilized and often demoralized. They note the efforts made to provide equal opportunities for black men and white women in higher education, while they somehow are left behind in the wake of both the black and feminist movements."[9] Fortunately, by the 1980s, Black American women scholars, especially in Black Studies, the humanities, and social sciences, insisted on gender as a topic of analysis and began to place Black Americans and women of the Africana diaspora at the center of their research.

That was what I had hoped for. But the university's political atmosphere exhausted me as I tried to avoid contentious situations. Some semesters, I simply came to campus, taught my classes, and went home. I found solace in my research with Fulbright and Rockefeller awards to the Caribbean.[10] And

I finally compiled my dossier for submission for full professor. I became the second woman[11] in the department to receive this promotion.

To my consternation, the number of Black American faculty at Pitt dwindled. When I first started teaching, three clusters of Black American professors existed. Nine were in Black Studies, eight in the School of Education, and seven in the School of Social Work. In 2013, the largest number was seven in Africana Studies with perhaps four in the School of Social Work.

Consequently, I continued to nurture my global connections and remembered the higher purpose of Africana Studies as a discipline. I loyally attended the African Literature Association conferences. I even organized one of the conferences in Pittsburgh, with the blessing of the then Black American provost, and brought in writers such as Ngugi wa Thiong'o, Maryse Condé, Marita Golden, Merle Collins, and Buchi Emecheta as guest speakers over the years.

Under the guise of an economic crisis at the end of the 1970s, university administrators mandated hiring freezes, reduced the faculty by 50 percent, and falsely stated that Black Studies departments lowered academic standards. As we say in the Black vernacular, "Let's get real." How can newly conceived departments without proper funding and staffing be expected to compete in less than ten years against established departments that had been in existence for one hundred years or more? Currently, Black Studies isn't offered as a major "at 83 percent of the more than 2,300 four-year colleges and universities throughout the United States. Black Studies programs have almost no presence in the course catalogues of universities in the southern states."[12] Only 9 percent of four-year colleges and universities have full-fledged departments, with an average of seven full-time professors.[13] Harvard, Yale, Princeton, Emory, and Columbia, with more than adequate external and internal funding, are hiring academic superstars for their Africana or African American Studies departments and are being viewed by outsiders as the strongest with the most majors.

There were times I considered leaving the university altogether. But, in the end, I held onto the hope that the cultural attitude about Black American female and male scholars would improve so much that meetings about "the diversity question" would no longer be necessary.

NOTES

1. For further information, read Fabio Rojas, *From Black Power to Black Studies: How a Radical Social Movement Became an Academic Discipline* (Baltimore, MA: The John Hopkins University Press, 2007) and Noliwe M. Rooks, *White Money/Black Power: The Surprising History of African American Studies and the Crisis of Race and Higher Education* (Boston, MA: Beacon Press, 2006).

2. The first-ever Black Studies Department was inaugurated in September. Shortly thereafter, one of the graduate activists, George Murray, was suspended. The students called for a strike and Murray's suspension to be lifted. The strike was the longest in U.S. history, lasting from November 6, 1968 to March 20, 1969.

3. Read Tamara Beauboeuf Lafontant, *Behind the Mask of the Strong Black Woman: Voice and Embodiment of a Costly Performance* (Philadelphia, PA: Temple University Press, 2009) and Melissa Harris-Perry, *Sister Citizen: Stereotypes and Black Women in America* (New Haven, CT: Yale University Press, 2011).

4. Among the many sources, read "Lori Latrice Martin, Biko Mandela Gray and Stephen C. Finley, "Endangered and Vulnerable: The Black Professoriate, Bullying, and the Limits of Academic Freedom," *Journal of Academic Freedom* 10 (2019). http://www.aaup.org/AF10/ endangered-and-vulnerable-black-professoriate -bullying-and-limits-academic-freedom#. XOpimMhkjlU; and Madeleine L. Daut, "Becoming Full Professor While Black, *The Chronicle of Higher Education,* July 28, 2019. http://www.chronicle.com/article/becoming-full-professor-while-black/.

5. The National Center for Education Statistics (NCES), Digest of Education Statistics Fall 2017. http://www.nces.ed.gov/programs/ digestd18/ tables/dt18_315 .20.asp.

6. Nellie Y. McKay, "Remembering Anita Hill and Clarence Thomas: What Really Happened When One Black Woman Spoke Out," in *Race-ing Justice: En-gendering Power: Essays on Anita Hill Clarence Thomas and the Construction of Social Reality*, edited by Toni Morrison (New York: Pantheon Books, 1992), 277.

7. Ann Petry, "Like a Winding Sheet," in *Miss Muriel and Other Stories* (Boston, MA: Houghton Mifflin, 1971), 198–210.

8. Baldwin, *The Fire Next Time*, 140.

9. Constance M. Carroll, "Three's a Crowd: The Dilemma of a Black Woman in Higher Education," in *But Some of Us Are Brave: All the Women Are White, All the Blacks Are Men: Black Women's Studies*, edited by Gloria T. Hull, Patricia Bell Scott, and Barbara Smith (Old Westbury, NY: Feminist Press, 1982), 116.

10. In my dining room, four women professors and I founded the Association of Caribbean Women Writers and Scholars and the journal *MaComère*. For five years, I was the book review editor.

11. Barbara A. Sizemore was the first woman to be promoted to full professor in the department.

12. Read Stacey Patton, "Black Studies: Swaggering into the Future," *The Chronicle of Higher Education*, April 12, 2012. http://www.chronicle.com/article/ black-studies-swaggering-into-the-future.

Chapter 17

Gender Politics

In an Indiana University restaurant, over the faint clinking of dishes, I sat alone at a table, saving seats for other women at the conference. I circled names and presentations in the conference program in my hands. There were sessions on "Portuguese-African Literature," "African Versus Western Audiences: Problems of Language, Form and Theme," and "The Literature of North Africa: The Writer and His Audience." I smiled and circled the presentation entitled, "Harlem Renaissance Poets and Their Influence on Négritude, by Brenda F. Berrian." I was anxious to see how my dissertation topic would be received, how it might contribute to the field. I had just taken the job in Pittsburgh, embarking on the new and exciting Black studies field as a debutante. The sun was at my back, the road ahead straight and smooth. It was my first-ever African Literature Association conference.

As my female colleagues, professors from various universities across the U.S., settled in at the table and began debating what to order, I began reading the titles of the talks I would be going to see if others were planning to go to the same ones. I figured we could tag team, and some of us could share notes on the sessions that others couldn't attend. But as I read aloud the titles of the talks, the authors they were researching and giving speeches on, my voice began to fade: James Ngugi, Ahmadou Kourouma, Camara Laye, Mbella Sonne Dipoko, Charles Mangua, Richard Rive, Wole Soyinka . . ."

I stopped. Looked up at the faces of bright, highly educated women around the table. These fellow scholars would become my close friends, allies, and sisters through the coming years. We were quiet. A colleague said aloud what I couldn't yet put into words, "It's all men." It was like we had walked right into a huge glass door and fallen flat on our backs. "Women writers should make up half of the topics!" I said. The silence was right there in front of our faces.

119

"We've all been so programmed to read men, men, men," someone said. "It's not right," said another.

"What is this? *We* are part of this nonsense." Out of 100 speeches, 99 were about male writers, including mine. Embarrassed, I blurted out, "We've been brainwashed!" Someone laughed. The words of Maryse Condé came back to me, that day in Paris as we watched the sunset while talking in the *Présence Africaine* bookshop. "It's all about the men," she had said about *négritude*. I made a mental note to slip some details about the Nardal sisters, who worked behind the scenes to ensure that *négritude* flourished and never received much attention or acknowledgement, into my presentation. "Women hold up half the sky."

Here we were at the biggest and most respected conference in our field, and there was a hole in our lineup. For a group supposedly at the forefront of "diversity," we had been caught wearing huge blinders. Privately, I kept thinking, *I'm a woman—what's wrong with me?*

Our lunch lasted over an hour, and after the plates were cleared away our discussion lingered. We agreed that if we were going to help build this organization, we had to be the ones to help balance it out. Today you won't find a conference that doesn't showcase a mix of women and men in terms of speakers and topics, but back in the 1970s it wasn't at the forefront of planners' thinking. We made a pact to seek, read, teach, and critique creative works by African women writers

Some African male scholars, who had been sitting at a nearby table and overheard our conversation, offered this, "Do not trouble yourselves. There are no African women writers." My immediate response—without stopping to consider what my next statement would entail—was, "Oh yes there are! I'll prove it!"

Loving a challenge, I realized what my contribution to my field would be. Had to be. Through the next year I performed a dramatic reading of Harlem Renaissance poetry in Jamaica. Neither Harlem Renaissance poetry nor its cousin, the poetry of *négritude*, would marshal the roads I paved in my field like I expected. My first goal would be to find out who the African women writers were to compile a comprehensive bibliography. I spent the next six years searching, calling publishers, ordering books, reading and teaching the books, expanding my friends and colleagues' connections in Africa to lead me to the writers. Two post-doctoral grants—the Southern Fellowship Fund to do research at Howard University and the Social Science Research Council (SSRC) to interview African women writers and journalists—led me to the writers in Kenya, Zambia, and the Seychelles. My first major book-length publication came out from Three Continents Press in 1985: *Bibliography of African Women Writers and Journalists*, followed in 1989 by *Bibliography of Women Writers from the Caribbean*.

When I organized the ALA Conference and brought it to Pittsburgh in 1988, the stars of the event were three women writers: Buchi Emecheta (Nigeria), Ama Ata Aidoo (Ghana), and Micere Githae-Mugo (Kenya). I thought we had really turned it around in terms of representing women. It may seem like small peanuts that this single event became more diversified, but it signaled ripple effects in dissertation topics and in college classrooms throughout the country. Women's contributions to literature were being recognized beyond the university as well, and some critics were none too pleased.

During the 1980s Henry Louis Gates, Jr., Houston A. Baker, Jr. and other men dominated Black American literary criticism and theory. The presses had decided the men's voices represented every Black American professor of Black American literature. Those who participated in it would deny it, but we all knew there was a concerted effort to exclude Black American women. The men felt threatened; they thought their power was somehow being twisted away, wrapped in a winding sheet.

Joyce A. Joyce published a 1987 essay about "The Black Canon" and, in part, how Blacks had a responsibility to write in a way that would be understandable to the "common" reader, and that Black critics needn't bend to Western ideologies of criticism when critiquing Black American literature. They should remember the stories in connection with real lives. Joyce wrote, "Since the Black creative writer has always used language as a means of communication to bind people together, the job of the Black literary critic should be to find a point of merger between the communal, utilitarian, phenomenal nature of Black literature and the aesthetic or linguistic—if you will—analyses that illuminate the 'universality' of a literary text."[1]

Joyce's essay sparked a furious debate, and Henry Louis Gates responded with an essay of his own, "What's Love Got to Do with It?" followed by Houston A. Baker's commentary "In Dubious Battle." All three arguments were flawed, but what I remembered most about the debate was the vitriol expressed toward Joyce. Baker's parenthetical remark was more than parenthetical, "I have found myself in conflict with other Afro-American critics. (The fact that both were Afro-American women may be altogether fortuitous.)"[2]

Then Alice Walker and Toni Morrison's works became more popular. Mel Watkins of the *New York Times* and the writer Ishmael Reed, instead of congratulating them, went on attack. They were mad about the way Black American males were portrayed in fictional works of Black American women writers. Watkins wrote, "There has been a concomitant tendency for some black women writers to portray black males in an unflinchingly candid and often negative manner."[3]

In his review of Toni Morrison's 1987 *Beloved*, Stanley Crouch accused Morrison of writing a "blackface holocaust novel."[4] He then stepped into the realm of personal attack when he called her a "literary conjure woman [who] has been paid off quite well."[5] Many Black American women writers and critics began to publish in response to the Black American male backlash, and Morrison and Walker sold even more books. Walker was awarded both the National Book Award for Fiction for the 1982 *The Color Purple* and the 1983 Pulitzer Prize. Morrison won the Pulitzer Prize for *Beloved* in 1988 and later the Nobel Prize for Literature in 1993.

Instead of Black American men being excited for the women, some framed their responses with anger and jealousy. And it was all happening in the public sphere. It was like what they were really saying was, "Don't explore social problems involving Black American males. You're airing our private laundry for Whites to see!" Sexist men. They didn't hesitate to air their negative or positive opinions about Black American women in their fictional works.

I appreciated how the Africana (African, Black American and Caribbean) women writers explored, through story, the range of experiences in their lives such as financial mobility, the foibles of relationships, navigating sexism in a racist world, the male gaze, infidelity and beauty. I didn't understand why the men took the stories from women so personally, unless they had believed, on some level, the stories were directed at them. I stayed out of the debates, but I watched them closely.

Once, at a women's studies conference, a surprising question of identity, one that I hadn't experienced nor seen explored in literature, sparked a lasting curiosity for me. Speaking on a panel about African women, I delivered a speech about a Buchi Emecheta novel. A White woman in the audience stood to ask a question.

"Professor Berrian," she proceeded. "When you wake up, are you a Black or a woman first?"

I stared at her. Didn't she *hear* me? I couldn't believe an educated woman had asked such a ridiculous question. One that bore no relevance to my speech. What had happened to enlightened sisterhood? Should I assume the woman had never read any of Emecheta's novels and was embarrassed? Was she subconsciously trying to put me where she *thought* my place ought to be since she was out of her comfort zone?

I responded, "Let me turn the question back to you. Tell me whether or not you were White or a woman when you woke up this morning."

The woman quickly turned red.

"Ohhh," she responded. "I suppose my question was silly. I can't cut off my White skin from my femaleness."

I was grateful for her answer, which was honest and captured my point perfectly. How could someone ever think one's gender and race could be compartmentalized? I thought of the famous 1979 speech by the Black feminist, lesbian, socialist Barbara Smith at a women's studies conference

"Racism and Women's Studies." Before a predominantly White female audience, Smith advised, "You have to comprehend how racism distorts and lessens your own lives as White women; that racism affects your chances for survival too and that it is very definitely your issue. Until you understand this no fundamental change will come about."[6]

In the years following the conference, something nagged at me, quietly. Something about the woman's question, the idea of separating one piece of identity from another. It sung like a red-breasted bird from a tree outside my window, softly, beckoning. It followed me on my travels abroad, my road trips to Jersey and Maryland to visit family, as I wrote about women writers and taught their work, as I lived my full and bustling life. It skirted at the edges of my conscience.

South Africa! I thought about the "honorary White" status Black American women adopted in order to get visas to live in the country. They maintained their "female" status but had to become White, under the vestiges of apartheid. How did that fracture work? Was it more than a formality? I'd experienced how the Black American identity held a status seen as elevated by White South Africans because of the "American" part. Could the story of these Black Americans resettled in South Africa form the true "full circle"? A diasporic journey realized in the culminating return to Africa? After forced extraction from Africa, enslavement in the U.S., freedom, the battle for civil rights, the flourish of expression and literature giving voice to their experience and that of other oppressed peoples around the world, and then the final return to the Rainbow Nation governed at last by a Black South African?

I had to find out. I had to dig into what that woman had asked me at the conference. There were no books to guide me. I wondered why there was such a paucity of autobiographies by or historical texts about Black American women's experiences in South Africa. I had to go there. [One of the women I interviewed, Bonnie Fitzpatrick-Moore, has since written *My African Heart* (1999), an autobiography which directly addresses her experiences as a Baha'i pioneer in three former Black homelands.]

I returned to South Africa in 1998, my fourth trip. There I interviewed twenty-eight Black American women expatriates and shaped their oral stories into an unpublished book-length manuscript called "Between Two Homes: Black American Women in the New South Africa." Out of the twenty-eight women interviewed, only two lived in the former Black homelands, and four lived in mixed areas. The rest resided in the former predominantly White suburbs of the urban centers of Cape Town, Durban, and Johannesburg. They had relocated, most of them permanently, to South Africa because of their own or their husbands' jobs, for mission work, for teaching opportunities, for diplomacy. Defined as members of a minority in the U.S., they searched afar for the ancestral African homeland, always a mystical place in the psyche of Black Americans, to answer the old identity question, "Who am I?"

Born and raised in the United States, remembering the Civil Rights Movement, they felt empathy toward Black South Africans who struggled under apartheid. Yet, many of the women expatriates expressed the feeling of not belonging. I listened to the women confess that since the pigmentation of their skin is Black, they assumed they would be able to blend in with the Black South African majority. To their surprise or annoyance, their manner of personal grooming, dress, posture, walking, and their way of speaking English alerted South Africans that they were foreigners. Kimberly, a lecturer in Mechanical Engineering at the University of the Witwatersrand (Wits) in Johannesburg, was astounded when a Black South African male told her that she was not Black. "I don't know what you are," he said. "But you are certainly not Black."[7]

"A real eye-opener," said another woman. "Is that some South Africans make no distinction between Black and White Americans. I am always lamenting about that fact. It's both scary and funny to realize how American I am to South Africans."

The importance of language and kinship came up frequently in interviews. Bonnie, who migrated to South Africa in 1978 for the Baha'i Faith and lived in the Xhosa homeland of the Transkei with her husband and four children, described how an elderly Xhosa woman once told her, "You are a White, Black woman. You have Black physical features, but you have a White tongue."[8] Like Kimberly, Bonnie did not speak Xhosa. She also was not a member of a Xhosa family. The elderly Xhosa woman saw Bonnie as an embodiment of two races and her "White tongue" as an indication of untrustworthiness.

Not only was "honorary White" a South African government euphemism, but it was a reality in the eyes of some Black South Africans. A Church of Christ missionary told me that even after years of being in South Africa she still did not belong. She explained, "South Africans aren't afraid to point this out to me. They only tolerate me because I have something to offer them such as hope and an education." Another woman said, "When I arrived, I felt South Africa was my home. To my surprise, when I went to work in the townships, I quickly learned the Blacks were not accepting me as one of them. First of all, they saw me as a 'Coloured.' Second of all, I was an American."

What differentiated the Black American women expatriates from the Black South African majority was that they were primarily from the middle class, held academic degrees, and were accustomed to a higher standard of living. The majority of Black South African women did not have the economic wherewithal to move even if they desired to. Therefore, the expatriates' claiming of homes on South African land forcefully taken away from the original owners three hundred years ago symbolically duplicated the British and Dutch settlers' seizure of the land when they colonized South Africa. By bringing in the almighty American dollar against the constantly devalued South African rand, Black American women expatriates could buy large homes with swimming pools and unattached cottages when it was impossible for them to do so in the States.

In becoming members of the privileged upper class in South Africa, they had also become, in a way, the colonizers. Though they could afford to hire domestic nannies and housekeepers, the Black American women felt uneasy hiring Black South African women for these tasks. It hit too close to home. I remembered how Aunt Anna worked as a domestic for a White family in Virginia. She never once talked about it. I remembered what it felt like, as a Black American family in the 1960s, to have servants while we were in the Congo.

Several of the Black American women I interviewed had adopted *ubuntu,* dedicating their lives to improving the level of education and employment opportunities for South Africans. A few of these women seemed to feel as though they were fully accepted, in contrast to many others who expressed the feeling of not belonging. One was given a Zulu name. She explained, "Students call me Professor and Granny and speak to me about their lives and dreams. Whenever I'm invited to share a meal with a Zulu family, the invitation brings about an indescribable feeling of complete acceptance in me."

A civil rights lawyer reported, "White South Africans, hearing my American accent, often approached me. One of their most common questions was, 'It's not as bad as they say it is, is it?' They disliked the lingering reputation of South Africa as a racist country." Another talked about the possible collaboration between Black Americans and South Africans. "A Black South African woman owns an emerald mine. Can anybody name a Black American woman who owns a mineral mine, or anything approximating that kind of resource, in the States? The key to the liberation of Black South Africans and Black Americans is the joining of their expertise and resources." Then an IBM executive reconsidered her American nationality, "I feel more American in the New South Africa, an African country, than I do in North America."

In February 2002, I gave the keynote address on this research for the first African American Studies: Interdisciplinary Perspectives Conference co-sponsored by the U.S. Embassy and Bogazici University in Istanbul, Turkey. These women's experiences fascinated me. During my keynote address and the speeches I gave at universities throughout Turkey and France as a scholar for the U.S. Department of State, I could relate in small measure, remembering my own time living and working in South Africa. Feeling guilty about seeing Black Africans on the margins. Amused and frustrated by the way people read me, I could understand theoretically, but not emotionally, the pervasive colorism and the colonized mentality. *Not one of the Black American women ever woke up in South Africa and forgot she was Black.* Each felt her "honorary White" status differently. Each was challenged in her beliefs about race and the complexities of identity. Their narratives trilled the birdsong of my curiosity, adding threads to the woven tapestry of my own becoming—the becoming of an Africana diasporic woman.

Back at the University of Pittsburgh, I became known as "the Iron Lady." My reputation as a demanding teacher preceded me into the classroom, and on the first day I would face rows of nervous faces. I used to lock the door the minute class started, shutting out latecomers. I demanded good grammar on response papers. I generally don't read online teacher reviews of myself. (It's too often simply a space for former students to complain about grades.) If I did, I would see comments like these currently on ratemyprofessor.com:

"She may be tough, but you learn soooo much!"

"Only take this class if you are an extremely good writer. She grades very hard and you must read all the books and come to class prepared to discuss or she'll murder you."

"She challenged me like no other teacher has and to her I'm thankful. Don't expect an easy A."

"She was very knowledgeable about the topics and was very funny too. You can tell she is very worldly. The class had a lot of reading, but they weren't too challenging of books."

Most of the students who enrolled in my African Literature classes had never been to Africa. They had never been taught about Africa, except maybe a basic, glancing history in high school.

Some of them may already recognize the holes in what we commonly teach our students in high school, but many do not. What is the university for if not to compel critical thinking? I determined my students would leave my class with a greater understanding of and respect for the Caribbean and Black American experiences and Africa with its many countries and cultures. Beyond what they've learned before, beyond the slanted messages mainstream media feeds them. More about a woman's experience, too.

I started by promoting Africana women and what they were writing about. Reading requirements for my classes included works such as Zora Neale Hurston's *Their Eyes Were Watching God* and Winnie Mandela's memoir *A Part of My Soul Went with Him.* The latter was a painful portrait of Winnie's marriage to Nelson Mandela, his and her imprisonments under apartheid, the constant police harassment, and the inability to raise her daughters due to her constant bans by the government. I focused on Mrs. Mandela's strength and resilience and migration from a rural Xhosa homestead to an urban Jo'burg.

For many years I assigned Buchi Emecheta's *The Joys of Motherhood*, about a Nigerian woman who raises numerous children and pointedly favored her sons, who then ignored her in adulthood. I taught the book because it also deals with early twentieth-century Nigeria under British colonialism and the migration from the rural village to the city.

I toted a bag full of books and objects from my travels to show students—a traditional wood-carved mask, a photograph of Léopoldville in 1961, traditional African clothing and CDs, etc. I told anecdotes of my experiences living in various African countries.

"An Italian diplomat I tutored in Gabon, who was also a taxidermist heading to Uganda to work during the Idi Amin regime, tried to give me an elephant foot as a gift!" They enjoyed my tales.

We read *Desert Flower*, a Somali book about a female teenager moving from a rural, desert area to an urban London, how out of sorts she felt about not knowing how the toilet on the plane worked, because before then she'd urinated in a hole in the ground. I described how I encountered the Turkish toilets in Paris, in the building where the African street sweepers lived. I had looked at the hole in the ground and thought, *What in the world am I supposed to do with this? Squat?*

I asked the students, "What happened in your life and what kind of adjustments did you have to make?"

Having left home to attend college in Pittsburgh, my students were surprised to find they could relate to stories like J. Nozipo Maraire's *Zenzele*, a novel about a daughter who leaves home to attend medical school in the States and begins favoring American customs and comforts over those of her native Zimbabwe. The mother writes her daughter about the importance of knowing her history, customs, and culture and how her aunt and father had fought for independence. The mother wants her daughter to return and contribute to Zimbabwe's future.

The topics we discussed were real; human things students knew and could relate to. Perhaps they thought before then that the White male canon was the only true voice of experience. We explored the artistry of the literature. I did not teach theoretical approaches which turn students off from books rather than getting them to read closely and look deeper. I brought in articles on history and sociology to help explain the book's context. I found critics who examined language and imagery. In my view, students needed to know the use of proverbs in Chinua Achebe's *Things Fall Apart* and Okot p'Bitek's *Song of Lawino*. Or how an Ousmane Sembène film duplicated the structure of an oral story on screen. How the Trinidadian Samuel Selvon employed Creole within the narrative of *The Lonely Londoners*. I wanted them to really understand the sociopolitical and linguistic messages in the film and books.

But there was danger in what we were doing too, what it opened up for students. Occasionally, a young female student would linger after class, her classmates already packed up and gone, and tell me she appreciated how a certain writer showed the sacrifices women are asked to make, and choose to make, for love. Like how Marita Golden's cross-cultural autobiographical novel *Migrations of the Heart* described a failed marriage between Marita, who had been a Black American journalist in the 1970s, and her Nigerian husband, when they moved to Nigeria and suddenly her husband expected her to be a submissive Yoruba wife, giving up her personal identity. Sometimes a student would be near tears, and I could tell she wanted to confess something. I let her. It became too much, at times, and I had to remind students I was not their mother. Instead, I was their teacher.

I wanted their worlds to open up, for them to travel, to meet people, and to see how expansive life can be, the many choices they had for how to live their lives and how they chose to *see* their lives.

Wisdom always presents itself in literature, for it is where truth is shown best, not preached, not lectured. I know students learn the most not from my lectures but from the novelists who paint, in a real way, the lives of Africana people. Literature has a way of inviting readers in, letting them encounter the story at their own pace, revealing the complicated, imperfect lives of people who are like them even if they live in circumstances completely foreign to them.

One day we were reading closely a section of Toni Morrison's *The Bluest Eye*, a novel about internalized racism through the perspective of Pecola, a young Black American girl who wants, more than anything, to acquire blue eyes. In one scene, her father, overcome with confusion and lust, rapes her. I urged students to find the moment when the father's stray thoughts turn to action. The room was quiet, as it often was when we discussed taboo topics that came up in novels, like incest.

Suddenly, a female student fell out of her seat onto the floor laughing. The book slipped out of her hand as she whooped and squealed, rolling around on her back as though someone were tickling her. Open mouthed, she covered her face with her hands and her whole body shook.

Other students looked at me, worry in their eyebrows, unsure about what to do.

"Let's take a quick ten-minute break," I said.

The student calmed as the others quickly filed out of the room. She kept her head down as I approached. With jittery movements, she began gathering her notes and books strewn on the floor. I picked up a few papers and handed them to her. Then she said, very quietly, that she had been raped by her father. She had never told anyone until then, and when we were reading the passages in class it suddenly gripped her and then tumbled out. She was so embarrassed.

I knew the book had changed her, had moved something out of her, and I hoped the story healed her some. I never found out. She withdrew from the class despite my objection.

Over the years, the student demographics began to change: more White students and students of the Africana diaspora enrolled. The appreciation for literature, or the sense that students felt connected to the literature, did not change. There is a moment in life when one arrives back at the same place one had been long ago, and the place hasn't changed but the person has. One arrives at the precipice of one's memory, grown and knowing.

How humbled I felt, again and again, to see the great influence of Black American culture, music, art, politics, and literature on foreign lands. Hearing Stevie Wonder's music in a commercial on French television. Reading how Winston Churchill, the late prime minister of England, read the Harlem Renaissance Claude McKay's "If We Must Die" poem during one of his famous World War II–radio speeches. Getting to know over the years the eldest son of the Senegalese novelist Abdoulaye Sadji, who was named Amadou Booker Washington Sadji after Booker T. Washington, the famous Black American educator and orator, because his father had admired him so much. Learning how French-speaking African and Caribbean writers and critics had founded a literary movement (*négritude*) after being exposed to the powerful words of Langston Hughes and other Harlem Renaissance writers.

I passed this on to my students. I recognized the change in myself, too, from a girl who drew her life story with pictures of herself and her family as White characters, not yet associating published stories about and by Black people, to a woman who found and taught works by women writers of the Africana diaspora and became a writer herself. Living here and abroad shaped my development. Even as an outsider in the foreign countries, I absorbed some of the customs, studied and adopted some of the cultural beliefs, and appreciated my racial heritage more than before. I remembered my father's urgent assurances that education was the key to betterment in society. Forty years later, President Mandela was to reinforce my father's words with the statement, "Education is the most powerful weapon which you can use to change the world."

NOTES

1. Joyce A. Joyce, "The Black Canon: Reconstructing Black American Criticism," *New Literary History* 18, no. 2 (Winter 1987), 343.

2. Houston A. Baker, Jr., "In Dubious Battle," *New Literary History*, 18, no. 2 (Winter 1987), 363.

3. Mel Watkins, "Sexism, Racism and Black Women Writers," *The New York Times*, June 15, 1986. http://www.nytimes.com/1986/06/15/books/sexism-racism-and-black-women-writers.html.

4. Stanley Crouch, "Aunt Medea," *The New Republic*, October 19, 1987, 40.

5. Ibid., 43.

6. Barbara Smith, "Racism and Women's Studies," *Frontiers: A Journal of Women's Studies* 5, no. 1 (Spring 1980), 48.

7. Kimberly Battle, quoted in "Between Two Homes: African American Women in the New South Africa," edited by Brenda F. Berrian, unpublished manuscript.

8. Bonnie Fitzpatrick-Moore, quoted in "Between Two Homes."

Chapter 18

Residues of Apartheid

The woman holding a sign with my name on it was White. *Dr. Brenda Berrian*, it said, and I looked back and forth between the sign and the woman in disbelief. She wore a dark green business suit, and she scanned the baggage claim area, looking this way and that for me. I might have watched her for a while without identifying myself to let the moment sink in, but I knew I had to come forward. I had traveled enough to know it would not take long before someone recognized me as a foreigner, whether by my accent or skin color or hairstyle or attire.

Here I was in South Africa for the first time to visit my friend, a Black American scholar and who picks me up at the airport, but a *White woman*?

I took a deep breath and approached her, introducing myself as the woman on the sign. She smiled wide and friendly and said, in a vaguely Dutch accent, "Welcome to South Africa."

It was June 1993, and I had read and heard so much about the persistent evil of South Africa's apartheid system that I almost expected her to say, "Welcome to apartheid." I might have viewed South Africa at that point as the most racist place on earth. Curious and nervous at the same time, I had planned to stay close to my friend Adele during my month-long trip, guarded against any danger or issues of discrimination, and here I was, a Black American woman, alone with a White woman in apartheid South Africa.

This was only the first of many shocks to come.

"Brenda!" I turned to see a familiar face, a gladdening sight, my friend Adele rushing toward me. We hugged and laughed like teenage girls. Adele had run quickly to the bathroom and missed my arrival. She introduced the woman as Annette, the chair of the English department at the University of Potchefstroom (now North-West University), where Adele, a Black

American, was teaching as a Fulbright scholar. Adele mentioned Annette was Afrikaner and spoke both English and Afrikaans.

It explained the accent I couldn't quite place: it wasn't British or even South African British but Afrikaans. And this was my next discomforting surprise, that Annette was actually Afrikaner. Of the two main groups of Whites in South Africa, Afrikaners were known as the ones who officially orchestrated apartheid, pushing through legislation that ensured Blacks could work only low-wage jobs for White-owned companies and live only in slums and poverty-stricken settlements close to those companies on land the Whites didn't want: a myriad of other oppressive rules. Blacks not only had to contend with discrimination at a social level, the general racist attitude of those in power in a White-ruled society, as we did in nearly every country, but on a political level too—you were actually *breaking the law* if you did not enact rules of apartheid. The law of the land not only justified but enforced supreme separation of races to the overwhelming, absolutely devastating, detriment of Blacks. I thought Afrikaners were the ones to blame for poor Hector Pieterson, murdered by a bullet of hate, his small body held in the arms of a fellow student in Soweto, an image I could recall in my mind so easily still, seventeen years after I'd seen it. And even more recently, I had been hearing news of these Afrikaners killing people.

As we walked through the Jan Smuts Airport (now O.R. Tambo International Airport), Adele explained the university professors had organized a reception for the two of us visiting her. (Another friend of Adele's from the United States—a White American—had traveled on the same plane as me, which I had not realized until after we landed.) As Adele talked animatedly about all the things she had planned for us to do, I noted she was acting normal as though nothing were amiss, and I wanted to stop and demand that she tell me what was going on. I liked my friend but thought she had a lot of nerve coming to the airport to pick me up with an Afrikaner in tow, no advance warning either.

When we stepped outside to the waiting car, I was still so unsettled that I barely noticed the cold breeze that whipped my scarf into the air. South of the equator like the Congo, South Africa's June was wintertime. Annette opened the car door for me with the courtesy of a chauffeur, then went around to the driver's seat.

I watched out the window as we drove from the airport to Adele's house in Potchefstroom, sixty-eight miles east of Johannesburg. The sky was overcast and in the grey light I watched tall, wheat-colored grasses blowing in the wind. Flat land stretched for miles and miles, with patches of neatly trimmed green grasses and clusters of trees whose bare branches stretched out like arms to greet you. Every time I visited a different country in Africa, I was reminded of how vast it was. (I constantly had to remind my American students that Africa is a continent, a huge landmass several times bigger than the U.S. and rich with many languages, cultures, and people. Not a country.) It always felt good to come to Africa, and a small part of me still took pride in a place where the majority of people were Black, just as I had as a teenager on my move to the Congo.

I also felt pangs of loss, as my father had passed away four years prior. He had been such a presence in my life that I felt a hollowness that seemed to have no end and, if I thought about his passing too much, it threatened to swallow me. I wished he could be here, in South Africa with me.

I was now a tenured professor at a research institution in the U.S., and my CV was ten pages long. Someone once said to me that I never let the grass grow under my feet, and that maxim held true long after I finished school. Since receiving my doctorate in Paris, I had presented at and organized several conferences on African literature, taught at the Freie Universität de Berlin (Free University of Berlin, or FU Berlin) in Germany, and traveled all over the Caribbean, to South America, and to Kenya, Ghana, Benin, Togo, Nigeria, Tanzania, Seychelles, Senegal, and Zambia in Africa. But I had not yet been to South Africa.

Just before the 1994 election, which would officially mark the end of apartheid, Adele was the first Black American awarded a Fulbright fellowship to teach in South Africa.

And where did they send this woman?

Potch, in what was considered the headquarters of apartheid.

I should have known.

I had done my homework; I read historical and political texts alongside fiction and biographies. I watched the films *Cry Freedom, A World Apart, Mandela,* and *Sarafina.* Each film dealt with the evils of apartheid and the Black South Africans' ability to survive against brutality. I spoke at length with South African students who were studying at my university—they all described the immense wealth of the White minority and the wretched poverty of most Blacks. Despite these conversations, the films and books and news reports, and my own imagination, I was still unprepared for what I was to see and encounter.

"It's nice—much better than you think, come on over!" Adele had said. She said the university administrators had given her a mansion to live in, and as we pulled into the driveway, I saw she had not exaggerated. A huge, sprawling house. A Toyota in the driveway. It was so over the top. The message they were trying to send was clear, *Look at how liberal we are!*

When we went to the bank to exchange money the following morning, the teller said to me, "Ah, the professor's sister! How do you like South Africa?" I was becoming quickly familiar with the Afrikaner accent which made "South Africa" sound like "Souf Efrikey," but it alarmed me that this person

I had never seen in my life, in a foreign country, knew who I was. There was a constant eerie feeling of being watched, and Adele confirmed our movements were being closely observed and monitored. Each time we went to a restaurant or shop Adele frequented I would be greeted with, "Hello Professor N's sister! How do you like South Africa?"

I did not know how to answer the question honestly.

I thought I might suffocate.

In this town of 120,000, there were White people everywhere, the market, the store, the school, and I kept searching for dark faces. Accustomed to staying with Africans and being in their company in other African countries, I had a hard time understanding how difficult it was to meet and have decent, long conversations with Black South Africans. In a country of 80 percent Blacks, it should not be this hard to meet Black people!

After an entire day of seeing not a single Black person other than Adele, her two children, her servant, and my reflection in the mirror, I asked, "Where are the Blacks?" Adele confessed she was the only Black who could live in the town legally, and she had told her colleagues at the university I was her big sister so there would be no problems or questions. Just the year before Black Americans could only enter South Africa with a special visa labeling them as an honorary White. They could only stay in certain hotels—hotels where Black South Africans could not stay—and they were followed by the secret police. I said never in life would I do that, and luckily the apartheid government officials discontinued the requirement just before Adele invited me. Yet, our station in the town felt something like an honorary White—we were treated with either over-amplified or cautious kindness that never let us forget our skin color.

Adele was the experiment. A test for how a Black person would fare at the university and in the town. She was not fazed by the arrangement. Since she had to deal with racist Whites in southern Florida where she worked, it wasn't much of an adjustment for her to work with Afrikaners in Potch. Annette had bent over backwards to welcome her, complete with a rent-free home and a shiny Toyota. She welcomed us with an elaborate dinner four nights later, while her Black servant ate and rested outside in her one-room brick home. Now I wondered if part of the reason Adele had wanted me to visit was so she didn't have to be so alone.

In 1993 South Africa was in the process of dismantling the four standard racial classifications: Blacks, Whites, Indians, and Coloureds. Indians had migrated to South Africa from a laboring class in India to cut sugar cane in Natal. English-speaking South Africans, the descendants of nineteenth-century British colonialism, comprised a third of the Whites. The Coloureds, aka the "brown Afrikaners," were descendants from mixed parentage (Khoi-Khoi and San people, enslaved Malays, and Europeans) and generally speak

Afrikaans as their first language. Traditionally, the Afrikaners (descendants of Dutch, French and German settlers) dominated the political arena whereas the English ruled the economy. Since light-skinned Coloureds were almost impossible to differentiate from Afrikaners, the Population Registration Act of 1950 emphasized association and ancestry as the way of establishing who was White. It was like a reverse one-drop rule.

In Potch, the rigid segregation of the four races affected me. I was appalled by how blatant and visible the demarcation between the lives of people of various races was. The former apartheid laws that governed housing along racial lines had been strictly enforced—city housing and the best land were allocated to the Whites. Adele and I drove outside the city to see the townships and informal settlements that were mandated for the other races on arid land without proper sewage, electricity and water. They were ten miles or farther outside of the city center. It was one thing to read about apartheid practices and another thing to see them with your own eyes, to move within this system as a person of color, knowing that if by chance you happened to have been born in this country your life would be the polar opposite of what it is.

Of course, there was still racism in the U.S., but no one could deny Black Americans had made progress. Discrimination had not been totally eradicated. One only needed to look no further than the Rodney King beating.[1] Part of the reason the King beating got such wide attention is it was a case of unusually overt, visible, violent racism. Years before racism settled into covertness. Invisibility. We had laws to prevent the visible stuff. Affirmative Action, for example, kept workplaces and universities from rejecting minority applicants or enforcing overtly racist ideas upon minorities. Here in Potch the uneven playing field was glaringly obvious, magnified by the difference in population numbers of Blacks versus Whites, and it felt like a Jim Crow South!

What was most unsettling was that when I finally found Black South Africans in the city, I realized they were always on the margin: the street sweepers, the gardeners, the janitors, the maids, and the street vendors. My contact with them was limited, because they were the invisibles, and they were there to work, not to talk to a foreigner.

If they were not scheduled to work the night shift, Black and Coloured workers had to vacate the town's premises by dinnertime or else they would be arrested. Reminiscent of the U.S. sundown towns. As the sun began to ease toward the horizon, a sense of haste filled the air. You could hear the movement, the change, in hurried footsteps and voices hailing taxis. If you were in town, sometimes you could see it, too—people running to the taxi stands and bus stops to catch the last rides back to the townships. By six o'clock in the evening, the streets of Potch were emptied of Blacks, leaving a feeling of abandonment. It saddened me. Blacks were only in Potch to work. They did not live there, love there, sing there, or learn there. It was not their home.

It was like a reverse "White flight" that happened decades before in the U.S., when Whites began moving out of cities to suburbs, where they had bigger, nicer houses and schools, and they did not have to live next to minorities. They worked in the city by day and commuted home to the suburbs at night. It was a move of privilege. Here in South Africa it was the opposite—the working-class Blacks came into the city to work and then went home to poorer, less-privileged areas where they lived involuntarily.

One afternoon Lynne, Adele's White American colleague, and I stepped into a restaurant in the town center to eat a late lunch. The place was empty. Not one customer. Before we could call out for service, we heard a woman's voice singing, in the melodic rolling tongue of Tswana. We turned to see a Black woman backing through a door into the dining area toward us, carrying a tray of glasses. When I said "Hello" as she turned around, she stopped singing and out of her hands fell the tray, glasses crashing to the floor.

I knew in the way she looked at me and not at Lynne that she had never seen a Black customer in the restaurant. My presence and *my voice* had thrown her out of sync. The restaurant was for Whites; she had never served a Black customer.

In another ten months, the apartheid government would be defunct. The newly elected ANC government in April 1994 would grant the Black South African majority freedom from the oppressive system that had set a low ceiling over their lives. Years of being treated as a third-class citizen were deeply ingrained in this woman. I saw how difficult the transition would be.

I kneeled down and picked up some of the broken glass pieces, a way of saying without words that I understood where she was coming from. With all the kindness I could muster, I gently told the woman, "Sisi, it's all right." She was shaking, clearly disconcerted and unsure of what to do. While she regained her composure, an embarrassed Lynne announced we were hungry and asked if it was too late to get something to eat.

"You are Americans," the woman said slowly, "Yes. Lunch can be served."

I shook my head and spoke quietly to Lynne as the woman swept up shards of broken glass and hurried to bring us menus. It will take the server a long time to feel like a first-class citizen, which was no fault of her own but a sad thing to recognize all the same.

One afternoon Adele and I decided to have a little fun with our "quasi honorary White" status to see what would happen if we got our hair done. She called an Afrikaner beauty parlor to book appointments for us. The Afrikaner salon was in the town center with a big display window in front. We looked at each other and said, "What would they do if we sat in that spot? We liked to be spontaneous because we knew we were under the microscope. So, we walked into the salon and sat in the two chairs by the window, side by side, and asked for a touch-up. At the time we both wore our hair perm-straightened.

There were several White female beauticians and two Black South African assistants. One of the Black assistants washed my hair and combed out the tangles. I had noticed several White patrons being served by White beauticians in the same way. When a beautician walked over to us, the assistant did not step away. In the mirror I watched as the Black assistant parted a section of my hair with a comb and held it up for the White beautician to dry it with the hair dryer and curl it with iron curlers, careful not to touch my hair with her fingers with hideously long plastic fingernails. The beautician carefully held the curler as the assistant smoothed my hair around the tube, then the White beautician waved her hand away just in time to avoid contact. As though my hair would pollute her skin. Could she truly believe my hair, just because I was Black, was tainted with something that could harm her? Was she afraid of being arrested for not following such a trivial rule? Did they truly take skin so seriously here?

Ironically, the White beautician's short haircut was dark at the roots and a garish bright red throughout. I wanted to tell her she needed someone more talented than herself to fix her duo-color hair problem. The Black assistant looked like she had just rolled out of bed—her permed-straight hair was haphazardly swept back away from her face but without a tie or clip. It just hung in the air. It looked brittle and dry, like she did not care or did not have time to condition it. I would learn that in many of the townships there were no mirrors—people could not afford them. They could not afford a reflection of themselves! The sight of the Black woman's hair just made me sad, while I resented the White woman's clownish coif as she refused to touch my hair.

I watched as the pair repeated the same don't-touch process with Adele's hair. They knew who she was and who I was too—everyone did. But what could they do with our strange status that didn't fit into any of the four boxes they put everyone in? What do you do with "honorary White" hair? It mattered none. We could live in a town Blacks weren't allowed to live in. Adele could teach at an Afrikaner university. I could be served at a White restaurant, but when it came to our hair, we were Black and that was all.

Apartheid showcased on our hair!

The beautician and the assistant taking great pains to gather and curl without touching each other or my hair were too many hands and made a job more complicated than necessary. Suddenly it struck me that they looked like a comedy sketch. Something Richard Pryor would imitate with an exaggerated, wide-eyed look on his face.

I wanted to hold my laughter until we were outside but I could not. I laughed until I nearly cried. It was ludicrous—the length they went to in order to keep the status quo. My laughter sent Adele into a fit and we got louder and louder, shaking our upper bodies, and the beauticians had to stop what they were doing because we could not sit still. Didn't we know they could have burned our hair! The two women attending our hair did not laugh—they didn't get it. I turned to look at the Black South African woman, tried to meet her eye, but she gave me a puzzled look. To them, nothing was strange; this was of course how they would handle the hair situation of a Black woman. Everything had to be separate. I had discovered at the library they had separate card catalogs for White, Black, Coloured, and Indian writers. Even names could not touch.

It was funny because it was so petty, and it was sad because it was real.

Even the White beautician suffered, in a way, having to be on alert. She endured the tiny aches that came with benefitting from another's affliction.

When I finally got myself under control, I remembered hair had been a marker for racial classification to distinguish a Coloured person from a Black person. An apartheid government official would tell the person to insert a pencil in his or her hair. If the pencil glided and fell from the hair, the person was classified as a Coloured. If it got stuck in the hair, the person was Black. Hair was racially charged in a way that made me feel I was back in the 1960s.

The United States had imposed deep economic sanctions on South Africa since 1986, demanding the end of apartheid. Still it took years to come to an end. Adele and I paid the beauticians for their services.

Before we left, I sat back in the styling chair, the beautician and assistant gathered in, and I handed Adele my camera; I wanted a reminder of this moment, something to show my students to explain the real, practical ways apartheid affected the daily lives of every person of every race in South Africa.

Though these antics were fun and I enjoyed spending time with Adele, it was exhausting to be under such surveillance. I wondered if this was how Angela Davis had felt when she returned from her studies abroad and the FBI interrogated her about her Communist views and put her on a watch list. Or if it was a tiny fraction of what Black South Africans felt as they had to carry passes with them everywhere they went. I did not think I could take it for the entire month of my stay.

"This is not working," I told Adele. "I have got to *go*." There were many other areas I wanted to see in South Africa anyway, like Cape Town and Johannesburg. I needed a real city; I needed to be able to move freely. Adele reminded me she had planned for all of us to fly to the Eastern Cape for the Grahamstown National Arts Festival and to drive to Durban for an American Studies conference at the University of Natal.

Freedom on the horizon!

As we left the flat fields and quiet buildings of Potch, I felt a lifting of my soul.

Like a typical American tourist, I compared each South African city to an American counterpart. Johannesburg with its tall skyscrapers, heavy traffic, clogged freeways, and crowded housing reminded me of Chicago. Durban, in the coastal Natal area, reminded me of both Miami with its beachfronts and San Francisco with its hills. Cape Town, based in the Cape Province, could have been Santa Barbara, Santa Monica, and Carmel rolled into one city. Durban captured my heart, for it was the only city that had almost a West African flavor with its tropical climate and smells of mold, dirt, and spices—earthy, honest smells that brought with them nostalgia for the Congo and Gabon.

When I saw Black South Africans at last, I went wild. I approached a Black man with a familiar countenance at the Holiday Inn's front desk and said, "Hey! You look like my *brother!*" He said he was Brian from Cape Town, and I replied, "Well, Brian I am going to Cape Town and I'm calling YOU!" He blushed and said he was married and I replied, "I don't care."

At the conference in Durban I eagerly approached Black South African men and women, meeting and greeting them and asking them where they were from. Once I said, jokingly "Where are your people from? Tell them I'm coming!"

Their reactions were warm and generous. That was the thing—no matter where you were in the world, Blacks formed a community with each other: a mutual understanding and quest for advancement. The long history of oppression that forced Blacks into the margins gave birth to kinships and networks within those margins. I grew up witnessing that web of connection with my father—all the people he knew and met through other people, people of political power and influence. As a scholar I had many contacts in the arts world this way. It was a jewel in the stone path of hardship. A jewel that began to fade as freedom arose, a triumph that carried loss alongside victory.

While approaching a stranger and making an immediate connection was certainly not the norm, for Blacks across the world it was not altogether unorthodox. I exchanged addresses with many scholars at the conference, and professors from Cape Town insisted that Lynne and I visit their city. We went, and I called Brian from Cape Town and his wife to pick us up, and we had a delightful visit. Another professor from Johannesburg gave me her phone number and urged me to call her and her husband when I arrived in that city, and I did. When someone was added to my "web" of connections, I never knew how or even if they would emerge in my life again.

In Cape Town I kept seeing people wearing colorful soft leather shoes. They looked comfortable and stylish, like decorative slippers. A shoe junkie, I asked one woman about the brand and where I could find them. She explained the Angel shoes were handmade locally in Cape Town and I could find them in all different colors at the upscale Victoria & Alfred Waterfront Mall.

One rainy afternoon I went in search of the shoes. I wore gold earrings and my shimmery raincoat that had tiered gold-and-black fabric, a coat that always garnered compliments and was undeniably classy enough for the Victoria & Alfred. Sitting right on the harbor with the backdrop of the majestic Table Mountain in the distance, the mall lived up to its reputation as the most gorgeous and expensive tourist attraction in town.

I entered a shoe store that displayed Angel shoes in the window, and the lone Coloured salesman was busy assisting two White women customers. I looked at shoes while he hurried back and forth retrieving different shoe sizes for the women. I ran my fingers along the soft fabric of the Angel shoes. They were sturdy and yet they had some give, and I knew they would form to my feet comfortably. Unique and resilient, they could represent, I imagined, the South African people to me, and I wanted to hold an emblem of that spirit when I returned home. I loved the turquoise ones that looked like the color of Caribbean waters, the orange ones bright as a summer sunset, and the red ones that reminded me of Mother. They were delicate and stitched in a feminine ballet-slipper style.

After trying on many shoes, the women left without buying anything. The man's shoulders sank as they walked out the door, and I sensed his salary was tied to sales commission. I knew I would make up for it by buying at least two pairs. He slowly placed the discarded shoes into their respective boxes, ignoring my presence. At last he looked up.

"May I see some Angel shoes in my size?" I said. By instinct, when traveling I always spoke slowly and clearly in case someone's first language was not English.

The man said, "Madam. Angels are upmarket," and he went right back to packing away shoes as though the conversation were over. Upmarket meant "expensive." I went on alert, knowing immediately he read my skin and put me in the Coloured racial box.

"Yes. And?" I pressed on. "Please show me what you have in size thirty-nine." Now I was set to prove him wrong.

Not moving an inch, the salesman repeated, as though I was the one who might not understand what he was saying,

"Madam. The shoes are upmarket."

He next dismissed me with a wave of his hand.

I felt a smallness come over me. I remembered being a young girl holding Mother's hand in the shoe section of Rich's department store in Atlanta, Georgia. In the early-1950s, Jim Crow ruled the land. Ignoring what she saw as a crooked law, Mother marched Toni and me over to the seating area designated for Whites and waited for assistance with the foot x-ray machine. Immediately, an agitated White sales clerk approached us and looked back and forth between my mother, Toni, and me, clearly confused as to why this woman who might be White was with these dark children. He then said we had to move next to the machine, which was in the Black seating area. Mother smiled calmly and told the man we would remain right there. He protested, though he would not name the reason. My mother pulled out of her purse a customer appreciation letter from the head of the company, who had sent out letters to names—not knowing of course what color the recipients were—and she told the man she would go upstairs to Mr. Rich's office and lodge a complaint if he refused to serve us. Quickly, the salesman kneeled down and put my foot in his hands to place it on the x-ray machine, and my mother sat down next to me.

I channeled Mother right then and calmed my breathing. I understood the code and why this Coloured salesman assumed I could not afford the Angel shoes, even though I was dressed sharply and wearing gold jewelry. My hair was straightened. Racism coming from a man who looked just like me was sharper, crueler. There was no alliance, none of the immediate connection between Black people, no web building. I hurt deeper, because I hurt for this man. The fact that he could disrespect me so easily meant he was full of self-hatred and that he held in low regard his own race and his own face.

I decided this was one of the reasons I had chosen the field of Africana Studies. Instead of reacting in anger, I would put my professor hat on. I was glad it was only the two of us in the store. With a deep, sad sigh, I told the man again to fetch me some shoes. "And when you come back, you and I need to have a private talk."

"What?" he said abruptly. It sounded like *Vut?* in that Afrikaner accent. "Oh shame. You are American!" I wondered if I had absorbed some of the local intonation, because he had only just now placed my accent. His face visibly changed, as though his boss had just walked in. He began apologizing and hurried to the back of the store.

He had just devoted twenty minutes to two White women who had purchased nothing. How dare he judge me and not the White women! I fumed.

He returned, still apologizing and saying he did not realize I was American.

I snapped, "What difference does it make? You didn't decide the White women couldn't afford shoes in this store." I chose two pairs of shoes, paid for them, and then sat down on the bench and motioned for him to sit. I forced myself to calm down because I wanted to teach him a lesson. Our experiences were vastly different, and I knew this wasn't even my country. My own background was more privileged than his, and I could offend him by trying to relate to him, but I reminded myself this wasn't about me. It was about him. It was about the future.

He and I had a similar history to share, I told him. I quickly compared apartheid and segregation before the Civil Rights Movement in the U.S. and advised him to start feeling good about himself, for things were about to change in his country. That he no longer needed to categorize himself or others according to which race box they looked like. He no longer needed to serve Whites over others, over himself. I paraphrased the Rev. Jesse Jackson's motto, "You are *somebody*." The man nodded, though I could not tell if he took it to heart.

I doubt my little lecture raised his self-esteem much other than for those few minutes, but as I walked out of the store with my new, colorful shoes that would protect and beautify my feet as I continued along my journey, I felt hope for him and his country.

South Africa in transition. Soon it would earn the nickname "Rainbow Nation," as the world watched the country take remarkable measures in healing its racial strife. Words like "forgiveness" and "reconciliation" formed a new and exciting story for South Africa. Yet still, in 1993, glimmers of apartheid would spring up in surprising ways.

White South African men walked the streets with guns holstered to their waists, as nonchalantly as if they were pocket handkerchiefs, unaware of how threatening the weapons could be. I never got used to seeing that scene. Once I approached a White policeman to ask for directions; his hand immediately touched his gun. I had forgotten what I looked like and how much that meant. He was looking at a Black woman, not a lost Black American. From his perspective, no Black South African would willingly approach a White policeman, and he saw danger. In a split second of panic, of imagining being shot, my awareness of the situation piqued and I raised my voice, using a heavy American accent tinged with adrenaline. As he lowered his hand, he uttered the usual, "Oh, you are an *American.*" Then, "How do you like South Africa?"

One morning I took a walk to explore Adele's neighborhood with its big houses, large gardens, double bar metal gates, and high concrete walls plastered with the warning signs: "Beware of the dog" and alongside an illustration of a cocked gun, "Armed Response."

A White couple walked toward me on the sidewalk. During apartheid in South Africa and segregation in the Deep South, the rule was for Blacks to jump into the street to let Whites walk by. Since I wasn't a Black South African and this was the transitional period before the end of apartheid, I continued to walk in the middle of the sidewalk. I had never jumped off the sidewalk in the South—certainly Mother didn't let us if the situation arose, and I wasn't going to do it now, decades later. I was not going to play by those stupid rules that were officially out of date anyway. I was not going to reroute my path because of the color of my skin. There were, no doubt, many Whites who would agree with me.

Grumbling with indignation, the couple stepped into the street rather than to walk near me on my left or right side. It was not the first time. I thought, *some of the same things that happened to me as a kid are happening here. It's like I'm back in the 1950s!*

It was going to be a difficult transition for them, I thought.

It occurred to me that during these weeks I had been more than a witness, more than a recipient; I was participating.

I continued walking.

"Sisi!" I turned to see a Black man who was cutting the hedges of a home nearby.

Having observed this short game of upmanship, he shook his head and remarked, "You should not have done that."

My response was a sharp retort, my mother's feisty, impatient spirit within me. "Yes, I should have! Why didn't you clap for me?"

He slowly shook his head again but did not speak.

I wanted to tell him he shouldn't be jumping off the sidewalk either, siding with the oppressors. He was free now, free to put down the shears and go make something of himself. And yet, in the silence I saw in his eyes that he simply did not want me to get hurt. He was scolding me in order to protect me, and I glimpsed the layers of complexity that as an outsider I would never fully understand.

Maybe it echoed, in a way, what it was like when the enslaved Blacks in the U.S. were told they were emancipated after the end of the Civil War. Some eagerly left the plantations; others stayed behind, scratched their heads, and wondered what would happen to them. Some had to stay. They did not have the economic power to make it on their own. Whites still owned the businesses that hired employees; Whites still ruled the government; Whites still held power. While the rules had changed officially, the strictures of society would hold intact for years to come, crumbling slowly.

In Johannesburg, I met up with Miriam, a friendly Mozambican teacher of history and wife of a Black South African worker I had met at the conference. She, her husband, and their son showed me around the city. Having seen documentaries that had featured the Johannesburg train station, I wanted to see what it looked like inside, this largest, most trafficked station in the country: tall arches holding up windowed walls, modern-looking sand-tiled floor. I remembered that much of it must be new, repaired within the last few decades.

When I reached out to open the main door of the station, Miriam, her husband Daniel, and her son who were directly behind me, came to an abrupt full stop.

Miriam spoke softly, "We were whipped or arrested if we went through the front door during the apartheid era."

The train station had been a site of strict segregation—a central public place visible to those entering and leaving the city. Blacks, Coloureds,

Indians, and Whites each had their assigned pathways. In the Whites-only section, a bomb was set off in 1964 by John Frederick Harris,[2] a White teacher and anti-apartheid activist. He was a member of the nearly all-White African Resistance Movement that sought the dismantling of apartheid and the creation of a free nation that embraced all races. He never wanted the bomb to go off; it was meant to demonstrate that Whites, too, opposed racial segregation and were willing to fight for its end, eschewing their own privilege for an equal society. He phoned in a warning but it was too late. The explosion left one elderly woman dead and several others injured. Harris was prosecuted and hanged.

The first and only White man executed for an act committed in resistance to apartheid.

Reports say he sang on the way to the gallows.

Brave and unafraid was his song, I imagined. Maybe a march or battlefield hymn. I knew his act had rattled many people, but I didn't know what that looked like. I imagined it made people more on edge, and that the policing was fiercer for a while, with the ghost of the White man swinging in front of every White who walked through the front door. In front of every police officer with a gun on his hip and the law on his side, a reminder that no matter how much force you use to control people's lives, you cannot control those who are willing to die for what they believe is right.

Taking a deep breath, Miriam crossed the threshold with me. Daniel and their son came next. Their steps through the front door erased some of the ugliness of apartheid. At least that's what I felt as I witnessed them move into a space where they had been formerly forbidden. They were forbidden no more.

Miriam continued, saying there had been separate entrances for each race and the trains never came to a full stop for Blacks. I felt a kinship with her at that moment. If I had lived in South Africa at that time, I would have experienced it, too.

Miriam was brave—you had to be brave living here. I could not imagine all that she had weathered. All the revolution in the 1960s civil rights movement back home and the demolition of Jim Crow South separation—Whites-only signs everywhere that dictated where each body could move. Here in South Africa the same sort of terror went on and on. Years beyond what I had witnessed in the U.S. No wonder apartheid's remnants remained in the psyche of those living through the transition, making their first steps shaky and tentative.

Afterward, they took me on a tour of Soweto, a township of more than 1.3 million people divided into many districts with a combination of shacks and middle-class brick homes. They showed me where the students had been shot in June 1976 and the memorial erected in Hector Pieterson's memory. There was the enlarged photo—the one seen around the world, seared into my memory since that day in Jackie's apartment in Paris—Hector, slain, his small body carried by a fellow student, carnage in the background, his distraught sister running alongside. Next to the photo, a huge red marbled headstone: *In memory of Hector Pieterson and all other young heroes and heroines of our struggle who laid down their lives for freedom, peace, and democracy.* I approached the headstone in silence. It was a place where quietude spoke louder than words.

Later I saw the exterior of Winnie Mandela's home and the Baragwanath Hospital where she had worked as a social worker; people garbed in white, blue, or green robes on their way to their independent churches; and a cemetery. Barber shops everywhere: tiny shacks with tarps strung atop for makeshift roofs; small tin buildings, all adorned outside with colorful paintings of scissors and razors; and price lists for relaxers, braids, S curl treatments, and various styles. Walls decorated with posters of Black South African women and famous Black American rap artists.

It would be much different to get my hair done in one of these places—none of this business of a woman holding hair while a second woman cuts, making sure nobody touches anybody they shouldn't.

I stood in awe of the painting of the Black "Madonna and Child in Soweto" in the Regina Mundi Church. The largest Roman Catholic Church in South Africa; it was known as "the people's church" during the anti-apartheid struggle.

Bright as neon, the Madonna's blue headdress and shawl and the child's elegant poppy red robe lit the space before it. The mother's arm encircles her son, who holds a cross in one hand and makes a peace symbol with the other. The scene is framed by a golden circle, and below it is an eye with two black forks on either side pointed toward the pupil. The pupil represents the township, and two black forks running across the eye represent the pain inflicted on Black South Africans. The forks never reach the pupil, which holds in its center a lighted cross. Hope in the midst of crisis. People fled to the church during the riots of 1976, and I imagined how the image of the Black savior dressed in red, rimmed in gold, holding a symbol of suffering in one hand and peace in the other, comforted their souls.

Overcome with nostalgia as I walked through history, witnessing memorial sites, seeing finally the places I had heard about for so long, I wished Daddy could have been here. He had wondered if South Africa would achieve its independence during the twentieth century. It would, five years after his death. Feeling his presence within me, I whispered, "Here we are." That evening I called Mother back in Maryland to relate what I had seen and how Daddy's spirit had been there. Silence on her end.

"Yes dear," she said softly, "I know."

I had witnessed moments of joy edged in anguish.

Adele, Lynne, and I had a ball at the National Arts Festival in Grahamstown—the largest arts and culture festival in all of Africa with two weeks full of opera, jazz and folk music, drama, dance, film, poetry readings, and arts and craft.

Sibongile Khumalo's sold-out concert highlighted the trip. A classically trained singer, Mrs. Khumalo had won an award in 1993 for her repertoire of traditional and jazz songs. Her name was mentioned so often that I couldn't wait to hear her voice. She became my favorite musician; I would return to South Africa four years in a row to hear her concert and greet her backstage.

Opening her program with the song "Untold Story," Mrs. Khumalo's rich, golden voice transported me to a place of bliss. A bathing of the soul, the kind that seemed to happen more readily when I was traveling. A joy undergirded with the excitement of being in a new place. It was impossible for the mixed audience to stay seated. They kept standing up to applaud her and move their bodies to the music.

Afterward, I insisted we go backstage to meet the singer. Mrs. Khumalo was as gracious as her voice and welcomed us. Two Black South African actresses whom I had met the day before approached Mrs. Khumalo who immediately screamed in surprise and joy. The three women had been school classmates. Mrs. Khumalo, who remained in South Africa during the apartheid years, hadn't seen the two actresses for many years, for they had fled to the States to escape apartheid. The crying, the exchanges in rapid Zulu and the breathless hugs among the three women brought me to tears. Their mood was raw, unfiltered, like a beat of silence in a mournful song that cracks emotion wide. It was joy and beautiful sadness at once—like soldiers returning home to their loved ones with wounded bodies and haunting memories.

Apartheid had broken up many relationships and families. People had scattered all over the world. In fear of imprisonment or murder by the apartheid government officials, the two actresses hadn't returned to South Africa to visit their families and friends for eighteen years. Not until 1990, when Nelson Mandela was released from prison, just three years ago, had it been safe for them to return to their homeland. A silent observer of the very emotional reunion, I thought about the thousands of Black Americans who had fled their homes and families under the cover of darkness to escape a lynching or an unlawful imprisonment. Sacrificing love for life, in hopes of a better day ahead.

That evening the women's reunion was a step toward an optimistic future.

NOTES

1. Rodney King, a Black American construction worker, sustained a brutal beating by the police of Los Angeles, California, which led to the L.A. riots in April 1992.

2. "1965: John Harris, White Anti-Apartheid Martyr," *South African History Online,* April 1, 2010. Accessed March 14, 2013. http:/www.sahistory.org.za/ people/Fredrick-john-harris. Harris walked to the gallows, singing "We Shall Overcome," a popular song performed by the civil rights activists in the United States.

Chapter 19

Going to Fort Hare

Fast forward two years to September 1995, and I arrive in South Africa again, this time to consider an offer to teach at the University of Fort Hare.

At the 1994 African Literature Association conference in Ghana, I was personally invited by the vice chancellor and English department chair at Fort Hare to be a visiting professor. I was excited. A return to South Africa! To teach at the famous historically Black university where distinguished members of the ANC like Nelson Mandela, Govan Mbeki, and Oliver Tambo had studied. Even my University of Pittsburgh colleague, poet Dennis Brutus, had earned his bachelor's degree at Fort Hare.

On the plane ride I started reading Mandela's 751-page autobiography *Long Walk to Freedom*. I had bought the book months in advance, but I wanted to wait until I was on my way to South Africa to read it so the place would feel more real when I arrived. I wanted to walk where Mandela walked, see what he saw, go where he went, and know the land he lived and struggled for.

This trip would be different. Mandela was president, having been elected in 1994. Apartheid was officially, fully abolished on paper. Yet the vestiges and the psychological effects of apartheid would affect the people's behavior and decisions for many years to come.

I wanted to see if the rainbow had emerged from the rain.

However, I had to reckon with going to Alice, South Africa, the town that housed Fort Hare, which I later discovered, was an hour's drive from any decent city. A full ninety miles from East London and forty-five miles from King William's Town (referred to as "King"). I became alarmed, as vast swaths of isolated countryside dotted with cows and goats filled my view. When my South African Indian friend Narissa, head of the ANC archives, described the rural area and how there wouldn't be much in the way of restaurants, movie theaters, grocery stores, or shopping, agoraphobic spasms kicked

149

in and I nearly gave up on the idea of living in Alice. I was getting too old to be "a pioneer" in the wilderness.

Mother encouraged me to go. Though she would never go herself, she knew I could handle it. "Tomorrow isn't promised," she said. "Live life to the fullest."

Then something else pulled my heart to South Africa and I had to go.

My friend Flora and her husband Ridley lived in Midrand, a town between Johannesburg and Pretoria. They wanted me to come, inviting me to visit them on the weekends. Flora was a Black South African who had studied at Fort Hare, but Ridley had grown up in Jamaica. The pair had met in Germany and agreed that after they completed their graduate education at the University of Pittsburgh they would move to her country if apartheid ended. But, when they finished their degrees, and when it came time to go back, Ridley admitted he was afraid. Afraid of the crime statistics in South Africa. All of the violence. And anger. Anger that had been lying dormant like a sleeping lion.

Yet, Ridley was joyfully surprised when he arrived in Johannesburg in 1994. He opened Crackers, a popular Jamaican restaurant on Rockey Street in the Yeoville neighborhood, which had always been a "gray" area, mixed with all races, not just White or Black or Indian or Coloured. It was multiclass, too, which would have surprised its original founder, England native Thomas Yeo Sherwill, who imagined it as a utopia for the rich. During apartheid it had been a sort of liberated zone as Blacks and Whites met and ate and listened to music together in defiance of prevailing separatist laws. Some Blacks even lived in flats rented to them by White owners.

Ridley's authentic Jamaican cuisine was a hit. The minute aromas of jerk spice, curry chicken, and sweet coconut filled the air, people started trickling inside the restaurant. The tables were full, every night. He loved it. He was popular in the community; they liked his big smile, his big heart. Sometimes homeless men would come by after the dinner rush, and Ridley would give them food.

"South Africa will surprise you," Ridley told me. "Come."

One November morning Flora was shopping for Christmas presents and stopped into her friend's clothing boutique. There she found the perfect red dress, held it up to her frame, ran her hands along the soft fabric, and smiled imagining Ridley's reaction when he saw her wearing it. After buying it, she hurried home to change. Her son Tabi dashed out of the house crying, "Mummy. Daddy has been stabbed." Flora cried out in disbelief. She rushed into the house, leaving the key in the car's ignition and the motor idling. Her brother held the phone in his hand and handed it to her. The cold voice of a policeman said, "Your husband is dead."

She immediately left with family members for the restaurant. Ridley's body had already been taken away to the morgue. A distraught employee explained that a known street corner drug dealer had come into the restaurant during the lunch rush. That morning Ridley had reprimanded the man for selling drugs and beating his wife or girlfriend in the street. Still fuming, and wielding a large knife, he stabbed it into Ridley's heart.

She learned later he had yelled at Ridley accusingly, saying *"How dare you come to this country and make so much money."*

Ridley was the victim of the emerging xenophobia primarily directed at foreign Africans by Black South Africans who were embittered with the persistent poverty and unemployment they were experiencing even after apartheid ended.

When Flora drove to the morgue to view and claim Ridley's body, she had to wait an hour and a half because, as she was told, the van with Ridley's body was picking up other murdered victims throughout the city. Finally, the curtain at the window was drawn back. His feet were closest to her. She touched the glass. With their heads at opposite ends, she sorrowfully stared at her husband. He looked like he was sleeping peacefully.

The red dress was out in the car, tags attached. Ridley would never see her in it.

Ridley's death made the headlines in the newspapers and on television. The Yeoville community was up in arms and led mass protests. Ridley had been one of their own, an adopted son who had been head of the Yeoville Trader's Association.

Out of my sorrow, I vowed to teach at the University of Fort Hare as a tribute to Ridley, who had grown to love South Africa and had encouraged me to come. I remembered the joy in his voice when he said, "South Africa will surprise you." I remembered the way he described the people, the vibrant life and creativity found on every corner. I saw how he had been welcomed and beloved by his community, how quickly the country had become his home. He would not want me to fear South Africa or shy away, let the gloom of his death overshadow the overwhelming goodness and strength of the people there. People who lived their regular lives, refused to define others according to the way the government might say they should. People who lived and laughed and delighted in the food of other cultures and welcomed neighbors as family.

Flora wore the red dress to her husband's funeral. Bright as a rose blooming against a grey sky. Red would not be the color of blood to her, or hurt and pain. It was, and would forever be, the color of love.

Founded in 1916 by Scottish missionaries, the University of Fort Hare is situated in the fertile Tyhume River valley, below the Amatola mountains in the central part of the Eastern Cape Province. On the site of a former fort, the university is located in Alice, a town with one traffic light. Rural as can be! When a roaming cow stopped in the middle of the road in front of my rental car, turned its head to look at me, swished its tail and let out a big "moooo!" I had to laugh. It was clear who was in charge here.

A serene campus greeted me. Wide paved streets, trapezoidal stone structures, white buildings with red-tiled rooftops. A library housed the African National Congress (ANC) archives. The famous theology building with its steeple-like design at the top where a person could lean on the windowless ledge and view the entire campus. A museum with some of the best Black South African art.

The energy of youth filled the walkways and halls. I watched clusters of students walking around. I overheard the chatter of languages, the Xhosa "clicks" and the British-accented voices, laughter. The staff was clustered with people, of all different colors, and not because they were trying to make a political statement. The student body was Black, unlike in Pittsburgh, where most students were White and did not seem to mix much among racial groups (and did not seem aware or concerned about it either).

Of course, a campus provided a particular view of social workings. The University of Pittsburgh is a part-public and part-private university, boasting "the best of both worlds" with resources and education like a private university but tuition costs similar to government-subsidized state universities. For the most part, students there came from middle class or working-class homes. So even though my Africana Studies classes were often filled with students of color, they were not less privileged than other students on campus. When class status came into play, questions of racial disparity were more salient.

Outside Fort Hare's main campus in Alice (a second campus in Bisho, next to King William's Town) and in the countryside toward the White town of Fort Beaufort, thirteen miles away, the Xhosa people lived in either two-room brick homes or *rondavels* (huts) without electricity and in-door plumbing. It used to be that all races lived together in Alice, but the apartheid government restricted it to Xhosa only. Although outspoken staff members were expelled from Fort Hare, the college became a stronghold of the student-based Black Consciousness Movement during the 1970s. At present, the university, with campuses in Alice, Bisho, and East London, consists of over 8,500 students from South Africa and neighboring African countries with a teaching and research staff of 260.

Naturally, I made comparisons between Fort Hare and the University of Pittsburgh, but there were more immediate parallels between Fort Hare and historically Black colleges in the U.S. Fort Hare had been established originally for Africans, not just those living in South Africa but as far away as Uganda. Similarly, Hampton Institute was originally meant for Native Americans and Black Americans. Fort Hare was rural, like many historically Black colleges in the U.S. that were built through land grants by the government in the mid-nineteenth century. They emphasized agricultural and trade education, something Booker T. Washington had endorsed. Soon liberal arts study was incorporated as well, with the influence of W. E. B. DuBois who thought vocational training only "perpetuated the servitude of slavery." My own time at both institutions intersected with important anniversaries. I arrived just after the eightieth birthday celebration of the University of Fort Hare, and I was at Hampton for its centennial milestone in 1968.

Chapter 20

Redemption and the TRC

It was April 1996, and no matter where you were in South Africa—in rural areas or cities—there was an air of tremendous angst.

Still mourning Ridley's violent death, I arrived in time to watch the first nation-wide televised hearings of the Truth and Reconciliation Commission (TRC). The TRC was established by the Government of National Unity, under the newly elected democratic President Nelson Mandela. It had been enacted by the Promotion of National Unity and Reconciliation Act No. 34 of 1995, mandating the promotion of "national unity and reconciliation . . . by restoring the human and civil dignity of . . . victims and by recommending reparation measures in respect of them."[1]

President Mandela presided over a nation wracked with extreme anger and pain. "Truth is the road to reconciliation. Revealing is healing." These two slogans were to be repeated over and over. Mandela struggled with alternative leadership structures and with the immediate need to heal his people. For these reasons, among many others, and to avoid a bloodbath, he believed the path to healing was to confront the past and to make forgiveness central to the TRC.

"Look the beast in the eye," Archbishop Tutu declared. "Forgiveness isn't cheap. Forgiveness isn't easy."[2]

Its message was outrageous, shockingly offensive to many, like all messages that speak of peace, forgiveness, and nonviolence in the face of oppression and unpunished crime. People were hurt and angry, and rightly so, and they needed a place to put those emotions. As Martin Luther King, Jr. was, in a way, provocative in his message of nonviolence, telling the people not to succumb to anger. The way South Africa did it, creating a commission specifically for the sharing of stories, welcoming confession, providing pardon to offenders, and doing it all so publicly. The TRC took the world by surprise.

I was deeply skeptical. I could endorse an intellectual revolution—power through education: liberating the mind; empowering identity movements. But healing and forgiveness for the oppressors? Letting those criminals off the hook? It seemed an impossible task, and worse, self-abasing. Sycophantic. Since when did you tell someone who wronged you, spat in your face, held up signs barring you from entry, that all was okay now?

President Mandela appointed Anglican Archbishop Desmond Tutu to chair the TRC for the process of transitional and restorative justice. The TRC (1996–1998) was comprised of three committees: the Committee on Human Rights Violations, the Committee on Amnesty, and the Committee on Reparation and Rehabilitation for the victims and perpetrators of political crimes. President Mandela, Archbishop Tutu, and the other commissioners thought the Commission would give access to information otherwise obscured by the apartheid political regime. They especially wanted the voices of the "incredible small people" to be heard and for them to put their trauma on public record.

The commissioners chose to open the hearings in the Eastern Cape (where I was living) during the week of April 15, 1996. The Eastern Cape was the birthplace of Black resistance and political awareness and the University of Fort Hare, the first institution of higher learning for Blacks. "Of all those detained without trial in South Africa," the Afrikaner journalist Antjie Krog wrote, "one-third came from the eastern Cape. It was apparently assumed in security circles that whoever crushed the eastern Cape would control the country."[3]

Port Elizabeth, the coastal, automotive capital of the Eastern Cape, had been the target of some of the most horrendous attacks by the police death squads in the 1980s. One of the explosive cases was that of the Cradock Four. Four Black activists of the United Democratic Front (UDF) were driving back to Cradock from a meeting in Port Elizabeth on June 27, 1985, when they were abducted and brutally murdered by the security police. Everyone knew their names: Fort Calata, Sicelo Mhlauli, Sparro Mkonto, and Matthew Goniwe. On day two of the hearings, April 16, 1996, three widows of the Cradock Four appeared before the TRC Committee on Human Rights Violations in the East London City Hall in East London.

Each widow separately recounted hurtful truths.

Mrs. Sindiwe Mkonto spoke first. She described how her husband had been shot in the head, stabbed, and burned.

Mrs. Nomondo Calata followed, recalling her husband's detainments as well as hers. When the commissioners asked her to describe her husband's mortal wounds, Mrs. Calata leaned back in the chair, covered her mouth with a handkerchief, and emitted a heart wrenching wail.

Her wail went completely through my body. Alex Boraine, deputy chair of the TRC, later described it thus, "It was as if she enshrined in the throwing back of her body and letting out the cry the collective horror of the thousands of people who had been trapped in racism and oppression for so long."[4] Antjie Krog declared, "For me, this crying is the beginning of the Truth Commission—the signature tune, the definitive moment, the ultimate sound of what the process is about."[5]

Mrs. Calata's cry exhumed memories, made audible suffering yet unspoken before the world. She described her husband's wounds, "His hair was pulled out, his tongue was long, his fingers were cut off, he had many wounds on his body. The dogs had bitten him severely."[6]

Her wail and testimony also prompted a sudden silence in the hall. In the hush, rare in a world full of noise, was a mourning so deep no one could move.

The silence was broken by a call for a ten-minute adjournment. After the break, Archbishop Tutu sang the Xhosa/Zulu anti-apartheid protest and funeral song "Senzenina?" which means "What have we done to deserve this?" or "What have we done?"

Mrs. Nombuyisele Mhlauli testified next. She, like the other two widows, delivered her speech in Xhosa, and my attention began to wander as a woman interpreter on television translated in stilted English until I heard something about a right hand. I blinked to attention as Mrs. Mhlauli painfully described the condition of her deceased husband's body. He had succumbed to a total of forty-three wounds. Acid was poured on his face; his right hand was chopped off. Another silence ensued.

"What would you ask the Commission to do for you?" Commissioner John Smith asked. "Are you interested to know the identity of the person or persons who are responsible for the death of your husband?"[7]

Mrs. Mhlauli's responded, "Even if I say these people should be given amnesty, it won't return my husband, but that hand, we still want it."[8] I gasped, felt the urge to shut my eyes. I could see an arm without a hand. Already engrained as the acute symbol of brute suffering in Africa to me were those men with missing hands I had seen in the Congo.

"We know we have buried them [him], but really to have the hand which is said to be in a bottle in Port Elizabeth," Mrs. Mhluali said. "We would like to get the hand. Thank you."[9]

Archbishop Tutu, clearly choking up, thanked her and the other widows for sacrificing their husbands. His tear-streaked face displayed the emotion every person felt as they watched the unfolding of truth. Truth was only half of it. Reconciliation was next.

I was still skeptical of the forgiveness part. The women had spoken, let it be a healing for them. The people who had killed their husbands? This tribunal wasn't about those murderers, I thought. They still needed to be punished.

"Forgiveness isn't easy," Archbishop Tutu had said. The widows were being heard, honored and thanked; perhaps that was a start.

Then, I remembered being in the Congo, those White people in the car in front of us dragged into the trees and the *bap-bap-bap* of gunshots. Theirs was a brutal retribution. I reluctantly acknowledged that President Mandela was right about doing it this way, avoiding bloody attacks of angry, hurt people who wanted revenge. It would only go on and on without an end. Tears and truth seemed more difficult, but they were better than gunshots.

The women's testimonies and Archbishop Tutu's singing left me emotionally drained.

I've asked myself if I would have the capacity to forgive people if they had imprisoned and tortured me or my family. I honestly do not know the answer. What I do know is *The Cradock Four*, the long-awaited documentary about the Cradock Four, was released on June 25, 2010 to commemorate the twenty-fifth anniversary of the deaths of Calata, Mhlauli, Mkonto, and Goniwe. Their stories were made permanent in history. They were not men who died in vain, their loss discarded and left out of history books. They would not be forgotten.

It would take years for me to fully understand how there was a need for the healing that forgiveness, true forgiveness, can bring. I think it helped the country a lot, especially the younger generation. Now you can go see the overt motions of that forgiveness. Kids of all the races play together, the past distant—not forgotten, but not determining the present. The new South Africa is not perfect, but some of the Rainbow Nation's urban schools, for example, are integrated in a way that surpasses many schools I've seen in the U.S.

In response to the negative criticism about the TRC being immoral with their encouragement of impunity for the perpetrator and the questioning about amnesty being given at the cost of justice, Archbishop Tutu has written, "We have to accept that what we do we do for generations past, present, and yet to come. That is what makes a community a community or a people a people— for better or for worse."[10]

"Pardon me, Madam, may I have your autograph?" Two White South African children appeared at my elbow and nervously held out a piece of paper.

"Why would you want *my* autograph?" I said. My friends and I were eating lunch at a hotel in Sandton, a predominantly White upscale suburb of Johannesburg.

The mother rushed over to our table. "You must be Whitney Houston!" I laughed, and the three friends sitting with me also began laughing. Couldn't she see I was short, overweight, and bespectacled—nothing like the tall, rail-thin singer? I told the woman that no, I was not Whitney Houston. Not even related. (Neither a singer nor a model). Me, mistaken for the famed Whitney Houston. The hilarity!

It was one of those blinding "all Blacks look alike" moments in which the person is so unaccustomed to seeing people of color that the features of unfamiliar races become blurred as they only see skin tone. Usually, White people live in all-White communities. Depending on where you lived in the U.S., I expect it's fairly easy for a White person never to see a Black person, since they only made up 13 percent of the population. In South Africa, as a whole, the percentages were the opposite. Sandton, South Africa, though, was comprised of a cloister of Whites, and being in an upscale hotel restaurant and hearing our American accents convinced the young girls I must be famous.

My friends and I chuckled while the children stood there looking hopeful. I took their piece of paper and carefully penned my autograph. Guess what I wrote? "Whitney Houston / Brenda Berrian."

Working and living with my family of friends in the new South Africa was challenging and rewarding, but the deaths affected me physically and psychologically. There were *too many*. On Monday mornings, I hesitated to open my computer because messages of condolences for deaths that occurred over the weekend were posted on the university's web page.

During my African American Literature class, I asked a female student why she had been absent for over a week. She responded timidly,

"My father was late."

"What does his being late have to do with you missing class?" I said stupidly, hand on my hip. A hush came over the class, and I realized I had made a cultural faux pas but could not imagine what it could be. The stricken student bowed her head. A male student spoke up.

"Miss, 'late' means her father died." I felt like two cents. I wanted to crawl beneath the desk. I must have apologized to the female student more than three times. "Late," I learned, was one of many ways of expressing death, particularly death from AIDS. There was so much stigma and shame attached to the disease. South Africans would call it pneumonia or simply say "blood disease." They could not come out and say exactly what it was because, even in that day, the entire family could be stoned to death or excommunicated from their own village.

The particular silence and crippling fear of this ravage was not new to me. Two of my Black American colleagues in Pittsburgh died due to complications from AIDS in 1986 and 1989, during the height of the hysteria about the disease. Neither of the professors ever said what exactly they were suffering from—the sweats, the pneumonia, the constant hospital visits—but we all knew. They were both male and Black American, and one was bisexual— all descriptions which directly dismantled the stereotype that AIDS was a "White gay male disease."

The reaction to the disease was more pronounced and fortified by anger in Africa, where the majority of people in the world who suffered from the affliction lived, South Africa especially.

Some leaders in Africa took the position of AIDS-deniers; for example, President Mbeki refused to allow state hospitals to dispense antiretroviral drugs to save lives.

In December 1998, Gugu Dlamini,[11] a mother and AIDS activist, was beaten to death by her neighbors in the township of KwaMashu, north of Durban, after she bravely revealed her HIV positive status on Zulu television and radio. After the assault, one of her attackers sent her boyfriend a text message that read, "You can come and fetch your dog; we are done with her."

The reaction was shocking and vexing and heartbreaking all at once.

But when you thought hard about why the attitude in Africa seemed so close-minded, you had to think about history. Africa was under the gaze of the West. A gaze like the fierce, unrelenting sun in the hot desert, where there is nowhere to hide.

Though these African nations were free, their freedom was still relatively new, and the gaze of the West still controlled the perception of Africans to the world. The way that Europe and America—with their economic and financial power, political clout, and far-reaching media—saw Africans established the dominant global understanding of them. The image of Africans in the minds of Europeans and Americans determined the value-system attached to Africans and African nations' value-systems which were still very vulnerable. These African nations very much wanted to participate on the global stage—to be seen as partners and not charity cases, to be fully and universally supported and recognized for their contributions to research, discovery and art. For their humanity, they could not afford to ignore the West, and there was no shade from its gaze.

Africans were reacting to the gaze that was often hurtful and demeaning. It was a gaze that had long ago cast the African as overly sexualized and immoral. The notion of a disease most commonly transmitted sexually and which resulted in death caused overwhelming fear. In order for fear not to turn to shame—for the West was very much responsible for the spread of the disease—fear turned instead to hatred, and hatred had to find a scapegoat. Years later, this was the only way I could make sense of why Gugu Dlamini died.

It shouldn't have been so much of a surprise that African leaders might find it easier to ignore the AIDS epidemic. Even before there was scientific research to back it up, they must have known that to deal with HIV/AIDS head on; they would have to bring to light the fault of the West. They would have to hold up a mirror to the blazing gaze.

With righteous indignation I read the research that confirmed how Western colonization of Africa did indeed prompt the AIDS epidemic. Studies revealed the virus originated in chimpanzees living deep in the forests of Cameroon where Africans never ventured. In the early days of colonization, European companies forced entry, along with Africans taken against their will, into the remote forests in search of rubber and other riches to exploit, thereby encountering the chimps.[12] Starved and enslaved, Africans attempted to cook and prepare the meat like they had another kind of animal meat, which eventually made them sick. There is no way to describe what happened next without being frank: the sickness spread across Africa then into Europe and the Americas primarily because colonizers blazed across Africa, raped African women (many of whom had husbands), and then returned home in the West to be with their wives. Occurrences of promiscuous behavior on both sides didn't help the matter. But the true menace was colonialism; among its many other evils, colonialism spread—like a map of conquest unfurled across a king's table—a deadly infection that would have otherwise remained naturally quarantined deep in the Cameroonian forest.

Mother's closest "friend" to be affected by HIV was Earvin "Magic" Johnson. She was an avid NBA fan, watching as many games as she could, especially the LA Lakers or the Boston Celtics. She called me crying one October evening after Magic's public address when he announced his HIV status. She feared for his life and for his health—this man whom she loved to watch play ball. She was upset for days, as though her own son had been stricken with the disease.

While I was teaching in South Africa in 1996, elaborate funerals took place in the local cemetery on Saturday—the day the apartheid government had set aside for Black funerals. Busloads of people showed up, dressed in their finery. Not every death was a result of AIDS, of course, but even if the *cause* of death were taboo, the funeral was a major celebration, involving the entire community. Death was part of life. People did not hide from it in the way Americans did back home. It was painful, but it was true. Even at death, there was room for embrace and welcome. More than once, I received an invitation to attend the unveiling of someone's tombstone.

One day, I summoned the courage to drive alone to Bisho and King William's Town while praying no driver would make a sudden stop in front of me. It was time for me to pay a private homage to the anti-apartheid activists who had died and were buried in the area: Bantu Stephen Biko and the victims of the Bisho massacre. Bisho had been the capital of the former Ciskei, one of two Xhosa homelands or Bantustans established under the 1951 Bantu Authorities Act. It was reincorporated into the Eastern Cape Province after the April 24, 1994, post-apartheid elections. In September 1992, it was the site of a massacre when nearly 60,000 demonstrators demanded an end to the military government of Brigadier Joshua Gqozo and tried to cross the Ciskei Defence Force lines to enter into Bisho.[13] Without warning, the soldiers fired into the crowd for five minutes, killing 28 and wounding more than 100.

After visiting the site of the massacre, I continued on to King William's Town. (I first heard about King William's Town while watching *Cry Freedom*, the 1987 film about the journalist Donald Woods and the Black activist Stephen Biko.) I turned off a paved street onto a dirt road which led me to the cemetery where Biko and the Bisho victims were laid to rest. I got out of the car and slowly walked to the grave. Silently, I bowed my head in respect, remembering one of Biko's famous slogans. "It's better to die for an idea that will live, than to live for an idea that will die."[14] The gravesite was as humble as Biko. A simple engraving with Bantu Stephen Biko, Honorary President of the Black People's Convention and the dates of his birth and death on the tombstone.

The anti-apartheid activist Bantu Stephen "Steve" Biko was one of the most recognized founders of the all-Black South African Students Organization (SASO), Black People's Convention (BPC), and Black Consciousness Movement (BCM) with the aim of a cultural and political revival of an oppressed people. In 1973, Biko was banned by the apartheid government to King William's Town, which prohibited him from making public speeches before more than one person. In August 1977, he was arrested at a roadblock under the Terrorism Act No. 83 of 1967 by the Port Elizabeth security police. For twenty-six days, he was interrogated and brutally beaten, suffered a head injury,[15] fell into a coma, and died a martyr on September 12, 1977, in a Pretoria prison. More than 15,000 people (including 13 Western diplomats) attended his funeral and burial in the Ginsberg cemetery.

After a lengthy investigation, the Constitutional Court, the country's highest judicial body, refused to prosecute the suspected officers, but gave the Biko family $78,000 as compensation for his death. After the TRC compiled its results, 22,000 families were deemed eligible for reparations, which the government promised to pay.

So far, nothing like that has ever happened for Black Americans at the federal level in the post-slavery United States. On the state level, only two states—Florida and Oklahoma—have paid reparations to Black American victims, and their descendants, of race riots: the May 31 and June 1, 1921 riot in Greenwood, Oklahoma,[16] and the January 1923 riot in Rosewood, Florida,[17]respectively. In June 2001, the Oklahoma state legislature passed the 1921 Tulsa Race Riot Reconciliation Act, providing more than three hundred college scholarships[18] for descendants of the Greenwood riot.

Calling the Rosewood riot "a blind act of bigotry,"[19] Governor Lawton Chiles of Florida signed into law the Rosewood Compensation Act on May 5, 1994. The state legislature settled on $2.1 million, including a $500,000 property compensation fund and college scholarships for needy students with preference for the children of descendants of the Rosewood riot and $150,000 for each survivor.[20]

I wonder how much we have truly healed from our past. How many Americans know about the history of these riots? What we know is slavery existed. In January 1989, U.S. Congressman John Conyers of Michigan introduced Bill H.R. 40 (for forty acres) Commission to Study Reparation Proposals for African Americans Act. The Conyers Bill (now H.R. 891) presents findings that "the institution of slavery was constitutionally and statutorily sanctioned by the Government of the United States from 1798 through 1865"[21] and that slavery "constituted an immoral and inhumane deprivation of Africans' life, liberty, African citizenship rights, and cultural heritage, and denied them the fruits of their own labor."[22] Ironically, the Conyers bill followed the passage of the Civil Liberties Act of 1988 by Congress, which granted reparations to Japanese Americans who were unjustly interned in camps during World War II.

Over 151 years have passed since the end of the Civil War. Neither an official apology nor a payment from the United States government as an acknowledgment of slavery as a crime against humanity to 43.9 million Black Americans and their heirs has come forth. Each year Representative Conyers reintroduced the bill. Each year it failed to reach the Congressional floor. On the other hand, South Africa's reaction to apartheid was remarkably courageous. The ANC government held the TRC hearings just two years after independence, while memory was fresh and many victims were still living.

NOTES

1. Promotion of National Unity and Reconciliation Act 34 of 1995 was adopted on July 19, 1995. http://www.justice.gov.za/legislation/acts/1995-034.pdf.

2. "Tutu and the TRC," *BBC*, Video, 7:05. http//www.youtube.com/watch?y= ujOL8F52wv4.

3. Antjie Krog, *The Country of My Skull: Guilt, Sorrow and the Limits of Forgiveness* (Johannesburg: Random House, 1998), 47.

4. Alex Boraine, *A Country Unmasked* (Oxford: Oxford University Press, 2000), 102.

5. Krog, *The Country of My Skull*, 42.

6. SABC Truth Commission Special Report, Nomonde Calata Case EC0028 / 96, TRC Human Rights Violations Hearing Transcript, East London, Day 2, April 16, 1996. http://www.sabctrc.saha.org.za/documents/hrvtrans/east_london/55192.html. The statements by Mrs. Sindiwe Mkonto Case EC0029 / 96 and Mrs. Nombuyisele Mhlauli Case EC0079 / 96 are included in Mrs. Calata's transcript.

7. Ibid.

8. Ibid.

9. Ibid.

10. Desmond Mpilo Tutu, *No Future without Forgiveness*, 279.

11. Nondumiso Mbuyazi, "Fear Was the Killer," *Daily News*, December 1, 2011. http://www.iol.co.za/dailynews/news/fear-was-the-killer-1190629.

12. Craig Timberg and Daniel Halpern, *Tinderbox: How the West Sparked the AIDS Epidemic and How the World Can Finally Overcome It* (New York: Penguin Press, 2012), 30–31.

13. Tutu, *No Future without Forgiveness*, 149–50.

14. Khadija Patel, "South Africa: Remember the Black Consciousness Movement and the 1977 Murder of Steve Biko," *Pambazaka News*, September 7, 2011. http://www.revolutionaryfrontlines.wordpress.com/2011/09/17/south-africa-remember-the-black-consciousness-movement-of-steve-biko.

15. Lynne Duke, *Mandela, Mobutu and Me: A Newswoman's Journey to Africa* (New York: Doubleday, 2003), 114. Biko sustained a massive blow that caused his brain to shunt from side to side in his skull and to come loose.

16. Charles P. Henry, *Long Overdue: The Politics of Racial Reparations* (New York: New York University Press, 2007), 70–2.

17. Ibid., 85.

18. Peter Schmidt, "Oklahoma Scholarships Seek to Make Amends for 1921 Riot," *The Chronicle of Higher Education*, July 13, 2001, A22.

19. Karen Voyles, "Marking History: Sign Memorializes Those Who Died in Rosewood," *The Gainesville Sun*, May 5, 2005, B1.

20. Henry, *Long Overdue*, 78.

21. "U.S. Congressman John Conyers, Jr. Introduction Bill H.R. 40," http://www.conyers.house. gov/index/cfm/reparations.

22. Ibid.

Chapter 21

Ubuntu in Alice

South African *ubuntu*. Described as a philosophy, a way of looking at life, a worldview, this is what I remember most about my time in South Africa.

"In the old days," Nelson Mandela once explained, over the swell of children's singing in the background, "when a traveler in our country would stop at our village, he did not have to ask for food or water. Once he stops, the people give him food, entertain him. That is one aspect of *ubuntu*."[1]

Acquaintances were more than acquaintances in South Africa. I was part of a community of fellow professors, neighbors, and friends. The hospitality was so immediate and expansive that I realized how much I had been missing it in Pittsburgh.

In Pittsburgh, people in my department might occasionally say "we should get together sometime," but it would rarely happen, which was strange to me at first. It reminded me of the difference between the North and South—how Southern culture was often characterized as more neighborly than the North. Southerners sat on porches, visited their neighbors. I had felt lonely in Pittsburgh, and I realized the absence of this more distinctly while in South Africa.

Every other Saturday, Ismail, my Somali roommate and professor of accounting at Fort Hare, one or two friends, and I would jump in my rental car and take the ninety-minute drive to East London. At a small shopping mall, we bought two weeks' worth of groceries, ate lunch at a restaurant, and went to the movie theater. Other times, we did some sightseeing, browsed in Click's or the C & A store and always got back to Alice before nightfall. After we unloaded the car's boot (trunk), either Ismail or I would cook dinner and entertain our friends.

At Fort Hare, I engaged in serious conversations with Black, Colored, and White South Africans as well as Africans from other countries. Since my apartment was in an old house across from the main entrance to the university campus, it became the "Do Drop Inn." I cooked meals of chicken and rice with salad and always made extra because someone would inevitably stop by. I kept a lot of biscuits (cookies), tea for afternoon tea, and *naarjies* (tangerines) I'd get from the local farms. Two of my colleagues—Zulu male teachers from the Department of English—once paid me a surprise visit, singing and high-stepping a traditional Zulu dance in front of my door.

"*Ubuntu* does not mean that people should not enrich themselves," Mandela said. "The question therefore is: Are you going to do so in order to enable the community around you to be able to improve?"[2]

I assumed the role of "big sister" to three young women colleagues: Vuyi, Shamiga, and Patricia. Vuyi, a Zulu from Pietermaritzburg, taught in the English Department with me. Shamiega, a Cape Malay from Cape Town, taught Afrikaans; Patricia, a Coloured from Cape Town, taught social work and worked part-time as a dorm matron. I advised them about further studies to improve their chances of obtaining another job with advancement. I shared my experiences about living under segregation in the Deep South and living through the civil rights movement. Sometimes they talked to me about their personal matters, but I reframed from sharing my opinion. Three or more times a week Vuyi and I met at the gym to exercise together, encouraging each other to be as healthy and fit as possible. The four of us exchanged recipes, and Shamiega helped me to be a better left-handed stick-shift driver to cope with driving on the left-side of the road. In contrast to being a pretend big sister in Potch to Adele, as she told everyone I was her sister so my presence as a Black American woman in town would be more acceptable, I *truly* was a big sister here at Fort Hare.

Most of my colleagues in the Department of English were men. Some would drop by my office to chat. Professor Losambe, the chair of the Department of English, was from the Congo, and he and his wife went out of their way to make me feel welcome. A White former priest, married with children, invited me to his home in King William's Town. An Indian male offered to teach me yoga. A British couple who were at the university on a program similar to the Peace Corps was friendly. I found living in a small, rural town resulted in either quick superficial friendships or long-term ones. During the winter break, I got a chance to meet some of my colleagues' relatives in their respective hometowns. Shamiga, her mother, aunts, cousins, and uncles cooked a traditional Cape Malay meal when I was in Cape Town. They also invited me to attend their cousin's Muslim wedding. My closest male buddies were colleagues from Nigeria (Patrick), the Congo (Osei), and Somalia (Ismail). Next were Claudia and Stephen, a young Coloured couple from Port Elizabeth who were to become parents of triplets (two boys and a girl). On many cold nights, I shared a meal with one or more of my groups of friends.

I traveled around South Africa, too, renewing contact with my friends like Narissa from Durban. Flora was coping with her grief after Ridley's death, and I talked to her on the phone many times, sharing her sorrow. I did not stay with her when I went to Jo'burg, though, giving her space in her continued healing. Instead, I stayed with a Black American friend, Mae, who was on a five-year contract to manage an office to place American teachers and technicians in tertiary institutions throughout South Africa. Staying at Mae's place provided me with the opportunity to meet many Black American women expatriates. I became interested in their stories and began interviewing them about their experiences, the workings of a new book on my mind. I flew so often from East London to Jo'burg that the airline attendants on South African Airways (SAA) knew me as the American professor who traveled with a small portable heater in a Macy's shopping bag.

Professor Mbulelo Mzamane, the vice-chancellor, creative writer, and professor of English, invited me several times to his home whenever some dignitary came to town. Usually, Mrs. Tau, my next-door neighbor and director of the university library, and Losambe and his wife Bibi were there, too.

One evening I sat on a sofa next to an elderly Xhosa man and his wife. Although his face looked familiar, I couldn't place it. Very friendly, he first asked me about my background. He next reminisced about his youth and his imprisonment on Robben Island (the notorious prison where President Mandela and other ANC activists had been detained on political charges). His wife entered into the conversation, remembering her loneliness during her husband's twenty-four years in prison. Then it clicked—I realized I was sitting next to Govan and Epainette Mbeki, the parents of Deputy President Thabo Mbeki and very close friends of President Mandela.

The couple was so unassuming and natural. In fact, Mr. Mbeki tried in vain to encourage me to eat a Xhosa delicacy: a sheep's head. "My dear," he said. "It is so sweet and delicious, especially when you suck out the eyes." Getting queasy, I politely told him I preferred to eat chicken or fish. He certainly had a good time eating a sheep's head! In my opinion, he deserved some enjoyment in life after spending almost a quarter of a century in prison alongside Nelson Mandela, Walter Sisulu, and other ANC activists. Unlike my earlier encounters with the gardener and server in Potch and the Coloured salesman in Cape Town, Mr. Mbeki, a graduate of Fort Hare in 1937, reminded me of my admiration for the people's fortitude and belief in their liberation.

He was someone Ridley would have admired, too.

When my five-month stint at Fort Hare came to an end, I felt honored to have taught where so many famous Africans had studied. As described by President Mandela in his *Long Walk to Freedom*, Fort Hare used to be a "beacon for African students from all over Southern, Central and Eastern Africa. For a young black South African like myself, it was Oxford and

Cambridge, Harvard and Yale, all rolled into one."[3] I also felt honored to have worked in South Africa under Nelson Mandela's presidency. Although I missed an opportunity with Narissa to visit President Mandela in his Houghton home, my mother and I had previously met him in Pittsburgh. During our brief conversation, then, Mandela had encouraged us to come to South Africa. And I was to follow Mandela's advice by teaching at his alma mater. In the meantime, I finished reading my copy of President Mandela's *Long Walk to Freedom* while walking through the corridors of the campus buildings he had described. On December 10, 1996, Narissa presented my copy of President Mandela's autobiography to him. He kindly wrote "To Brenda, Best wishes to a wonderful lady" with his signature and the date. This book I will treasure forever.

During my stint at Fort Hare I realized my 1993 desire to meet and engage in serious conversations with Black South Africans and other citizens of the Rainbow Nation had been fulfilled. I had made lifetime friends. I had been a teacher to many bright and eager students. I had been a "big sister." In April 1996, I was alone when I landed at the East London Airport to begin teaching at Fort Hare, cloaked in sadness and thinking of Ridley. Five months later, in August, I departed with good-bye dinners, many hugs and kisses, and a three-car caravan of well-wishers accompanying me to the airport. No doubt about it. An expression of South African *ubuntu*. The term *ubuntu*, as translated by Archbishop Tutu, means, "I am because I belong." Or "I participate. I share."[4]

In attempts to describe all that is encompassed in the concept of *ubuntu*, people offer words like "helpfulness," "community," "caring," and "respect."

To me it meant this: Family.

Speaking of *ubuntu*, Mandela said, his voice carrying the wise rumble of story, "These are the important things in life."[5]

When Toni accompanied me to South Africa in December 2013, together we wondered if the Black majority was still able to hold to that ideal of *ubuntu*. Initially, we witnessed despair. Open public toilets and shacks looked like they would collapse any minute in the Imizamo Yethu township on the outskirts of Hout Bay, a suburb near Cape Town. Built on a hillside with a dumpster for people to leave their old furniture, two roomed houses are constructed side-by-side with corrugated roofs held down by cinder blocks.

"Isn't that a fire hazard?" Toni said. Indeed, fires had wiped out large sections of housing in the past.

Black children walk five miles to attend school in the Coloured area. Why? There is no school in their own neighborhood. Still they have no jobs, no decent housing, nor access to good health care or schools. Is this what forgiveness and reparation looks like? Aren't these important things in life, too?

Sometimes, stories of anguish are best told through fiction. In Chinua Achebe's novel *Things Fall Apart*, the Igbo ethnic group of Nigeria is slowly dismantled by the arrival of White missionaries who build churches and schools in various settlements. They demand that the Nigerians abandon their customs in favor of the missionaries. Otherwise, the Nigerians would be denied an education. No more sacrificing to false gods and wooden things. They must worship the White god and his wooden cross. They must be "civilized." Disintegration ensues. The people are fractured, unity and kinship bonds slip from them, and respected leaders of the clan are rendered powerless. From the outside, one might think the community has improved, for formal educational centers and more buildings have been constructed. But from the inside, the losses are greater, as the people are forced to assimilate to the powerful, often cruel, European immigrants on their land. The villagers disregard their culture. Children grow up in a world alien to their parents' experience. Elders fear the children will forget the important principles of their people: respect for elders and ancestors, tradition, the language of drumming and dance, and the concepts of love and generosity like *ubuntu* or the Igbo greeting *nno* (welcome).

I read this book many years ago. In 1988, I invited Chinua Achebe to a conference in Pittsburgh, and he graciously came and was the opening night speaker. Though *Things Fall Apart* was published in 1959 when many African countries were still colonized, the chilling lesson of the story hold truths that can be witnessed today. Through a series of unfortunate events and poor decisions, the ANC government in South Africa has become riddled with mismanagement, corruption, violence against women and children, and crumbling public health care and educational systems. On a superficial level, the four races continue to get along much better, but the grinding poverty and economic inequalities for the majority of poor Blacks make it hard to imagine that interactions are always smooth.

I am not an emotive person. I don't mince words. I am bold and confident, not easily moved. But as Toni and I climbed up a hill that overlooked the township with its tiny matchstick houses, the warm South African breeze blowing through our hair, I could not help but want to cry at the sight. Instead, my sister and I looked on in silence.

In her *Conversations with My Sons and Daughters*, Dr. Mamphele Ramphele, former anti-apartheid activist, academic and medical doctor, and mistress of the late Stephen Biko, writes that the youth must become pro-active. The sixteen to forty age group makes up the largest proportion of the South African population. By opening themselves up to transformative leadership along with a revolution of spirit and being engaged in a stewardship role, the youth have the possibility, according to Dr. Ramphele, to build a stable society by upholding "the values of the constitution"[6] and returning to the idealism of "a rainbow nation at peace with itself and the world."[7]

Maybe *ubuntu* is like a diamond. When diamonds are first extracted, they are dirty, dull, and commonplace. Only after they are processed and polished do they shine brilliantly, and only after exchange do they reap value, love, attention, cultivation. Perhaps the younger generation will take the *ubuntu* learned from their mothers and fathers and not only display it themselves, but boldly demand reciprocation from their government, too. *Ubuntu* cannot be a one-sided practice.

Diamonds are also one of the hardest rocks on earth. *Ubuntu* should be unbreakable, too.

NOTES

1. "The Ubuntu Experience (Interview with Nelson Mandela)," Interview by Tom Modise, *SABC*, November 1, 2006, Video, 1:36. http://www.youtube.cm/watch?V=OOQ4WiDSEBQ.

2. Ibid.

3. Nelson Mandela, *Long Walk to Freedom: The Autobiography of Nelson Mandela* (London: Abacus, 1994), 51.

4. Tutu, *No Future without Forgiveness*, 31.

5. "The Ubuntu Experience."

6. Mamphele Ramphele, *Conversations with My Sons and Daughters* (Johannesburg: Penguin House, 2012), 217.

7. Ibid.

Chapter 22

Teraanga in Senegal

On March 15, 1989, I stepped off the plane in Dakar, Senegal, in a rare moment of self-doubt and hesitation. Daddy was ill. He was dying in fact. Yet he insisted I go ahead with my visit to his favorite country. It was a country I had been hearing about and reading about and listening to Daddy commend since I was fourteen years old. I hated he was dying. I hated to leave him. But he wanted me to go to Senegal and, with filial respect, I did what I was told.

"Bienvenue à Dakar, Brenda." [Welcome to Dakar, Brenda.] A voice called to me from the crowd outside the gate. All around me were the patterned, rushed sounds of Wolof-accented French and the smell of incense and essential oils that the women in Senegal are known to smooth on their skin. Amid the bustle I found the source of the voice—my friend Mamadou, beside him his wife Fatou. A professor of English, Mamadou and I had first met a few years before when he was one of the many foreign travelers I hosted in Pittsburgh as a member of the Pittsburgh Council for International Visitors. When I told him I was writing about the Nigerian women novelists, Flora Nwapa and Buchi Emecheta, he said his wife also studied their works and encouraged us to correspond. Like pen pals, Fatou and I wrote back and forth about Nwapa and Emecheta. Three years later, we finally met.

We hugged in greeting. I was thrilled to finally meet Fatou, a person I had grown to admire through handwritten letters across the ocean. I already knew she was friendly and studious. Now, I saw she was fashionable, too. Of slim build and about my height, she was dressed in a bright purple patterned matching head scarf and dress, with eye-catching jewelry and sandals. She was much younger than Mamadou, and I remembered her story of how Mamadou, a young teacher looking for a wife, had met her at her classmate's house. When he quickly inquired with her parents about marrying her, a nineteen-year-old who had no desire for marriage, they agreed.

Thus, after being nagged incessantly by her mother, her fate was arranged. Two months after meeting Mamadou, and barely knowing him, they were married. Fatou was most unhappy about it at first, but soon adjusted. She had continued her education and now taught English at l'École Normale Supérieure de Dakar (ENS).

My friends did not yet know how dire Daddy's health was.

During the flight I had been in a daze, floating in the sky between past and present. Thinking of memories of Daddy, while moving toward the future, toward the continent where Daddy always hoped for good things yet to come. "Africa is coming into its own," he had said to us all those years ago. Dakar is the most easily accessible city in Africa from the States. After less than nine hours on a nonstop flight from New York, I touched down to a sunrise in one of the most electrifying cities in the world. I had been excited that this year's African Literature Association Conference was to take place in Dakar, a city of 1.45 million, but now I didn't know if I would have enough energy for the conference. Nor did I know if I would be able to experience Senegal fully, and the company of my friends. My heart was home in a Maryland hospital bed.

The first time I heard the word "Senegal" was when Daddy spoke it in the Congo in 1962. When I spotted men wearing loose-fitting, long flowing Muslim-style damask or wax-print *boubous* over matching pants and skullcaps on their heads walking in Léopoldville, I turned to Daddy for an explanation.

"Who are they?" They were taller and slimmer than the Congolese who had rounded faces and features. They carried pillows and prayer beads and rolled out their individual prayer rugs in the main square to kneel in prayer to Allah. It might have been the first time I witnessed Islam in practice, and this kind of worship had been a rare sight in Léo, where most people were Catholic. Daddy said the men were *les diamantaires* (diamond traffickers),[1] who the Congolese claimed to be from Senegal. Unfinished diamonds looked like plain old rocks and were easy to smuggle out of the Congo. I learned later these smugglers came to Léo either by *la vedette* (speed boat) or the ferry via Brazzaville, and that they were actually Malians and Guineans. Who knows why the Congolese called them *les Sénégalais*. Maybe it was because the West Africans stayed in the "Little Dakar" neighborhood of Léo, or maybe they wanted to be associated with the reputation of the Senegalese as kind and peaceful and thus unlikely to steal. (One thing they did right was their attire. The flowing robes were much the same as the true Senegalese style.) *Les diamantaires*, it was rumored, smuggled diamonds in their pillows. In 1965, more than 42 percent of the production of Congolese diamonds was exported illegally from Léo via Brazzaville to Europe.[2]

In the Congo, Daddy became friends with a man named Moussa, a Senegalese businessman of imports and exports. Of what? At the time we kids did not know or care. We only knew our father formed a friendship with this man that became lifelong. He visited us twice in Jersey City after we had returned to the States. Daddy called him each time he went to Senegal. Very tall with smooth dark skin, Moussa dressed in well-cut shirts and carefully pressed, tailored French pants that fell "just so" on the back of his shoes. He spoke French with a choppy accent I found delightful. After meeting Moussa, I immediately asked my parents about the accent.

"This child is so *nosy!*" Mother exclaimed. Ignoring her, Daddy responded it was a Wolof accent, Wolof being the lingua franca of Senegal. It's clipped, Arabic-flavored, heavy on the consonant sound. Like a sharp salute. When the Congolese would say "how are you?" it sounded like "mingy mingy linga leen," like a song. In Wolof it's a quick *"Nanga def!"* to which you responded *"Mangi fi rekk!"* I loved it.

Daddy adored Senegal. The word itself was special just by the way he said it, with a subtle hint of wonder in his voice. He was intrigued with the music, the dancing, and most of all the literature. He was always reading Senegalese novels and poetry. There was so much literature, even back in the 1960s, coming out of such a small country. In graduate school I read Abdoulaye Sadji's two novels: *Maïmouma* (1953) and *Nini, la mulâtresse du Sénégal* (1954), the first novels to feature central characters as women in a transitional society

Many of the African-produced stories, poems, and films that hit the international stage were coming out of Senegal. Ousmane Sembène, remembered as "the father of African cinema," produced and directed some of the best films about Senegal. I became his fan after viewing the 1968 *Mandabi* (The Money Order), which exposed corruption and greed among scheming family members and strangers. Later I would publish two essays about Sembène's works; the first on his short stories,[3] the second on his 1977 film *Ceddo*.[4]

Senegal was the home country of Léopold Senghor, the *négritude* poet who drafted France's Fifth Republic constitution. Senghor, the first post-independence president of Senegal, remained in power for two decades until 1980. In 1983, the retired president became the first African to be elected to l'Académie française,[5] the most prestigious cultural institution in France.

There was much to reflect on as Fatou and Mamadou drove me to the conference hotel after my flight. During the drive, I told them about Daddy's failing health.

"Senegal is your father's favorite country," one of them said, reminding me if I were to be anywhere in the world other than in the same room with him, it should be here. True.

Within minutes of being in the country, my sandaled feet were covered in a thin layer of fine, wheat-colored dust. Senegal is flat and sandy, with expanses of desert land reaching back from the coastal waters. The climate is hot and dry. I would not find the lush, green, humid climate of the Congo and Gabon. With the land so flat, the sky is bigger, more present, the motions of the sun more noticeable. I shook the sand from my feet, but knew it was no use. The sand infiltrated everything, everywhere.

I remembered the horrible sandstorm accident Daddy had while in Senegal in 1972. Although I was living in Paris at the time and did not witness the accident, from Daddy's recounting of the story I formed a picture in my mind that never faded. His experience became my memory. While associate commissioner for higher education in New York, he traveled to Senegal to plan an educational exchange program with l'Université de Dakar. Of course, he visited Moussa, too. They took a car to the neighboring country Mauritania, and on their way back they hit a sandstorm. Sand so strong it could pick you up. It had a life of its own. All Daddy remembered was a wall of sand descending on them and the driver saying, ominously, "We are in the eye of death." Daddy awoke confused, bruised, and battered in the hospital, his right arm bundled in a cast. The driver died. Moussa and Daddy were injured.

With a severe concussion, two black eyes, a banged-up head, and a right wrist that had been broken in nine places, Daddy boarded a plane back to the U.S. Mother screeched when she saw his bloody, swollen face.

"I ran toward him," she told me. "Then I ran away from him. I didn't know what to do." Daddy had to assure her he was okay. She found him an orthopedic surgeon who said the Senegalese doctors had done a beautiful job putting together his wrist but he would not be able to use his hand again.

"No," Daddy said, characteristically stubborn. "I *will* use this hand."

He went to physical therapy for seven months, and while I was home from Paris for summer vacation, I watched him arrive at the house, face blanched in so much pain from the physical therapy, and continually work his right wrist with a stress ball all evening until bedtime. The hand was smaller, weaker, fragile. To lose the use of a hand was dreadful, but to lose your dominant hand, the right hand . . .

Suddenly, I shuddered at the ghost-memory that popped up unannounced from time to time about the Congolese men and their missing hands. It had stayed in my subconscious waiting for the right time to haunt me. I wondered how close Daddy had come to losing his right hand. Of course, the connection between Daddy's hand and the hands of those Congolese men who had been brutalized by violence remained just the same body part. In all other respects the injuries were different—a completely different context, and with a completely different outcome.

Daddy had prime healthcare and physical therapy. He kept his high-ranking job with the New York Department of Education. He taught himself how to sign his name and eventually write with his left hand. He even wrote me letters with his left hand, for Daddy was determined to regain the flexibility of his right hand.

After about a year, he defied the doctor's prognosis and began to use his right hand. Yet, it was never as flexible as before. Never again could he bowl with his sons like he had every week before the accident. He could do small things, pick up light things and play a song or two on the piano before it began to hurt. Most importantly, he could write again, cut precious stones and become a certified gemologist. Amazing! Every day thereafter, he carried a stress ball and worked his right wrist to keep it strong. He would be having a conversation with someone, watching television, or reading, all the while working his wrist. For over seventeen years he kept it up. I wanted to see him clutching the stress ball again, squeezing strength back into his hand. Never giving up.

Daddy did not hold a grudge against Senegal for the terrible sandstorm. He went back and thereafter continued talking about Senegal the same way he had always talked about the country: a magnificent place. He always said the people were so kind. Senegal is one of the few African nations never to experience a coup, usually peaceful in the transfer of power. It is widely recognized in large part because of Senghor, who had ruled with the ideals of *négritude*. Senghor believed in art and culture and knowing his culture is transformative to healing and development.

There was relatively little violence in recent history of what was probably one of the least expected sites of peace. The shore houses a history of much horror: Senegal's l'Île de Gorée is one of the first places in Africa settled by Europeans, and it was literally *la porte du voyage sans retour* ("the door of no return") for more than a million enslaved Africans—their last stop before being packed onto ships and transported across the ocean in the TransAtlantic Slave trade. Now tourists visit the dungeon-like chambers walled with red or green stucco and follow a tour guide down the long-covered walkway that leads out to the sea. It is said this brick corridor was the path down which Africans were forcibly herded before boarding the ships. When I visited, I intuited the moans and screams of ancestors as the waves crashed against the faded red walls of the house.

And yet: Peace. Children today play soccer on l'Île de Gorée and bright magenta bougainvillea drapes the pastel-painted colonial houses.

It's not unusual for me to fall in love with a country in Africa and yet find the pervasive patriarchal attitude and social structure vexing to the point I could not imagine myself living there permanently. *Where are the women?* I often asked. *Where are their stories?* My angst is what sparked my idea to write about the expatriate Black American women in South Africa, to take down their stories of living as honorary Whites.

In Senegal, women and their contributions to society throughout history were not invisible. Directly across from la Maison des esclaves is le Musée de la Femme Henriette Bathily (The Henriette Bathily's Women Museum). Inaugurated on June 17, 1994, under the direction of Annette Mbaye d'Erneville, the Henriette Bathily's Women Museum is the first of its kind to be devoted to the popular and traditional art work, folk arts, and glass paintings of women from the urban and rural areas of Senegal.[6] It's also the first women's museum on the African continent.

Mbaye d'Erneville, Senegal's first woman journalist and author, launched *Les Femmes de soleil* (later changed to *Awa)*, the first Francophone African women's magazine in 1957. In her 1990s, she is also an active poet and an author of children's literature. Her friend, Henriette Bathily, for whom the museum is named, had been actively involved at le Théâtre National Daniel Sorrano in Dakar and les Ballets Africains de Keita Fodeba of Guinea. Second wife of Boubacar Bâ, former Minister of Finance (1971–1978), Bathily was also a journalist for Radio-Mali before working at le Centre Culturel Français where she helped to promote many artists. An activist, she was involved in the women's movement until her death in 1984.

I would come to know and recognize a sense of calm and respect among the people in everyday Senegalese life, not victimhood.

I sighed as I settled into my room at the hotel. Even thoughts of peace were laced with heartache. It was hard to accept the idea that Daddy would die soon. I suppose my mind held onto the fantasy that every girl has that her father is somehow immortal. He was such a strong person.

On that first visit to Senegal, as I slipped between past and present, surrounded with impending grief and nostalgia, my friends were gracious. It helped to have them around me: Fatou, Mamadou, Pape, Awa and my friends at the ALA Conference. My roommate was Debra, who had previously spent a year in Senegal as a U.S. Fulbrighter teaching a Senegalese Protestant choir how to sing Negro spirituals. Yvonne, whom Mother had befriended in the Congo and reestablished contact, was there, too. She served on the board of directors of Africare, a nonprofit dedicated to development and clean water initiatives in Africa, which had an office in Senegal. She knew how sick Daddy was and she comforted me. I showed a picture of Daddy to my conference friends one night at dinner, who recognized him and recalled him from the ALA in Pittsburgh the year before. He'd sat on a panel with the *négritude* poet Jacques Rabemananjara from Madagascar, about whom he was so excited. Daddy gave a speech, which turned out to be his last, on a panel called "Historic Witnesses: A Dialogue on *Présence Africaine*."[7] Over the next few days in Senegal, we friends gathered together and shared dinners and laughs, caught up on life happenings and literature, and for a few moments my worry over Daddy subsided.

Dakar opened up to me. I found myself engaged with the place in spite of everything, imagining that Daddy had gone to the very same places and seen the same things when he was here. In the aggressive, friendly, bustling city, the Senegalese easily strike up conversations with Black American strangers.

Nanga def? [How are you?]

Mangi fi rekk. [I'm fine.]

or—

Salaam alaikum [Peace be unto you.]

Malekum salaam [The same to you.]

After a greeting comes an inquiry about family. The Senegalese take the time to ask after the health and well-being of relatives, even of someone they have just met.

A predominantly Muslim city where one eats from a communal enamel-coated bowl, jumps on a colorfully painted *car rapide* (fast mini-van), and shares a ride on a *sarret* (horse drawn cart). A city where Lebu fishermen go fishing in their *pirogues* (canoes) in the Atlantic Ocean from 5:00 a.m. to 5:00 p.m.

A boisterous, polluted city with traffic jams, drivers who change lanes without signaling and cross through the gas station to merge into traffic, forging a lane that doesn't exist.

Taxi drivers, who never have small change, honk at me to declare their availability. Beggars approach me for money, and children ply the roads, hawking bottled water, chewing gum, light bulbs, coat hangers, newspapers, and sunglasses. Women stroll along the sidewalks with babies tied to their backs with pieces of patterned cloth. Women's heads are covered with scarves. It's not uncommon to see a *musoor* (headwrap) of the same material as the dress elaborately tied in angular shapes on their heads. Along the alleyways, women carry plastic tubs piled with fabrics or fruit on their heads. Beaches are dotted with fishermen's boats painted with chipping blues and reds. Here men run along the shore.

The various markets assault the senses. The smell of exhaust fumes, lemony cologne, and overly ripe fruit greet me at Marché Sandaga, the congested central market. In the enclosed Marché Kermel, I smell flowers, fresh fruit, and smoked or salted fish and the sharp odor of raw meat. And the pungent freshly caught fish such as *thiof* (grouper), *capitaine* (Nile perch or hogfish), and *gambas* (prawns) in Soumbédioune, the evening fish market along *la Corniche* (long boulevard parallel to the Atlantic Ocean) in the populous Médina neighborhood. At the less touristy, dirty, crowded Marché de Tilène, the fruits and vegetables aren't as ripe.

Under canvas-covered stalls in Marché Soumbédioune are baskets, jewelry, and leather goods. Gold and silver jewelry can be purchased at Cour des

Maures. Cotton fabric and silks in indigo, solids, stripes, or prints in vibrant colors on wooden tables from West African countries capture my fancy in Marché H.L.M. It's difficult to decide what *not* to buy. While I maneuver around the people, potholes, sewage, stray dogs, and wheelbarrows on narrow sandy paths in the Médina fetish market, the vendors hassle me about buying *téere* or *gris-gris* (amulets), cobra heads, and other fetishes. Dakar is the trading center for the whole of West Africa.

Friendly Dakar. The home of singers and musicians such as Orchestre Baobab, Wasis Diop, Coumba Gawlo, Ismaël Lô, Baaba Maal, Youssou N'Dour, and Omar Pene. Women initiate the spontaneous *tàan-béer* (improvised street parties) to the *sabar* drumming and dancing. The percussion laden *mbalax* music, created by Youssou N'Dour et le Super Étoile, is heard in all parts of the city. The Baye Fall, in their patchwork clothing, beat the drums while singing and asking for food and water or money for their *marabouts*. Live performances guarantee packed nightclubs, like Just4U, Thiossane, and Club Baobab.

The music uplifted me on that first visit. I expected to hear the famed Youssou N'Dour's voice often, and he did not disappoint me. He was by far the most popular musician in the country, maybe even in all of West Africa. N'Dour had been popular since he was fourteen, creating uptempo blends of African, Caribbean, and pop rhythms, using modern and traditional instruments like the djembe and tama drums and the harp-like kora. And always the balafon—the wooden instrument similar to a xylophone—with its deep and gentle bell tones that reminded me of wooden wind chimes blowing softly on a sunny afternoon porch. You had to dance or at least nod your head to the music. On the street, amid choke-hold traffic and vendor tents spilling with bright-colored fabric, people in those flowing robes walking by, the scent of perfume and sweat and rotting trash, the music would emanate from somewhere. Like the sound of the Iman's voice announcing prayer, it was ever-present. Everywhere I went I kept hearing the same song, N'Dour's voice singing "Bamako, Bamako." It must have been his newest hit. I was humming it along with him without even noticing, but I had no idea what the song was about. I assumed it was a tribute to the city Bamako in neighboring Mali.

When I visited Fatou at home, I watched as she would stop in the middle of a task, get out her prayer rug, place a wrapper that covered her head to her chest, and begin to bow and murmur the prayer. Outside, the Iman announced prayer in Arabic over the whole city and read scripture. The voice echoed throughout the city. This ritual happened five times a day. I said nothing as she prayed; out of respect and embarrassment I gazed out the window at the bright blue sky. My opinion of religion is neutral at best and scorn at worst, knowing how much destruction and pain has resulted from the way people have twisted religion throughout history. Missionary conquest and colonial oppression were frequently parallel forces, I felt, especially in Africa. One paved the way for the next.

Perhaps because of my vulnerable emotional state, there was a moment I felt a tiny flash of envy at Fatou's belief and trust in God, in some higher force full of so much goodness it was worthy of bodily worship. A higher force that could control the uncontrollable.

I wished I had the power to make Daddy well.

When he was first diagnosed with cancer of the colon in 1985, he was depressed. I had never seen him like that. Lethargic. I drove four hours down the Pennsylvania Turnpike to Silver Spring, Maryland, every other weekend to help Mother and take him to chemotherapy and radiation treatments. When he was too weak to eat, Mother spoonfed him. When he could not shave close enough, Mother took the razor and shaved for him. Subsequently, I left to teach for six months at the Freire Universität Berlin. Before leaving I told him to hurry up and recover from his operation because for his sixtieth birthday, I had bought him an airline ticket to visit Germany. Mother later told me my words were like magic. Daddy's spirits rose and he doubled his gumption to fight. He recovered, and he and Mother spent three weeks with me in vibrant West Berlin.

Now, three years later, the cancer had returned, and there was nothing I could do. He had taken to sleeping almost all day in a hospital bed at home. He feared the cancer would spread to his brain, and when he talked, he often stared with a steady, unrelenting look at me, Mother, and Derek and asked if we understood what he had said. We reassured him again and again he was speaking clearly enunciated English.

I thought of him bathing in the golden sun. As soon as he told me he only had a few months left to live, a sudden ray of sunlight shot across the room. The late afternoon light was soft and warming, a sharp contrast to his gloomy news.

"Daddy, I wish I could be a fairy tale princess and wave my wand over your body to get rid of the cancer," I said.

"Oh, Brenda. How I wished you could be a fairy tale princess," he said in a voice barely above a whisper. We were quiet for a long while.

My heart was aching when I asked him if I should cancel my trip to Senegal. "I want you to go," he said. I crawled into the twin bed next to him and together we slept through the night. The next morning, I kissed his forehead.

After I had been in Senegal for four days, on a Sunday, two friends from D.C. arrived.

They told me Daddy had passed.

Mother hadn't wanted to tell me the sad news over the phone and sent friends to break the news instead.

I had worn a yellow dress the day they told me—the color of sun and friendship.

Daddy had died on Friday, March 17. Knowing that there were only a few flights from Senegal to the U.S. every week, Mother scheduled the funeral for Wednesday instead of Monday to see if I could get home in time.

After all of these years, it is still very difficult to describe how I felt: my throat hurt from the pain; I couldn't see for the tears; I could barely croak out a word; I struggled to gather my composure.

I dialed Yvonne's hotel phone number to relay the tragic news. She jumped into action, emanating comfort. In her calm, soothing voice, she called the Black American director of Africare to ask if I could make an international call to Mother from his office. He collected us at the hotel; drove us to his office; granted me permission to call Mother; and kindly offered to lend me money for the purchase of a one-way ticket to return to Washington, D.C., for the funeral.

I had just met him two days ago!

Through my cloud of pain and bereavement, I was struck by this man's generosity.

"You can pay me back when you have the money," he said. "It doesn't matter if you take two or three years." Unfortunately, at the time, daily flights between New York and Dakar didn't exist. You had to catch it on the right day of the week. Even after layovers in Morocco and France, I still would not have arrived in time for the funeral. So, I declined his offer. The director offered to let me use his office phone to call Mother.

"Talk as long as you need to," he said gently, leading me back to his office. I asked if I could please give him some money. He refused. It was one of many encounters I had that week with Senegalese *teraanga*, the Wolof term meaning "hospitality" and "gracious welcome."

I don't know exactly when the reality of Daddy's death sank in. The week was a blur. Time was fluid. Past, present, and future seemed to merge. I was a zombie. Sometimes I felt outside my body viewing myself. I could not stay in my hotel room and cry. I kept moving. When people asked how I was doing and how my family was, I told them honestly my condition.

The Sunday I learned Daddy was gone, Mamadou, a member of the Sufi Mouride brotherhood, said he wanted to take me to visit la Grande Mosquée in Touba where Cheikh Amadou Bamba Mbacké, the founder of the Mourides, is buried. A two-and-a-half hour drive inland, it is the Muslim holy city of Senegal. A Mecca. *Daru Salaam* ((Land of Peace). I agreed, and soon I stood before the marbled entrance of one of the biggest and most magnificent structures I had ever seen. The castle-like mosque had five minarets and large domes of green and purple.

Everything had meaning to me then, so I could appreciate the dome painted in purple, the color of triumph and royalty. It felt important. It was the largest structure for miles around. As I always do when visiting holy temples, I stood outside while Mamadou went in to pray. I gazed at the monument, sweating in the hot sun, and I felt a calm and quiet sadness.

Daddy was gone.

As I stood back far enough from the mosque to get a good view of the whole structure, the people going in and out seemed as small as grasshoppers, miniature in their billowing white robes. It felt right to be at their holy place. I thanked Mamadou.

I decided what I was going to do: plan a memorial for Wednesday, to hold at the same time my family held Daddy's funeral back in Washington, D.C.

Yvonne, a practicing Unitarian minister at that time,[8] helped me to organize the program. On my behalf, Debra asked Pierre Loby, the director of La Chorale des Martyrs de l'Ouganda, if he and some members of the choir would be able to sing at the service. I invited Abena Busia, a Ghanaian poet at the conference whose work I had read. She said she would be honored to read a poem she had written at her father's death. South African Dennis Brutus, who was my colleague in Pittsburgh and came to the conference as well, agreed to read a poem. The Ghanaian Kofi Anyidoho, too. My Senegalese friend Pape, who had studied in Pittsburgh, agreed to talk about how he had known Daddy. Yvonne officiated. The kora player we met at the United States embassy agreed to play.

Thousands of miles and an ocean removed from family, I had friends near me. Daddy was gone, and I felt shell-shocked, but I was still moving.

In just two days, we secured a banquet room at the hotel, a few singers, a kora player, and a full program. Printed on the first page of the bilingual (French & English) program was Daddy's obituary.

Wednesday came. At 11:00 a.m. in Washington, D.C., and 5:00 p.m. in Dakar, I pictured Mother, Toni, Albert, Derek, my nieces and nephews, and aunts and uncles, all gathered together.

On the day of the service, I walked into a packed banquet room. People were everywhere. Instantly overcome with emotions, I could barely see where I had to sit. I was surprised and shocked to see all those people, each of the faces I knew. I scanned the room for Moussa, wishing I had known how to find him. There were people to whom I had mentioned our quick memorial when I saw them at the conference, people I had just met on the street, my friends from D.C., the poets and musicians I had invited. A Supreme Court justice whom I had met the day before, the brother of my friend Pape was there, along with his friend I had met at the same time. I was touched, knowing they had canceled court to be there, these people who were strangers just a day ago.

The hotel management had decorated the room with candles and flowers.

I thought only a few choir members would come, maybe ten, but there was Pierre with the entire eighty-member choir, walking in one-by-one, dressed in their greenish brown robes. Their voices filled the room with sorrow and joy. The walls vibrated with memory and raw, unfiltered emotion. Negro spirituals summoned forth the souls of Black Americans who had endured so many trials. When the choir stood up to lead us into the Gullah spiritual song "Kum Ba Ya" (Come by Here), I felt my father's spirit and the love and friendship surrounding me from people from around the world. A song sung by both Gullah Blacks in the South and by White Boy Scouts gathered around campfires in the mountains. An ocean away from my family I was protected, enclosed in a cocoon. I could not have been in a better place.

I was too choked up to speak. Others spoke.

Abena Busia read "Testimonies for Father,"[9] a poem that brought nearly everyone in the room to tears. She had written it as a funeral poem for her father who had also been the former prime minister of Ghana. Then Dennis Brutus and Kofi Anyidoho each read a poem.

Yvonne described how she had known Daddy all those years ago in the Congo. She said that the best was what he always did, in everything he did—the best he possibly could. The last time she had spoken with him on the phone, all he talked about was his Mary and how she was doing. He was more concerned with his wife than with himself. When it came to himself, whenever anyone asked him how he was doing, he always said, "I'm doing the best that I can."

The kora player weaved a gentle lullaby.

It was a pan-African program, just like how Daddy would have liked. The service was gorgeous. I had honored my father in the best way I knew.

Daddy was the single greatest loss in my life, and yet as I looked out at all the people in the room, I felt more love than ever. I was cushioned by the love. All those people gathered to celebrate and mourn over the person most precious to me in the world, and half of them had never even met him.

The grief palpitated within me, and would be there for many years, but it was a grief shared.

Sustaining me was the kindness of the Senegalese Daddy had always talked about. For example, you had to be careful when you complimented a piece of art or jewelry in someone's home, because the next day they would give it to you. That was the expectation and it would be rude to refuse. It was part of their culture.

As Yvonne and I cleared away the chairs and blew out the candles, I asked the hotel manager for my bill that included the room rental, flowers, and candles. The hotel manager shook his head while saying there was no charge.

The kora player, packing up his instrument, said he couldn't take money for doing his part either.

"My daughter," he said. "You're not with your family—we take care of you now."

While the choir members filed out, I tried to thank them individually. (They had also refused to take any money.) Several of them looked at me shocked. One woman finally stopped and asked why I was thanking them.

"But you finally came home, daughter," she said.

Teraanga.

As always, when I experienced something noteworthy or compelling, I had the urge to call Daddy and tell him all about it. I couldn't.

I called Mother. We cried together.

Later that evening, I joined my friends, to their surprise, at the dance concert by Le Ballet National du Sénégal (a troupe my father admired) at le Théâtre National Daniel Sorrano in downtown Dakar. They had assumed I wanted to be alone after the memorial service or I would be too emotionally spent for an outing. As we waited for the dancers to come onstage, N'Dour's song "Bamako"[10] came on. The soothing, plaintive acoustic song was meant for me that week, apparently, because here it was again. With so many repeated encounters, the song itself felt like a friend.

The show was about to begin. Suddenly, stage lights beamed brightly onto the audience, and I squinted and turned my head to the right. When I opened my eyes, Daddy was sitting next to me. He was healthy, not skinny and fatigued like the last time I had seen him. His face was round and full. He wore his favorite suit. He was smiling, and happy. For a split second, before the analytical side of my brain kicked in, my heart lifted. He was so real and so close, I could reach over and touch him. Positivity blanketed me whole. I felt joy. He said—though I don't think he moved his mouth. "Don't worry, Brenda. I will see you again."

Quickly I turned to Mamadou on my left. "Mamadou!" I gasped. When I looked to the right again, he was gone.

"Daddy!"

Excitedly, I told Mamadou and Fatou I had just seen my father.

"*Bien sûr.*" [Of course.] Unfazed, they nodded absently, just as if I'd said the ocean was blue. They understood ancestors made visits all the time. People are not gone when they die, according to African cosmology. Ancestors are always with us, they say. In the trees, in the leaves. The dead are not dead but always living and breathing, still touching earth's realm. "The dead are in the paling shadows / and in the darkening shadows,"[11] writes Senegalese poet Birago Diop.

I am not one to believe in such things, but I know what I saw.

For those few moments my heart greeted my father. Then I sank back into an even deeper sadness. How I missed Daddy already.

I am not one to believe, but right then I made a decision about what was true. Daddy had visited me. There was no way to prove it, but it was true.

I am not one to believe, but then I was reminded of faith's magnitude in Dakar. Sometime during my stay, I had witnessed the city en masse praying outside. Women prayed indoors, or in upper rooms in the mosques, hidden. But outside all these men, as far as the eye could see, in all different colored robes flowing in the wind, all prayed at one time to Allah. On Friday afternoons after the Iman's announcement, everything stops. Cars, taxis, and buses halt in the middle of the street. Suddenly, the roads and sidewalks are filled with men, shoulder to shoulder, before their prayer mats. Shoes off to the side. Together they stand, bend, and kneel in unison toward the same direction. What an awesome sight! Standing, bending, kneeling, faces to the ground. Rows of bare feet bottoms, the soft pale flesh so intimately exposed. The feet all look the same. The soles of feet, so vulnerable, so integral, so rarely seen.

I was swept into the vastness of it all. The togetherness. Nothing mattered to all those people except paying honor to their God. A sandstorm could rise up on the horizon and no one would quit.

My God, I thought, *look at the power.*

Senegal is the poorest country I've been to. People are starving, begging on the street. There is poverty in places like the Congo as well, but the country itself is rich in other ways; with diamonds, gold, bauxite, and other minerals. There is wealth and unlimited potential right there on the land. What does Senegal have? Peanuts! Fish and music. Sand. FAITH.

Since I began visiting Senegal, the number of beggars and homeless people has increased twofold. The CFA franc was for many years tied to the French franc and later to the euro. In 1994, the CFA franc was devalued 50 percent in foreign currency terms,[12] and the economy has never recovered. When you research this fact, you will read only that it turned out positive for Senegal. The CIA World Factbook records that after the devaluation, "Senegal's inflation went down, investment went up, and the gross domestic product rose approximately 5 percent per year between 1995 and 2007."[13] But Senegal's debt doubled overnight and the average Senegalese citizens' savings were wiped out. The cost of living continues to increase, eroding the standard of living. Many become migrants and work abroad to send money home to Senegal, and it's often the only thing that keeps the unemployed afloat.

Fatou and Mamadou feed their extended families every day. A homeless woman rings their doorbell every morning and Fatou hands her a *baguette*.

Yet, Senegal is the richest place on earth. It harbors a spiritual richness unlike I had ever witnessed before or since.

I did not envy the bowing mass of praying people, individuals who became united as one body, moving in supplication, of their own will, carried by the hope and obedience of those around them. I felt in union with them, and a great peace descended upon me. I could have stayed there all day. I was not in the past or the future—I was not concerned with what was next nor what had happened before. There was no need for words.

I relayed to Mother how Daddy had visited me. She, too, understood. "You were where he wanted you to be. He knew you wouldn't be able to handle his death in the States," she said. "He wanted you to experience the mysticism of Senegal."

Only later did I learn the full lyrics and meaning of Youssou N'Dour's "Bamako" song, and the symbolism struck me immediately.

The song opens with N'Dour in Bamako, the capital of Mali, where he briefly meets Maky, a female stranger in the train station. Later the woman appears before him out of nowhere, dressed in a wrapper from head to toe. At his approach, she proceeds to engage him in a conversation, expressing wonderful things about his future and giving him advice about the ills of the world. A captivated N'Dour departs, relates his meeting with Maky to friends, and returns with them to the train station. *Hélas!* They can't find the mysterious stranger. Maky has disappeared, but what she has told him keeps coming to his mind. It makes him cautious and causes him to think twice before doing something. N'dour realizes she was dead, a *djinn* (spiritual creature). She was an ancestor who came to visit him, and he sings this song for her. She is with him, because he is able to see her spirit. N'Dour cries in the high keening voice of a *griot*, "*Ah mani. Ah mani Mane douma fatté Bamako.*" I say. I say. I'll never forget Bamako in my life.[14]

Maky seemed to deliver a divine message. For N'Dour, the advice came true: In 2004, *Rolling Stone* described N'Dour as "the most famous singer in Senegal and much of Africa."[15] From April 2012 until September 2013, he served as Minister of Culture and Tourism under Maky Sall's presidency.

The song seemed, somehow, to give a divine message for me, too.

Rarely do I believe that happenings in the world have anything to do with me. I often find that the most interesting things happen to other people. Sometimes, I happen to be in the vicinity of some important event, but usually I am on the outside, observing. I like this position of the outsider, feeling like a student, learning something about myself, my country of birth, and the foreign countries and people I have met. In fact, I've often thought that if I weren't in academia, I would have chosen a career behind the camera: filming movies about the lives of Africans or working at a production studio behind the scenes. I like to observe and participate, but not necessarily in the spotlight or as the one with the microphone. However, on that first trip to Senegal, it was different. I felt that something or someone was looking out for me, could hear the inner workings of my heart. Too many things aligned for me in ways that could not be explained.

Later, back home in Pittsburgh, when I described my mystical encounter and the significance of N'Dour's "Bamako," some people openly questioned my state of mind and assumed I had turned "religious." A few colleagues told me later they were worried I was headed for a nervous breakdown. In Africa, belief in more than what you can see is unquestioned. It is necessary. It is part of why, I believe, Africa has been able to heal and hope, at all, in the wake of such debilitating, ongoing oppression. Senegal would not be a place of peace without faith. In the West we do not see miracles or commune with our ancestors. I wonder if it's not because those celestial moments don't happen, but because we refuse to see them when they do.

In the 1980 *Une si longue lettre* (So Long a Letter), the first novel in French by Mariama Bâ, a Senegalese woman, the protagonist Ramatoulaye mourns the death of her husband. In a letter addressed to her best friend, she writes poignantly, "One does not fix appointments with fate. When it moves in the direction of your desires, it brings you plenitude. But more often than not, it unsettles, crosses you. Then one has to endure."[16] Not only does Ramatoulaye endure the mourning period but also matures, displays a dignity and courage to emulate, and seeks happiness and hope once again.

When Senegal comes up in my conversation with other Africana scholars and friends who have visited the country, we all concur—even those of us decidedly non-religious—that it's a wondrous place. Something beyond the sum of its parts. The catchy, soothing music. The notion of *teraanga*. The kindness of the people, the way they welcome you in until you feel a part of the whole. Even the open sewers and stinking trash and extreme poverty and the sand that perpetually covers your feet. All those faithful bending in tandem, honoring a force much larger than themselves, a force for good and peace.

"There's something about Senegal" someone might say, and we all nod in agreement.

My friendships grow deeper as I return and continue to cultivate my connections to Senegal. Fatou's second son visits me in Atlanta and calls me "Mama Brenda."

In recounting the first trip during which my father left this world for the next, I have searched unsuccessfully for words to describe the country of Senegal. It is the place where my father's footsteps guided mine; a place that held a special place in his heart. It is a place that enveloped me in love at a very difficult time in my life. It is a place where life and death exist in tandem for me, where the past, present, and future converged. It is a place of universal faith, where I have felt God.

All I can say are words borrowed from N'Dour, "*Ah mani. Ah mani. Mane douma fatté Sénégal.*" [I say. I say. I'll never forget Senegal in my life.]

NOTES

1. Sylvie Bredeloup, "L'Aventure contemporaine des diamantaires sénégalais," *Politique Africaine* 56 (1994): 83.

2. Jean Sylvie La Fontaine, *City Politics: A Story of Leopoldville, 1962–63* (Cambridge: Cambridge University Press, 1970), 52.

3. Brenda F. Berrian, "Through Her Prism of Social and Political Contexts: Sembène's Female Characters in *Tribal Scars*," in *Ngambika: Studies of Women in African Literature*, edited by Carole Boyce Davies and Anne Graves (Trenton: Africa World Press, 1986).

4. Brenda F. Berrian, "Manu Dibango and *Ceddo*'s Transatlantic Soundscape," in *Focus on African Films*, edited by Francoise Pfaff (Bloomington, IN: Indiana University Press, 2004).

5. Eric S. Ross, *Cultures and Customs of Senegal* (Westport, CT: Greenwood Press, 2008), 28.

6. Le Musée de la femme Henriette Bathily has been moved to Dakar at the Place du Souvenir Africain et de la Diaspora.

7. Albert H. Berrian, "Historic Witness," in *The Surreptitious Speech: Présence Africaine and the Politics of Otherness, 1947–1987*, edited by Valentin Y. Mudimbe (Chicago: University of Chicago Press, 1992), 367–69.

8. Brooke Bryan, "A Lifetime of Making a Difference," *Yellow Springs News*, July 16, 2009. http://www.ysnews.com/news/2009/07/07/a-lifetime-of-making-a-difference.

9. Abena Busia, "Testimonies for Father," in *Testimonies of Exile* (Accra, Ghana: Woeli Publishing Services, 1978), 29.

10. Youssou N'Dour et le Super Étoile de Dakar, "Bamako," *Gaindé*, 1988.

11. Birago Diop, "Breaths," in *Talking Drums: A Selection of Poems from South of the Sahara,* ed. Véronique Tadjo (New York: Bloomsbury, 2004), 58.

12. Pierre Van Boogaerde and Charalambos Tsangarides, "Ten Years after the CFA Franc Devaluation: Progress toward Regional Integration in the WAEMU," IMF Working Paper W/P/05/145, July 2005. http://www.ssrn.com/sol3/papers.cfm?abstract_id=88014.

13. "Senegal," *2016 CIA World Factbook*. http://www.allcountries.org/world_face_book_ 2016/senegal/index.html.

14. N'Dour, "Bamako."

15. J. D. Considine and Michaelangelo Matos, "Biography: Youssou N'Dour," *The Rolling Stone Magazine*, 2004.

16. Mariama Bâ, *So Long a Letter* (London: Heinemann, 1980), 2.

Chapter 23

Childhood Sweethearts and Colorism

In most episodes of the popular family-centered television shows, make-believe parents reassured their spouses and children they were loved. They were White families, mostly, as was the status quo for television. Daddy and I would deconstruct this constant reassurance of love. Why did the characters need to say it so often? Why didn't they just know they were loved? Was fear beneath the surface that caused a sense of love to disappear? Was this true for many White families in reality?

The opposite could be seen on *The Cosby Show*, which featured an upper-middle-class Black American family of five children. One knew intuitively the Huxtables loved one another although they rarely uttered the phrase, "I love you." Daddy and I pointed out how the Huxtables teased each other, laughed at each other, and got angry with each other. How Claire, the wife, would get angry with her husband Cliff or one of her children, but even then, you could see, in the way her lips suppressed a smile and how her eyes shone with affection that the undercurrent was always love. The special scenes were ones that reflected my own parents: Cliff and Claire cuddling on the living room sofa to the accompaniment of music. Cliff and Claire kicking off their shoes and dancing around the house, laughing and flirting with each other. They stole these moments after their children were in bed, and they relished in their time together after their children were grown.

My parents, Albert and Mary, lived those scenes in real life. No video camera to record them, no witnesses except for the occasional notice of their children.

Albert would interrupt Mary in a household task, take her in his arms and twirl her around the living room. Through the record player crooned Etta James, Ray Charles, Nancy Wilson, the Whispers, the O'Jays, and Sam Cooke.

When I would visit home after all four of us kids were living on our own, I caught a glimpse of their daily life. Music streamed through the open windows of their house as I pulled into the driveway—the kind that would lift any mood. Luther Vandross's greatest hits or Patti LaBelle's "New Attitude" on CD, or other high-beat contemporary Black American music from the local WHUR-FM radio station. Mother's voice singing along at top register, and Daddy's faint laughter beneath it.

Mary rose early and cooked a hearty breakfast of grits, eggs, and sausage for Albert before work. The minute she called up the stairs, "Babe, come to breakfast," he leaped out of the bathroom, dollop of shaving cream still on his face or not, and practically ran downstairs to be with her. Through the floorboards in my room upstairs I could hear their laughter and snippets of conversation. I listened and watched, not wanting to interfere on what felt like a private moment. They were on a honeymoon that lasted forty-four years.

Their story began as family.

Mary Miles, the fifth child born of her parents' union, lost her father Edward at age one. It was 1927 in Virginia. Her mother Josephine remarried and had three more children, then her second husband died, leaving her widowed twice over. She couldn't take care of eight children on her own with only a third-grade education and house cleaning job, so she asked her eldest daughter, Sarah, and son-in-law, Percy, who didn't have kids yet, if they would take Mary in.

Mary had inherited her mother's take-no-disrespect attitude, so her mother knew she'd be all right. Mary would grow into a self-assured Black woman, and she might even fare better up North anyway.

Still reeling over her stepfather's death and distraught over leaving her mother, eleven-year-old Mary arrived in Jersey with one small suitcase and a growing hole in her heart.

Her sister and brother-in-law lived around the corner from a family of five, the Berrians with two little girls, one the same age and the other two years younger than Mary and a boy one year older. Mary became very close friends with Rena (called "Sister") and Carrie, who loved Mary's boisterous attitude and the way she made even the most boring task fun. They played hopscotch and jumped rope on the sidewalk. They walked to school together. They slept in the same bed. They whispered about when they might grow hips and breasts. They giggled about boys.

Rena and Carrie's brother Harry, whom everyone called "Bubba," was quiet and studious, and Mary thought he was stuck up. Only a grade ahead in school, but too good to hang around silly young girls, always busy reading, and when he'd say smart things Mary was never sure whether he was showing off.

Mary was around these neighbors so often she quickly became part of the family. Mr. Berrian, especially, was glad to have her. He called her one of his daughters, and Mary loved him with the intense loyalty of a girl who lost her own father too soon. He would gather all the kids in the car and toss Mary right in, and they would head to South Jersey for gatherings with the large extended family.

"Mary knew all the relatives," Aunt Sister told me. "She knew the family better than *I* did."

Mrs. Berrian, however, was none too pleased to have Mary in the house. She could have easily identified with her, because she herself had been given up by her mother and sent to live with an aunt and her daughter as a child, but she had no sympathy for Mary.

Because Mary was a little light-skinned girl, Florence Berrian did not appreciate her and other light-skinned girls.

Even if the nasty phrase "You little light-skinned this-or-that," never came out of her mouth (which it often did), Mary would have known the woman resented her. Mary was no fool. She could see it in Florence's every move. The way she stiffened around her, cut her eyes in her direction, served her food at the dinner table with an air of inconvenience. She was a color struck woman—herself dark complexioned and plain-looking. Like Pecola in Toni Morrison's *The Bluest Eye*, Florence had probably been told she wouldn't amount to much. Nevertheless, she had gone to Daytona Normal and Industrial Institute (now Bethune-Cookman University) for cooking and could cook like no other. She had married "up," she thought. The youngest of ten kids, her husband Neal was light-skinned and came from a long line of people who could pass for one of his brothers did live as White. Not only was he light skinned, he had curly hair and golden-brown eyes, undeniably handsome. He came from a higher class, too. His family owned land, which was important in the Deep South. His mother was Jewish with hair so long that she could sit on it. His father was mixed with Cherokee Indian blood.

Neal Berrian paid no mind to Florence's disdain for Mary. He loved Mary openly and generously the same way he did his own daughters. But he had his own color issues. There were these good-looking men who would marry someone they considered unattractive so they wouldn't be "shown up" in the looks department, and Neal was one of those. His wife looked up to him. He could take his pick of women, and Florence knew it. He might have preferred a light-skinned woman so he could continue for his kinfolk the privilege of all that almost-Whiteness, but he did not. He wanted it for himself only. Neal married Florence, a sturdy, strong, dark brown woman who nearly worshipped him and whose plainness would never be in contention with his handsomeness.

Their kids were brown, shades between their mother's and father's. Fortunately, they did not inherit their parents' color consciousness. They grew up in a different generation, after all.

Florence's scorn did not temper Mary's sense of self. In fact, it probably made the girl child fight for confidence even more. Maybe it hardened her some in the process. The two females would bicker from time to time when they happened to be alone in the same room, then grow hushed if someone else walked in.

Figure 23.1 My parents Mary and Albert H. Berrian, 1985 (author's collection).

Sometime around age fifteen, the world began to shift for Mary. One day she looked at Bubba and realized, with a start, that he was cute. He had taken up boxing, so his body was lean and muscular, and he carried himself with an earned confidence. All that piano practicing also had paid off; he could tickle the ivory like a pro. One day Mary leaned on the piano while he practiced a song they both knew, and his eyes wandered to meet hers. He didn't seem so stuck up anymore.

Right under Mary's nose was a good-looking, smart man, and her stomach suddenly did a flip when he walked into the room. He must have noticed, too, for he began paying special attention to Mary, looking at her with a new shyness in his eyes. One summer, during his sisters and mother's absence, they began dating. Florence and her two daughters had traveled down South to see their relatives. "A letter arrived from my friend Helen," Aunt Sister recounted. She wrote, "Guess who's dating? Bubba and Mary Miles!"

There was something special about having known each other since the fifth and sixth grades, growing up side by side, from bony kids to blossoming teens. It was like they had been destined to spend their lives together, and it was too easy and fun.

To the delight of Neal and his daughters and the chagrin of Florence, the couple got engaged. Albert signed up for the Coast Guard, and Mary's five brothers all joined different branches of the military. The young couple wanted to be sure everyone could be there to witness their vows. At ages eighteen and nineteen, as World War II neared its end, they held a small, private wedding.

The GI bill financed Bubba's undergraduate and graduate education at New York University and part-time jobs. While Mary also worked to support the family, Albert earned bachelor's, master's, and doctoral degrees at New York University. When Mary got pregnant for the first time, she knew half the joy of having a child would be to watch her husband become the loving, doting father his own father had been to her. It was like the two ends of a string held by a young fatherless girl had intertwined to form a perfect circle.

Bubba was calm, Mary was excitable. They complemented each other that way. Whenever we were naughty as kids, Mother would be the one to come after us with a strap, whip our butts, and move on. Daddy would lecture us on what we did wrong and deliberate for an hour on our detailed punishment, while we would groan from the torture. In different ways, they modeled for us how to be confident and demand respect, no matter if society didn't agree with how much respect a Black person deserved.

My parents challenged us to be proud of ourselves, to hold our heads high and not let discrimination go unpunished. They ensured we took our education seriously. They dedicated their lives to educating us, moving around the country for Bubba to teach at historically Black colleges. Still, they knew education wasn't the only tool to fight oppression; they admired the way others resisted discrimination in the United States and around the world. For example, Nelson Mandela captured their hearts from the beginning. I recall many times when they mulled over the question of whether they would have the commitment and courage to do what Mandela did—remain in prison for decades until the apartheid government met his terms for a non-racial democracy.

"Now, it's my turn!" Mary told Bubba after he finished all his degrees. She started taking classes toward a home economics degree and made straight A's. She started making clothes for everyone in the family. But Bubba kept getting job offers, and every time he accepted a new position in a different city Mary had to transfer and lose credits. After retaking the same class for the third time, she said of her attempts to get a college degree, "Forget it!!"

In the end, she completed three years of college. All five of us regretted she wasn't able to finish. After all, she and Bubba paid for all four of their kids to go to college.

When Bubba got sick, Mary cared for him at his bedside, not only cooking for him and shaving him, but also giving him the everyday affirmations of love that must have kept him alive just a little longer—I would walk in to find her holding his hand, soothing his brow, kissing him.

He told me he was awed by her strength.

Punctilious person that he was, Bubba began to get his affairs in order. He made sure Mary would be taken care of. He bought her a new car and insisted she write the checks for the monthly bills.

Mary did not need to say aloud, "I love you."

Though I have never married, to witness such great love—the real, not fictional, Black American story of two childhood sweethearts who lived through war and civil rights and the many Black intellectual and cultural movements within the United States and Africa, moved fifteen times and raised four children, and still looked across the table at each other with such ardent affection after fifty years—was enough. And there isn't a day they aren't missed.

Chapter 24

A Tribute to Ma Berrian

At age eleven, I suffered from severe pains in my left leg, and my parents and I feared it might be the beginnings of polio. There were days when I could barely stand up. I imagined being trapped for the rest of my life in an iron lung: the coffin-like metal chamber that helped polio patients to breathe had begun to punctuate my nightmares. Mother massaged my left leg daily to ease what the doctor hoped was simply "the growing pains" of oncoming puberty.

"If this turns out to be polio, Brenda, you'll be just like Wilma Rudolph," Mother said. Rudolph, who recovered from childhood polio that had rendered her temporarily without the use of her left leg, went on to earn three gold medals in track in the 1960 Olympic games, the most gold medals in a single Olympics by a Black American female.

My mother believed I could be just like Wilma Rudolph, and I believed her.

Within a couple of months, the pain gradually ceased.

My mother was a mother to many.

Though her children called her "Mother," others addressed her as "Mary, Ma Berrian, Mama Berrian, Mother Mary, Mrs. B, Mary B and Grandma." She answered to all of them. My girlfriends in Pittsburgh affectionately called her "Ma Berrian." She would arrive in Pittsburgh, draped in gold: chains around her neck, bracelets on both wrists, and rings on every finger to show off her manicured nails. More bling bling than the rappers wore.

"Mother," I often warned her. "Be careful. Someone will knock you in your head."

"Well, he had better move out of my way then, or I will knock the you-know-what out of *him*," she replied. My friends got a kick out of her brazen defiance and confident mannerisms. Into her seventies, she was always the life of the party.

My friends laughingly and fondly proclaimed, "Ma Berrian is a hot mess!"

They looked forward to their one-on-one outings with her. They would take Mother to lunch, who listened carefully to their tales of heartbreak and hope and struggle, and gave them sound advice. They would tell me they loved how they could talk more openly about private or taboo topics with her than with their own mothers. If you can laugh about things like sex, it's easier to talk about everything else. For instance, Mother took pleasure in sharing raunchy jokes.

Mother would lean forward, gently pat their hands and complement them on their hair, clothes, and make-up. She would remind them they didn't need a man to make them feel good about themselves. Though she never dated after Daddy died, and he had been her only love, she knew how to help women navigate the ups and downs of dating, romance, breaking up, getting married, and making it through the long stretches of struggle in strong and lasting relationships.

She made a list of their birthdays and sent each of them a birthday card as the months rolled by with the same closing, *Love ya. Ma Berrian.* Her message endeared her even more to them.

"How lucky you are to have a mother like Ma Berrian," they would tell me in wistful voices. "She's a lot of fun."

Born just four days before my mother's twentieth birthday, I often drove down from Pennsylvania to Maryland to celebrate our birthdays after Daddy's passing. On one occasion, Mother, Toni, and I joined Florence and her mother at a strip club in Southeast Washington, D.C., where Black American men danced and stripped to their underwear. It was Ladies Night Only. The club was packed to the hilt with Black American women. A well-oiled, handsome man danced and gyrated behind Mother. Another one crawled on his knees underneath our table to slide his hand up my left foot and then to remove Florence's mother's shoe. Gay men standing at the entrance demanded to be let in to "Ladies Night Only." When the bouncers closed the front door, the gay men started pounding on the door and pleading "Leeeet us in. We wanna see the male dancers." The five of us hooped, hollered, and doubled over in mirth while the lively music rose in tempo and the show became raunchier. What a night!

"Look what you made me do," Mother told Toni and me when we returned to her house. "Trying to corrupt an old lady!"

"The club was *your* idea!" we said. That was our mother.

When we relayed the story to Derek, he laughed and said what he had always said about Mother, "She's off the hook."

One of my former students worked at Capitol Records in Hollywood. Once when Mother and I were visiting in Los Angeles, we paid her a visit and she told us the identical twins, Walter and Scotty, members of the R & B group The Whispers, were downstairs in the recording studio.

"Would you like to meet them?" she asked. Before I could respond, Mother squealed with delight. I had to go outside to pay for parking, so it wasn't until I stepped off the elevator that I saw Mother hugging one of the twins like he was a long, lost son.

All I could hear was a muffled voice. "Ma, please. Let me go." The man's face was pressed into her chest, and he could barely breathe.

"Mother," I admonished. "Let go of the man!" Luckily, Walker or Scotty (I don't know which one) had a good sense of humor.

By chance, they had a scheduled performance in Washington, D.C., a week after our return, so they offered us complimentary tickets.

On the evening of the Whispers' performance, Mother, whose skin was much lighter than that of the twins, bragged about coming to see "her boys" to the Black man seated next to her in the front row.

"Sure. And I suppose I'm their brother," the man replied in a sarcastic tone.

"Just you wait and see," Mother said.

When Walter and Scotty walked down the aisle singing one of their hit songs, they spotted Mother and shouted, "Ma!" and ran to hug her. Mother turned to the man next to her with a smug smile and asked, "How do you like that?"

Raised in the overtly racist Jim Crow Richmond, Virginia, and the covertly racist Jersey City, New Jersey, Mother developed a tough exterior. She refused to allow someone—male or female, White or Black—to run rough-shod over her. She insisted that she, her husband, and children be treated fairly. When we lived in the South and had to use the public facilities, Mother played the look-out role. She encouraged us to drink from the Whites-only cold-water fountains and to use the Whites-only clean bathrooms while watching out for a White person's approach. Not sure about her race because her skin tone was a light golden shade, the Whites sometimes gave her the benefit of the doubt. I felt sorry for the White salesperson who snubbed her or the teacher who wronged one of her children. And I am not sure if Toni's eighth-grade teacher ever fully recovered.

Mother's idols were five Black American women who had faced and defied enormous odds: her mother Josephine Frooks; the educator Mary McLeod Bethune; the tennis player Althea Gibson; the activist Fannie Lou Hamer; and the sprinter Wilma Rudolph. Having grown up in a working-class environment like the five women, she was inspired by their accomplishments. Like Mother, the five women had been born in the South. Like Mother, three of them eventually migrated up North (Bethune, Gibson, and Rudolph). Though Mother admired male revolutionaries too, like Dr. King, Malcolm X, and Jesse Jackson, it was always the women she came back to again and again.

In 1968, the students at Hampton Institute staged a sit-in with demands about courses, dorm regulations, and cafeteria food. They barricaded the dean (my father) and the president in their offices, but Mother shoved her way through the crowd to bring Daddy his dinner. My friend Florence was among the students who were protesting. She closely watched Mother's arrival with Daddy's dinner on a plate wrapped in plastic. She reported to me that some of the students respectfully said, "Mrs. Berrian. We can't let you in." Mother looked them in their eyes and shouted, "You had better move out of my way because my husband is going to eat his dinner! He's on your side. Now, move your a**." Accustomed to seeing her prim and proper in a hat, suit, and gloves, and always speaking with eloquence, the students were shocked at her sudden vulgarity.

"Whoa," a few of them reportedly said. "Mrs. Berrian, don't take no s—t." Florence recalled, "It was like looking at Charlton Heston playing Moses in *The Ten Commandments*." The students quickly moved aside, like the parting of the Red Sea.

I got to know my mother even more the thirteen years she lived after Daddy's death. We traveled together. After I finished my dissertation defense in 1976, I took her on a trip to Guadeloupe, Martinique, and Trinidad to thank her for the many letters of encouragement she'd written me over the years as I toiled on that doctoral degree and even thought of quitting once or twice.

I'm so proud of you, she would write, every time. *You have such courage, to leave and go off on your own to Paris. We know you can do it.*

During our first trip to Martinique in 1976, we found out that ignorance wasn't always blissful. One hot afternoon Mother and I, sweaty, hungry, and thirsty, entered a café from which the rich, spicy smells of curry chicken wafted. A friendly waitress beckoned us to enter and seated us at a table. After we quickly drank the cold fruit drinks the waitress served us, we glanced around the café and only saw men seated at the other tables. Suddenly, a man caught Mother's eye, winked at her and lewdly moved the zipper up and down on his pants. Stunned with indignation, Mother sputtered, "Look at that nasty man. What's wrong with him?" (To our discomfort, we later learned the café was the meeting place for local prostitutes and their prospective customers.) Without a moment's hesitation, we almost fell over each other in our haste to get out of the café.

When Mother came to Martinique for a second visit in March 1995, I introduced her to Jean-Paul Soïme, the violinist and director of the string band Malavoi. Mother and I had taken a public bus to have lunch in one of my favorite local restaurants. After we exited the bus, Mother stopped on the sidewalk and frantically searched her body, then started jumping up and down.

"I left my purse on the bus!" she kept repeating. While Mother was screaming and jumping like she was on a Pogo stick, Soïme approached to greet me on the sidewalk.

"My mother mistakenly thinks she's left her purse on the bus," I explained in French.

"Call Shawna (my landlady)," Mother interrupted. "Ask her if my purse is in the apartment." I called Shawna. Kindly agreeing to search for Mother's purse, she verified the purse was home safe on the hallway cabinet.

"Whew," Mother exclaimed. "My blood pressure shot up sky high." To Jean-Paul, she apologized in English for her over-reaction.

A month later, Jean-Paul teasingly asked me, "*Votre mère, comment va-t-elle? La femme qui saute?*" [How's your mother? The woman who jumps up and down?]

All I could do was to smile, then shake my head.

Though we loved to travel together, Mother would not return to Africa. Not even to South Africa, no matter how excited she'd been when Mandela personally invited us. "The plane ride is too long," she'd say. Or, "I had enough dealing with Africa when we lived in the Congo."

While I was teaching on Semester at Sea, Mother wrote to me in an e-mail: "I want you home safe and sound." It was a four-month voyage around the world with 650 students from American and Canadian universities in the spring of 2003. Halfway through the trip, President Bush declared war on Iraq, and the SARS epidemic broke out in parts of Asia. Thus, we could not dock in Hong Kong or Vietnam as planned, and many of the South Asian ports had closed. For over a week, the ship floated in the China Sea while awaiting word from the university about where we could go. To make it worse, pirates surrounded the ship with bows and flaming arrows.

When I sent emails to the States describing the pirates, family and friends asked if I were hallucinating about the pirates. "You know you have an active imagination," they said more than once. Mother instead encouraged me to catch the next plane back to the States as soon as the ship was cleared to enter a port. "The price doesn't matter," she wrote. "I'll pick up the tab."

"Thank you, Mother," I wrote back, though I would not take her up on her offer. I had a contract to abide by. She worried about me until I safely reached Seattle, Washington. She had planned on our spending Mother's Day together in Maryland, but didn't tell me about it. Since I wasn't privy to her plans, I had already made other arrangements to spend a week in Oregon. Mother exploded on the phone when I told her I wouldn't be spending the holiday with her.

Frankly, I couldn't understand her reaction because this wasn't the first time I wouldn't celebrate Mother's Day with her.

Two months later, Mother passed away. Her sudden death was incomprehensible to everyone.

How I regretted not spending that last Mother's Day with her.

Waking up thirsty in the middle of the night, Mother left her second-floor bedroom for the kitchen, which was downstairs. She slipped on the carpeting that covered the stairs and broke her left ankle. She pushed her body backwards up the steps and crawled into her bedroom to call me in Pittsburgh. Hearing her labored breathing, I told her to hang up with me and first call 911 and then call Derek who lived nearby. Derek rushed to Mother's house as the ambulance arrived to take her to the hospital.

The next day I left for Maryland to see about Mother, whom I found in good spirits. She underwent an operation to repair her ankle, was moved to the rehabilitation unit to learn how to handle a walker or a cane, and called me every morning at 8:00 a.m. before I came to the hospital.

On Wednesday morning, July 23, 2003, the phone rang at 8:00 o'clock.

"Good morning, Mother," I answered automatically.

"Hello. Is this Mrs. Berrian's daughter?" an unknown voice queried. "If so, your mother is having trouble with her breathing. Please come to the hospital."

When I arrived, her doctor was waiting for me.

He quietly said, "I'm sorry. Your mother didn't make it."

I gasped, held my stomach with one hand and clutched my heart with the other one. My body went into such immediate shock that I thought I was having a heart attack. I immediately called Derek, Toni, and Albert. Derek, his wife Cathy, and Albert's son rushed to the hospital. Albert, who was in Williamsburg, Virginia, with his wife, drove like a madman back to Maryland. Toni, overcome with grief in Jersey, couldn't gather enough strength to come until two days later.

It was a pulmonary embolism that took her life. It caused a blood clot to appear in her lungs, making it hard for her to breathe. A complication of her ankle's healing. I wished I could have massaged the hurt out of her, saved her somehow. Given her an encouraging word, like she had reminded me of Wilma Rudolph all those years before with my leg cramps. But I hadn't known she would need it. My mother had died from complications of a broken ankle!

Mother looked natural in her final sleep. Instinctively, I caressed her still warm right arm, kissed her cheek. I smoothed her hair, which had recently turned gray just around the temples. She was beautiful, as always. Still, somehow, full of life.

I wondered how I had the strength to stand with this growing void in my heart. I sensed already, with her body still warm next to me, that part of me had left this world.

A numbness spread through my body before, during and after the funeral. I sorely missed her twinkling eyes, mischievous grin, risqué jokes, and infectious laughter. The hardest part was being alone in my parents' house after everybody had left. A deep, deep silence. Many nights, with my body crouched in a fetal position, I chose to sleep on Mother's side of the king-size bed that she had shared with my father. Yet, a good night sleep was impossible for weeks. Consumed by grief, I yearned for my mother and soaked the pillow with my tears.

I often consoled my friends on the loss of "our" Ma Berrian rather than the other way around. Even Mother's doctor was heartbroken. "I feel like I've lost my own mother," he told me. "Your mother lit up the office whenever she came in." Mother had told me how he liked to call her "Sweetheart" and kiss her on the cheek. She had his personal cell and home numbers and claimed him as her third son. He even invited her, Toni, and me to his vacation home to meet his family. "I usually maintain a distance with my patients," he told me. "But I get a kick out of your mother."

As the eldest of my siblings and the executor of our mother's will, I knew I had to be strong for them. I therefore kept my head high and a false smile on my face. Derek, more than once, remorsefully called me "Mother" during one of our long-distance telephone conversations. He explained that he had heard hints of Mother's voice in my vocal delivery. "I understand," I whispered, my voice cracking. "I miss her, too."

Mother had taught me to look to others for strength when I needed it. For her, it was always her mother Josephine, Fannie Lou Hamer, Wilma Rudolph, and others. For me, it was the expressive work of musicians and writers.

During my attempts to shake off an oncoming depression after Mother had joined Daddy in the land of our ancestors, I re-read Birago Diop's "Breaths" and listened endlessly to N'Dour's "Bamako," the Senegalese poem and song that had given me so much comfort when Daddy had passed. This time, though, they weren't enough.

I listened to Patti LaBelle's soaring delivery of "If Only You Knew," during which she tenderly sang, "If only you knew / How much I do / Do love you."[1] The R&B vocalist found the song's theme of unrequited love to be relatable because she regretted not spending enough time with her two sisters before their deaths. In my case, I regretted not spending Mother's Day 2003 with my mother.

I next remembered how Lorna Goodison's poems, "I Am Becoming My Mother" and "For My Mother (May I Inherit Half Her Strength)," had touched something deep within Mother. I had played a recorded version of the Jamaican poet's reading during a 1994 speech I had delivered for the S.S. Universe Semester at Sea voyage to the Caribbean. I had invited Mother as my guest: a voyage on which I was known as "Mary's daughter" instead of the other way around.

Mother and other women in the audience had leaned back in their chairs and closed their eyes, relaxing into Goodison's lilting voice. The poet's words transported them to memories about their own mothers. In "I Am Becoming

My Mother," Goodison read, "I am becoming my mother/ brown /yellow woman."[2] Mother later told me that during the poem, she had pictured her mother Josephine feeding her chickens outside her home in Varina, Virginia.

In the opening stanza of "For My Mother (May I Inherit Half Her Strength)," Goodison recited, "My mother loved my father / I write this as an absolute / in this my thirtieth year / the year to discard absolutes."[3] Eyes closed, I could feel and hear Goodison's voice. I repeated the poem to myself. Not long thereafter, a peace descended on me with the remembrance of Mother's words, "Tomorrow isn't promised. Enjoy each day to the fullest." A general platitude, but it didn't seem cliché when she said it. Perhaps because she truly lived it.

Three weeks after Mother's funeral, Toni, her two daughters, and I traveled to Miami, Florida, a trip our mother had looked forward to going with us. After our arrival Vicki, a Jamaican friend, invited Toni and me to have lunch at a seafood restaurant, where she tried to cheer us up. Despite her efforts, our eyes swelled with tears and we left from the table to go to the women's restroom in search of tissues. While we were dabbing at our eyes, two elderly women entered the room, immediately asking us what was wrong. Upon hearing we were crying over the recent loss of our mother, they, in unison, shouted, "How lucky you are!" Their statement shocked us, causing us to ask them for an explanation. They venomously replied, "We are glad our mother is dead. We hated her. You two were lucky to have had a loving mother. A mother so beloved that you are mourning her."

The two sisters' stunning revelation brought our tears to a halt with the realization we were indeed lucky.

"The daughter is never fully a woman," Edwidge Danticat wrote in *Breath, Eyes, Memory*, "until her mother has passed on before her."[4] These days, Toni and I agree. We have survived; we're much stronger than we had thought; but Mother's loss is always within us. Often, we talk about Mother, at first with sadness but ending with laughter as we recall one of her jokes; the night at the strip club; traveling with her to the Congo or even within D.C.; the way she patted our hands and told us everything would be just fine; and the way she taught us to be bold in the face of bigotry and always to hold our heads high.

It's why I cannot be saddened for long when I think of Mother. Her presence is much stronger than her absence. Her spirit fills a room, fills the tapestry of my life. In fact, people frequently remind me that I'm looking more and more like Mother and taking on some of her mannerisms. I maintain that I am a composite of my mother and father, but still, my own self.

Mother hated social injustice with a ferocity that often took people by surprise. She drew strength from Black American women role models and became a role model to many. She believed in people, that any one of us could move mountains.

She was a woman who loved and protected her ever-expansive family.
A woman who lived out loud.
A woman who loved a good joke.
A woman who carried on.
A woman whom I admired.

NOTES

1. Patti LaBelle, "If Only You Knew," *I'm In Love Again*, Philadelphia International/ CBS, 1983.

2. Lorna Goodison, "I Am Becoming My Mother," in *I am Becoming My Mother* (London: Beacon Books, 1986), 38.

3. Goodison, "For My Mother (May I Inherit Half Her Strength), in *I Am Becoming My Mother*, 46.

4. Edwidge Danticat, *Breath, Eyes, Memory* (New York: Vintage, 1994), 234.

Chapter 25

From Whence I Came

Before I had lived in the Congo, my racial consciousness developed when I was a young girl in the United States. In 1957, when I was ten, I realized what it meant to declare being a Black person on paper. One of my first sixth grade assignments for Cook Elementary in Wilberforce, Ohio, was to write a story with illustrations. Unaware I was neglecting vital details, I labored over the narrative and carefully drew pictures of my cousins and me, playing in the school playground, eating ice cream, tossing marbles. As I scribbled away, I thought about how the story was a companion in these lonely times when I hadn't yet made friends in this new school. This story would be a way to show my new classmates who I was and where I came from.

I wrote and drew until my hand hurt. Finally, I brought my finished creation to Mother and Daddy in the living room and asked if they would read it. Proof of intellectual achievement was a quick route to affirmation from my parents, Daddy especially. My parents made it known that they were pleased I was reading well above the level expected at my age. But soon they would realize it wasn't what I *was* reading they should be concerned about, but rather what I *wasn't* reading.

When I handed my story over, immediately Daddy quit grading his students' papers and said he and Mother would look at it right away. Beaming, I went into the bedroom I shared with my sister Toni and waited. After a few oddly quiet minutes, Mother called out,

"Brenda?"

I ran back to the living room, ready for accolades. But neither Daddy nor Mother was smiling. They were looking down at my story, but they did not look pleased. I felt a stiffness in the air as I stood before them.

"Brenda, who is this story about?" Daddy asked. From the tone of his voice, I suddenly felt like I was in trouble.

"Me and my cousins."

"What color are you and your cousins? Your skin?"

"Brown," I answered without hesitation. Mother sighed. Daddy pointed to one of my drawings, perhaps it was the one of my cousin Elaine and me jumping rope outside the brick apartment building.

"What color are the characters in this drawing?" he asked. In the picture Elaine and I wore dresses—I in my favorite blue one, Elaine in yellow. But our skin? What color was our skin in the pictures? No color. The lines weren't filled in. Just the white paper beneath. Then, with growing alarm, I realized: I had drawn White people. These were not stick figures; they were fully outlined, and I hadn't colored the place between the lines on the arms and legs and faces of my people.

I knew I had brown skin, of course, but the skin color that had come from within me, from my imagination to the page, was left out. I was embarrassed, sensing that my crime, though I'd had no malicious intent, disappointed my parents, and my highest hope was always to please them.

What's worse (though I don't remember my parents reacting to it), I had drawn hair on the heads of the characters with straight lines, some of them yellow. Another false depiction charged with racial identity. We were not White people with straight blonde hair. Though society insisted that was what we should *want* to be, we did not.

I felt I was proud to be a person with brown skin. I needed only to look to my mother for example. Mother always said she was proud to be Black, that she wouldn't have it any other way. When people mistook her for being White or mixed, because she was fair-skinned and her hair was curly, she always told them right away where they could go, and she did it with righteous contempt in her voice that showed just how important it was to her to identify as Black. Black and brown were colors of delight. I recognized then that it was not just about the story I had within me, the story and the colors I had sketched about myself, but about the story I would show the world. It mattered not only whether I was proud to be Black but whether I carried that pride with me in full view of others.

It wouldn't be absurd to conjecture that my mistake was representative of my education: a curriculum that often left out stories of non-White people. Before then, I cannot recall ever reading a story about Black people at school. Although the laboratory schools I had attended on Black college campuses consisted only of Black students, the public schools I attended were populated mostly by White students. My parents hadn't seemed worried over this, at least not that I knew of. They were most concerned with the quality of education. I hadn't worried over this either, for I enjoyed school and eventually made friends. I was never bullied for my race by my classmates or teachers. I treasured my White and Black friends and had no qualms about it.

Yet, Toni and I gradually recognized subtle forces of racism in school as we moved between the South and the North. Several times when Mother would enroll us in a new school in New Jersey, the principal would force Toni and me to take an exam before being placed in our respective grades, despite Mother's insistence that we were right at pace for our ages. When Toni's eighth-grade teacher gave her an "F" in reading, Mother stormed into the school with Toni's report card to dismantle the teacher's racism. My parents carefully monitored all of our homework assignments and knew that Toni should have passed. She'd read all the books more than once because Daddy always put us to work in August, requesting book lists from our teachers and ensuring we read all the readings before school even started.

"How did Toni receive 'A's' in science, math, history and English if she can't read?" my mother challenged the White teacher, who was known to treat Black students poorly. "The 'F' in reading doesn't make sense. Didn't Toni have to read and comprehend the math and science questions and the information in the history and English textbooks?"

The teacher, of course, couldn't explain the "F" in reading. She seemed to shrink away from Mother, refused to meet her gaze. All she said, "Toni is an overall good student. Perhaps she has the potential to go to college in the future."

Mother coldly responded, "Toni *grew up* on college campuses; her father is a college professor."

Toni's next report card showed an "A" in reading. But Mother didn't let the teacher off the hook. She returned to the school and demanded to know, "How could Toni jump miraculously from being a 'F' non-reader to an 'A' reader in six weeks?"

More than once Mother yelled at a school administrator. Her raised voice always put people in a flurry and suddenly a stack of papers would slip from a desk, hands would be wrung. Mother was quick to anger, particularly when she sensed injustice.

My father, however, knew what it could feel like to be the only Black face in the classroom when people were against him, the pressure of having to prove himself again and again. As a young girl I didn't know the story, but later he explained how he'd had to chase down his thesis advisors for his dissertation defense at New York University (NYU), finally finding the group in an upstairs classroom. They hadn't shown up to the appointed room. Instead, they were lounging elsewhere, feet upon the table, as though they expected he wouldn't show up, laughing like *wasn't it cute this Black man was trying to attain the highest degree in the world.* As if it were preposterous—downright amusing—that he would be in the same league as they. Whereas Mother would have slapped every one of those jerks, Daddy completed his defense on the spot, calmly addressing questions from each committee member.

At ten years old, I hadn't felt racism directed at me. As I look back on it now, I know I felt I had a healthy self-identity, which is probably why it hurt so much when I realized my drawing error. I hadn't meant to deny the markers of racial identity in my story, skin or hair; I'd just, sort of, forgotten. The simple fact was this: I did not associate published writing with Black people.

After the incident, my parents started bringing home Paul Laurence Dunbar, Gwendolyn Brooks and Langston Hughes' poetry; magazines like *Jet* and *Ebony;* and pointing out the few Black people on television. I began to recognize that all the stories I'd been devouring up until then had featured White people. The Dick and Jane reader series. Louisa Mae Alcott. Laura Ingalls Wilder. *Nancy Drew. No images of people who looked like me, and I hadn't even noticed.*

Even *Rapunzel*, the story of a girl whose golden hair became a staircase for her prince to climb up, rescue her, and marry her, I now recognized as a story about only White characters. A Black woman was never pictured as being able to do that with her hair. It could never get that long, or that straight. Which was not a bad thing. Besides, I thought, the pain from someone pulling on your hair wasn't worth it just to have a man.

My eyes were opened. I learned the ability to see what was there and also what was not there. From then on, I became vigilant about noticing. I made sure that what I equated with stories worthy of print included the stories of people like me.

That day, I took my story back from Daddy and Mother and started anew. With great care I redrew the illustrations, detailing tightly curled hair and braided hair and coloring the skin to reflect reality. I mixed brown or black with other colors in my crayon box to create golden caramel (Mother's skin), cinnamon (my skin, Toni's, and our brother Albert's), chocolate (Daddy's), coffee (my brother Derek's) and all the many hues of people in my life—espresso, brown sugar, and cocoa. I worked right up until bedtime on those gorgeous colors, and that night I went to sleep without reading.

A few months earlier, another incident had seared an awakening within me and marked the birth of my Black identity consciousness: the day I first learned the danger of brown skin.

It was summertime in Virginia of 1956—the pavement so hot it steamed like the wake of an iron smoothing out wrinkles. I stood with Aunt Anna at a bus stop in downtown Richmond, shifting from one foot to the other, waiting. Toni and I traveled every summer to visit Grandmama Josephine and Aunt Anna in Varina, a rural hamlet outside the city. If we wanted to go to town, we caught a ride from a friend, or hitchhiked. It must have been too far to walk across town to hitch a ride back to Varina in that heat, for rarely ever did we ride public transportation, and soon I would learn why.

Today was just my aunt and me, which felt odd, because Toni and I, only seventeen months apart in age, did nearly everything together. But earlier that morning Aunt Anna had announced she was going to town to get her hair done and then shopping at Miller & Rhoads and she wanted to bring me along. Toni protested.

"No, I can't handle you," Aunt Anna responded. "You are too much and you don't know how to behave." There were times my aunt's frankness reminded us sharply of our own mother's bold way of speaking. The kind of tell-it-like-it-is manner that spares no feelings. She was a daring person in general—she'd gotten divorced years before, at a time when divorce was nearly unheard of.

In her own way, and like our mother, she took on some of Grandmama's spirit. Grandmama cussed like a sailor, kept mounted a rifle over her bedroom door, made her own blackberry brandy and dandelion wine, and raised a flock of chickens in the backyard. She never stopped moving and never apologized for it either. She was fun, through and through.

I had smiled big and shrugged when Aunt Anna refused my sister, knowing just what Toni was thinking because she said it all the time: I was our aunt's favorite, her little pet, because I was prissy. Toni was the tomboy, more inclined to play street stickball with a bunch of boys (and probably beat them) than to fuss with her hair or shop for dresses. But even if it were a prissy escapade, Toni didn't like being left out. I resolved to share every moment with her when we returned.

Aunt Anna had taken me with her to the salon, which we'd hitchhiked to. This wasn't as dangerous or unusual as it is today. Our most often used mode of transportation—a ride from one of my aunt's boyfriends—must have been unavailable that day. Men adored her. She was fair-skinned like Mother, her youngest sister, and had the energy of a girl who could dance to the mere sound of raindrops on asphalt. She wore Bermuda shorts on the weekends, pleats perfect, and it was a rare sight if she didn't have a cigarette dangling from her fingers or the corner of her mouth. She wore lots of makeup and liked to go out on the town any chance she got. Dazzled by her presence like Toni and I were, the men who vied for her attention probably hoped she'd settle down with one of them and make a family, though she remained single for many years and the closest she came to mothering was when her nieces arrived every summer. But maybe that didn't count because, as she confessed, she had too much fun with us, especially me.

People moved and talked slower and were friendlier in the South compared to those in the Northeast. The men carried handkerchiefs in their pockets to pat the sweat from their brows; the women carried fans in their purses to wave the heat from their faces. You also couldn't just say hello and be on your way. You had to talk to people. We stayed at the salon for what seemed like hours,

Aunt Anna chatting and laughing with everyone, and I wished for a book to read while I waited. Finally, we made our way to Miller & Rhoads, the biggest department store in the city, at the center of the White business district downtown. There were endless rows of dresses and brightly colored scarves and anything else you could ever want just as I'd predicted there would be, but now, waiting for the bus in the late afternoon sun, I was tired and ready to go home.

When the bus finally rumbled to the stop and we mounted the steps, I thought of how I might describe my first time on a bus in Richmond to Toni and to our parents. The sights, the sounds, the people. A real grown-up thing. A real city thing. Maybe I'd write about it; there was always an assignment the first week of school to write about our summer. Brenda on the city bus, out on the town.

Although there were two empty seats right there at the front of the bus, Aunt Anna motioned me toward the back.

"But why are we going to the back?" I asked. Aunt Anna said hush and nudged me forward.

"Why do we have to sit at the back?" I asked again. "I want to sit in front."

I usually never stopped asking why until I got an answer. I was known to pester relatives with incessant "whys," which everyone except Daddy scolded me for. "Let her ask it," he'd say to the exasperated relative, "she needs to know."

"Just do it! We're not gonna be on here long," Aunt Anna said, and by this point she was nearly pushing me ahead. I didn't know that at that time, on many city buses around the country, Blacks had to board, pay the fare, exit the bus entirely and re-enter at the back. On this one, we just had to keep walking after paying, but still I felt uneasy and knew something wasn't right. We settled into seats at the back. I wanted to know why Aunt Anna was acting strange too, quieter than usual.

Two minutes ago, she had been her usual confident self, looking cute like she knew it, hair set perfectly. At the hairdresser, she had the usual—wash, trim, hot comb and hot curlers. Toni and I always wore our hair in ponytails or braids, and for a moment I wondered what my hair would look like smoothed out and curled, Aunt Anna's style.

The bus was quiet, less than half full, and after a few stops, I looked toward the front at the still-empty three seats in a row. I just did not get it. Aunt Anna was not one to comply with foolishness, and there were perfectly good seats up there with more room for our legs so it made no sense to me why we'd passed them up.

If I had suspected it might have something to do with us being Blacks, I would reason that it wouldn't matter. If Daddy was there and he wanted to sit in the front then he certainly would do it. And Mother, too. Once in Houston,

Texas, she'd refused to sit in the Black-only waiting room of the White ophthalmologist's office, threatening to talk to the doctor to lodge a complaint if the nurse tried to remove us. Horrified, but clearly put in her place, the nurse left us alone. I decided not to ask Aunt Anna again, but until I got an answer, the "why" would rest at the top of my throat.

Briefly, I wondered if this were a side of Aunt Anna, a quiet, compliant side that existed somewhere un-witnessed by me. Aunt Anna worked as a maid for a wealthy White family in Richmond, but she never talked about her job. Once she was home from work, she hung up her apron and that was that.

The ride itself was forgettable, nothing special to show off to Toni about. Soon Aunt Anna said it was our stop and we walked toward the front.

The doors swung open and we stepped onto pavement just as a Black woman began to board. And then, a few steps later, a voice cried out. The timbre of the cry revealed itself such that I knew immediately that the woman who had just boarded refused to go to the back. Sure enough, as we stepped onto the sidewalk and turned around to look, we saw that what had erupted was an argument. The woman was standing near those empty seats at the front. A scuffle. Folks started to crowd around, trying to see into the bus, but through the high windows you could only see part of the motion. Three White men were standing near the woman, her arms now flailing like she was dancing or fighting. One of the men grabbed her arm. The bus driver rose from his seat and joined the man in restraining the woman who was clearly being attacked, her body jerking this way and that to break free. I had never seen anyone attacked except on television and wasn't sure what I was seeing was real.

Then, suddenly, the woman was horizontal, kicking and screaming as the men moved her wriggling body toward the entry door, where she came into full view of the hushed onlookers on the street. Her dark hair was pressed and curled, in a style like Aunt Anna's, only now it was sticking out every which way as she shook her head side to side. The men thrust the woman out the door, down the steps, and my jaw dropped as I realized they were going to drop her. *Oh, my God,* I thought, *her head is gonna hit the pavement.*

Just then, Aunt Anna grabbed my head and shoved it to her chest and held it there buried into her thin blouse damp with perspiration and fear. I shut my eyes. I did not fight to turn around. I heard gasps coming from all sides. Aunt Anna lifted my head and we must've locked eyes for a moment. How I wish I could remember her expression. It surely would have held a thousand words, explaining the sorry truth that this scene was how it was. That this was our story, too. That sometimes we Blacks had to move to the back of the bus even though it wasn't fair. But the only imprint of the moment that my mind remembers was the woman behind us whose head was so close to the pavement. Then we were walking away quickly, Aunt Anna gripping my hand so hard it almost hurt.

I never saw whether the woman's head hit the pavement, and it wasn't a question I asked as we hurried off. I felt shock and confused anger, and for once I was unable to form words.

I thought this: I had wanted to refuse to move to the back of the bus, too.

Would they have done the same to me? Certainly not. I was, after all, a child. But then, nothing was certain.

Would they have hurled Aunt Anna off the bus if she'd sat in the front like I begged her to? This was an answer I feared.

Daddy and Mother later explained to me what had happened. How Blacks had long been relegated to the back of the bus—partly why our family never used public transportation in Richmond. Just a twelve-hour drive southwest from Richmond to Montgomery, Alabama, a woman named Rosa Parks had refused to give up her seat on a bus the previous December 1955, thus launching a citywide boycott and igniting similar dissents around the country. People were tense with fear, Blacks and Whites both.

When Mother and Daddy explained things I always felt better, safer. But I sensed something bigger than what they were telling me. I *changed* that day. I had witnessed the danger of being a Black, the cruelty that neither my father nor my mother nor anyone else for that matter could stop. If my parents suspected this could be the "coming-to" moment for their little girl, that moment all Blacks experience when they first meet, face to face, the fact of "being Black"—not in a skin color sense, for even the smallest child notices chocolate and vanilla, but in the way the world shapes the meaning of Black—they didn't say. I myself may not have recognized it as such. But right then, an almost ten-year-old, when sirens of the Civil Rights Movement had begun to sound, my moment of reckoning came as a moment of witness.

My parents worked hard, as all parents, to cocoon their children with affirmation, love, and self-respect and to protect us from the outside world rolling with the fervor of civil rights. We stayed close to family when we lived in Jersey, and we built a web of community among other Black academics when we lived elsewhere. When we traveled down South, Daddy carefully planned the route with a map, a phone directory, the *Green Book* and specific recommendations from friends, ensuring we only ate meals at Black-owned restaurants and stopped to rest at Black-owned motels where we would not meet danger. We did not go to protests or marches. When confronted with the micro-aggressions of living in a racist world directly, they revolted in private, individual ways. Mother refused to abide by Jim Crow laws if we were in the South. She would waltz right into a Whites-only bathroom and challenge anyone who tried to stop her. Daddy would explain, even-tempered, what he wanted, and with his non-threatening, intellectual manner, he often got his way.

Yet, over and over, after we had returned home from our venture in downtown Richmond safe, hugged Grandmama, had dinner, went to bed, and rose with the sun the next day and all the days after that, I pictured the woman's head suspended just above the blacktop. Never did it touch down fully in my imagination, though I knew the contact with the pavement must have happened. Those people—those White men—had thrown her out onto the street just like that, like she was a bag of coal dust and not a living person who simply wanted to sit down.

The whole of my summer was contained on the sidewalk of that city street, at the foot of a bus where people whose skin looked like mine could not sit where they wanted. What I witnessed that day was a breaking point, when the world had penetrated the cocoon. And so, at the top of my throat, that "why" I never asked remained, long after I learned the answer.

My two earliest moments of reckoning with being a Black in America were joined by a third with an increased attention to the African continent. I learned about Africa through fellowship with an African friend and—even more alluringly—through story.

Africa was in the news, but only occasionally, after Daddy initiated a weekly routine involving the reading of news stories together. Regular newspapers that came in the mail were the Black *Pittsburgh Courier* or the local newspaper, but we always bought the special Sunday *New York Times* at the corner store. Daddy would instruct Toni and me to pick a section of the newspaper or sometimes an individual article, read it, and then give an "oral report" on what we'd read. Toni and I groaned at this new directive, another one of Daddy's ideas that felt a bit too much like school. "Brenda, you have the Education Section," he would say. Or, "Toni, you have the Business Section." We complied, and luckily Daddy didn't force us to act interested. Interest had nothing to do with it.

We needed to know what was going on in the world, he said.

In action and appearance, Daddy upheld an air of professionalism. He wore dress pants and a white pressed shirt, even at home. He rarely lost his temper. He valued the Arts Review section of the newspaper just as much as the front page; this was a man who sang opera songs as he was getting ready in the morning, played classical music on the piano, and brought all of us to New York, dressed to the nines, to see the New York Philharmonic Orchestra (NYPO).

One day we asked, or rather begged, "Can't we read the comics, Daddy?"

To our surprise he said yes, if we read them critically. We critiqued *Dennis the Menace*, about the little boy who was always up to mischief but never seemed to get in trouble for it. Or *Sad Sack*, about the bumbling military guy whose predicaments illustrated the absurdity of war.

Grandma and Papa Berrian were also avid newspaper readers. When they called us from Jersey, I would swap stories with Grandma. "Did you read the article in the *Courier* about the Pittsburgh NAACP chapter's campaign for new members?" I asked

Often, she would beam, "My grandchildren are *so* smart!"

Now eleven years old, I could see already the intellectual capital gained by reading the paper. The kind of critical reading none of my teachers at school had asked of me as yet. I would only fully recognize the value of it many years down the road in graduate school.

The newspapers also ensured that Toni and I were learning the stories not just of White people, but of others, too, especially Blacks. The front pages proclaimed stories of the mounting Civil Rights Movement. There was no way to avoid it. Toni reported to the family how the Montgomery bus boycott had finally ended after 381 days. (No more could a Black woman with hair like Aunt Anna's be thrown onto the street for wanting to sit in the front of the bus.)

Then I reported on the nine Black students who were barred from entering Central High School in Little Rock, Arkansas, and federal troops who were sent in to guard their entry in September 1957. I picked the article about it from the newspaper and described it to my family. I felt connected to the story immediately, because I no longer went to the lab school, but took a special bus from Wilberforce to the town of Xenia to integrate the school. It was the second year of school integration in Ohio. From the article, I understood the gravity of this act, though, for me, integration, so far, had been no big deal. I was used to going to school with mostly Whites. Public School #22 in Jersey City had been that way, and no one else seemed to mind either. I liked Central Junior High School, in fact, mostly because the homework was challenging. I had relaxed moments which were different from what the Black kids from the East End experienced in the newly opened, integrated Xenia High School. They were stigmatized and tracked into the non-college preparatory courses.

What I would recall later in life about my time at Central Junior High School was not racial strife and soldiers with guns and crowds with spewing hatred, but learning about the "Buckeye State" and practicing square dancing in gym class. White girls do-si-do'd with me just the same. I however felt awkward, not because I was Black, but because I was not developing a womanly figure like many of the other girls. With Daddy's constant prodding with the news, and simply by becoming more aware, I began to see my own story in relation to others' around the country, even when it didn't line up perfectly.

In the newspaper, occasionally a story about the African continent would appear, though rarely, as Mother pointed out, on the front page. Daddy paid special attention to stories of Africa. Africa was coming into its own, he said. Revolution fomented across the nations, a path similar in some ways to the Civil Rights Movement here at home. Africans were seeking independence from Europeans, who had colonized their countries and enforced a veritable slavery, only without the chains. We read about Ghana's independence in 1957, one of the first nations to gain freedom from British colonial rule.

"Where is Ghana?" Daddy asked his girls, and this was our signal to hurry over to the big globe and see who could find it first.

"I found it!" Toni called out, for once beating me to the punch. "West Africa, next to Ivory Coast!" She stuck her tongue out at me.

"Côte d'Ivoire," I pronounced the French colony's name with my best guess for a French accent. I'd planned to start taking French at school as soon as I could, which turned out to be two years later as a high school freshman. Little did I know how valuable those language skills would become when my family moved across the ocean to a French-speaking African country. Or how valuable they'd be in preparing me for graduate school. For now, it earned me a scowl from Toni and praise from Daddy.

Stories of Africa were indeed some of my favorites, though of course not the kind found in newspapers. The stories of Africa told to me out loud by African people: now *that* was a treat.

A man named Adeboye came over for dinner one night. As if in anticipation of my inquiries, my parents explained beforehand he was a student of Daddy's at Central State College. Daddy often brought home students, friends and colleagues from the college who were from Africa or connected to the continent in some way. Toni, our brother Albert, and I would probe him with questions until Mother told us to hush. Adeboye was from a country in West Africa called Nigeria. Daddy pointed it out on the globe. (We also had an atlas from the *Encyclopedia Britannica* and sometimes we'd have to consult both as country names were changing with independence: The Gold Coast became Ghana, Northern Rhodesia became Zambia, Tanganyika became Tanzania.)

Adeboye's presence was electrifying, and from the minute he walked in the door, Toni and I hung on his every word. We barraged him with questions— What was Nigeria like? Was it always hot? Was absolutely *everybody* Black? And goodness, was he black himself! Much darker brown than anyone in our family, and we figured the sun must shine harder in Nigeria. Adeboye seemed amused at our rapt attention, and right away he began indulging us in stories.

He said words like "Yoruba" and "tribe" and "chief" when describing his home. I remembered reading about tribes of Indians, at school and in *Little House on the Prairie.* I imagined groups of dark-skinned people who hunted and migrated by foot and set up teepees in a circle with a fire in the middle. But it wasn't quite like that, Adeboye explained. Groups were divided according to ethnic identity—like Americans who identified as Italian or Black or Irish.

When Adeboye told a story, he spoke slowly, as if letting the story come at its own pace, giving every word the weight of importance. He once recited a tale of two sisters, who lived beside the glittering ocean that lapped the beaches of Nigeria. Adeboye entertained us with this story and other tall tales: all containing a moral lesson at the end. The stories also bore the African sensibility of communal sharing and kindness.

Adeboye also told us the stories of his life. He had grown up on a cocoa plantation. His father was a chief in his village with several wives. At this, Toni and I almost fell out of our chairs in a fit of giggles.

"*Several* wives?" I said. "Are you kidding?" Mother shot me a look, the one that said *don't be rude.*

"Not at all," Adeboye replied with a smile. Toni and I looked at each other with wide eyes. We could not imagine Mother sharing Daddy with any other woman. Not without a fight at least.

"Did your father live with you?" we asked.

"Sometimes," he said.

He described how he'd traveled to the States on a big boat, a voyage that took weeks

"On the ship I was served tomato sauce on long, white worms for dinner," he said, raising his eyebrows for effect. Toni and I held back our laughter as Mother explained he had eaten spaghetti, and that it was a common pasta dish made from the wheat plant.

"Oy!" Adeboye laughed. He asked if Mother would make it for him some-day, winking conspiratorially at us as he said it. We kids did not dash away from the dinner table as long as Adeboye was there. Soon he became a regular at our house, eating white worms and babysitting when Mother and Daddy enjoyed the occasional film or dinner out. Toni, Albert, and I didn't mind being left home at all. We couldn't get enough of Adeboye.

"Tell us a story!" we'd say, again and again.

Adeboye enchanted us with more folktales of his home country. He described princesses who wore gold bangles on their wrists and styled their hair in big towers elaborately decorated with jewels. He told of mountains blanketed in vast, glittering green. He painted images in our minds of the big River Niger, the pulse of the land. He charmed us with these tales of Nigeria, true and storied. It was a country populated by Black people. Yes, just about *everyone* there was Black, Adeboye confirmed when Toni asked to be sure.

Right then, I decided I would like to visit Africa. A continent of lush beauty and people who looked like me and surely—*surely*—there were no racial troubles there. My naivety quickly dissolved when I learned about the legacy of Belgian colonialism, apartheid in South Africa and the ongoing ethnic rivalries among Africans. After living in several African countries and teaching in Africana Studies, I reached the conclusion that people of the African diaspora are spiritually connected with their differences.

Also, I would not be who I am without going to the Congo and beyond.

Bibliography

Abi-Saab, Georges. *The United Nations Operation in the Congo, 1960–64.* London: Oxford University Press, 1978.

Achebe Chinua. *Things Fall Apart.* Portsmouth: Heinemann, 1959.

Angelou, Maya. *And Still I Rise.* New York: Random House, 1978.

Bâ, Mariama. *So Long a Letter.* Translated by Thomas Modupe. London: Heinemann, 1980.

Baker, Jr., Houston A. "In Dubious Battle." *New Literary History* 18, no. 2 (Winter 1987): 363–69.

Baldwin, James. *Go Tell It on a Mountain.* New York: Alfred A. Knopf, 1953.

———. *Giovanni's Room, a Novel.* New York: Dial Press, 1956.

———. *The Fire Next Time.* New York: Dial Press, 1963.

Beauboeuf-Lafontant, Tamara, *Behind the Mask of the Strong Black Woman: Voice and Embodiment of a Costly Performance.* Philadelphia: Temple University Press, 2009.

Berrian, Albert H. and Richard A. Long, ed. *Négritude: Essays and Studies.* A Centennial Publication. Hampton: Hampton Institute Press, 1968.

Berrian, Brenda F. *Bibliography of African Women Writers and Journalists (Ancient Egypt- 1984).* Washington, DC: Thee Continents Press, 1985.

———. "Through Her Prism of Social and Political Contexts: Sembène's Female Characters in *Tribal Scars.*" In *Ngambika: Studies of Women in African Literature,* edited by Carole Boyce Davis and Anne Graves, 195–204. Trenton: Africa World Press, 1986.

———. "Manu Dibango and *Ceddo's* Soundscape." In *Focus on African Films,* edited by FrançoisePfaff. 143–55. Bloomington: Indiana University Press, 2004.

Berrian, Brenda F. with Aart Broek. *Bibliography of Women Writers from the Caribbean.* Washington, DC: Three Continents Press, 1989.

Biko, Steve. *I Write What I Like: Selected Writings,* edited by Aelred Stubbs CR. San Francisco: Harper & Row Publishers, 1978.

Boitten, Jennifer Anne. "In Black and White: Gender, Race Relations and the Nardal Sisters in Interwar Paris." *French Colonial History* 6 (2005): 120–135.

Boraine, Alex. *A Country Unmasked.* Oxford: Oxford University Press, 2000.

Bredeloup, Sylvie. "L'Aventure contemporaine des diamantaires sénégalais." *Politique Africaine* 56 (1994): 77–95.

Brooks, Maegan and Davis V. Houck, ed. *The Speeches of Fannie Lou Hamer: To Tell It Like It Is.* Jackson: University Press of Mississippi, 20.

Bryan, Brooke. "A Lifetime in the Making," *Yellow Springs News,* July 16, 2009. Accessed May 29, 2013. http://www.ysnews.com/news/2009/07/a-lifetime-of-making-a-difference.

Busia, Abena P. A. *Testimonies of Exile.* Accra, Ghana: Woeli Publishing Services, 1978.

Calder, Ritchie. *Agony of the Congo.* London: Victor Gollancz Ltd., 1961.

Carroll, Constance M. "Three's a Crowd: The Dilemma of the Black Woman in Higher Education." In *But Some of Us Are Brave: All the Women Are White, All the Blacks Are Men: Black Women's Studies,* edited by Gloria T. Hull, Patricia Bell Scott and BarbaraSmith, 115–28. Old Westbury: Feminist Press, 1982.

Césaire, Aimé. *Return to My Native Land.* Translated by Emile Snyder. Paris: Présence Africaine, 1968.

Condé, Maryse. *Le Coeur à rire et à pleurer: contes vrais de mon enfance.* Paris: Robert Laffont, 1999; rpt. *Tales of the Heart: True Stories from My Childhood.* Translated by Richard Philcox. New York: Soho, 2001.

Considine, J. D. and Michaelangelo Matos. "Biography: Youssou N'Dour." *RollingStone.com,* 2004. Accessed September 2, 2007.

Cooper, Anna Julia, 1998. "The Third Step: Cooper's Memoir of the Sorbonne Doctorate (1945–1950?)." In *The Voice of Anna Julia Cooper and a Voice from the South and Other Important Essays, Papers and Letters,* edited by Charles Lemert and Esme Bhan, 320–30. Lanham, MD: Rowman and Littlefield, 1998.

Crouch, Stanley. "Aunt Medea." *The New Republic,* October 19, 1987, 38–43.

Damas, L.G. *Pigments.* Paris: G.L.M., 1937.

Danticat, Edwidge. *Breath, Eyes, Memory.* New York: Vintage, 1994.

Daut, Madeleine L. "Becoming Full Professor While Black," *The Chronicle of Higher Education,* July 28, 2019. http://www.chronicle.com/article/becoming-full-professor-while-black/.

De Gregory, C. A. "Jacqueline E. Lawton's "The Hampton Years' Features HBCUArtists," *HBCUStory,* May 15, 2013. http://www.hbcustory.wordpress.com/2013/05/15/jacqueline-e-lawtons-the-hampton-years-features-hbcu-artists-biggers-and-lewis.

De Witte, Ludo, Renee Fenby and Ann Wright. *The Assassination of Lumumba.* New York: Verso, 2003.

Diop, Birago. "Breath." In *Talking Drums: A Selection of Poems South of the Sahara,* edited by Véronique Tadjo, 58–59. New York: Bloomsbury, 2004.

Dirie, Waris. *Desert Flower: An Extraordinary Journey of a Desert Nomad.* New York: William Morrow, 1998.

Duke, Lynne. *Mandela, Mobutu and Me: A Newswoman's Journey in Africa.* New York: Doubleday, 2003.

Edwards, Brent Hayes. *The Practice of Diaspora: Literature, Translation and the Rise of Black Internationalism.* Cambridge: Harvard University Press, 2003.

Ellison, Ralph. *Invisible Man.* New York: Random House, 1952.

Emecheta, Buchi. *The Joys of Motherhood.* New York: George Braziller, 1979.

Erickson, Mark St. John. "With Resistance." *Daily Press,* May 9, 2004. http://www.dailypress.com/dp.brown09-story.html.

Evans, Mari. *I Am a Black Woman.* New York: William Morrow and Company, 1970.

Fabre, Michel. *The Unfinished Quest of Richard Wright.* Translated by Isabel Barza. New York: Morrow, 1973; rpt. Urbana: University of Illinois Press, 1993.

Farnham, Willard, ed. *Hamlet Prince of Denmark* by William Shakespeare. The Pelican Shakespeare. New York: Penguin, 1970.

Fitzpatrick-Moore, Bonnie. *My African Heart.* Johannesburg: Bahai Publishing Trust, 1999.

Forbes, David, dir. *The Cradock Four,* South Africa / France: Shadow Films, 2010. 92 min.

French, Howard W. *A Continent for the Taking: The Tragedy and Hope of Africa.* New York: Alfred A. Knopf, 2004.

Golden, Marita. *Migrations of the Heart.* New York: Ballantine Books, 1983.

Goodison, Lorna. *I Am Becoming My Mother.* London: New Beacon Books, 1998.

Gordon, King. *The United Nations in the Congo: A Quest for Peace.* New York: Carnegie Endowment for International Justice, 1962.

Harris-Perry, Melissa. *Sister Citizen: Shame, Stereotypes and Black Women in America.* New Haven: Yale University Press, 2011.

Hélénon, Véronique. *French Caribbeans in Africa: Diasporic Connections and Colonial Administration, 1880–1937.* New York: Palgrave Macmillan, 2011.

Hennessey, Maurice W. *The Congo: A Brief History and Appraisal.* New York: Fredrick A. Praeger Publishers, 1961.

Henry, Charles. *Long Overdue: The Politics of Racial Reparations.* New York: New York University Press, 2007.

Hill-Collins, Patricia. *Black Feminist Thought: Knowledge, Consciousness, and the Politics of Empowerment.* New York: Routledge Chapman and Hall, 2000.

Hochschild, Adam. *King Leopold's Ghost: A Story of Greed, Terror, and Heroism in Colonial Africa.* Boston: Houghton Mifflin, 1999.

Hoskyns, Catherine. *The Congo since Independence, January 1960-December 1961.* London: Oxford University Press, 1965.

Hughes, Langston. *Selected Poems of Langston Hughes.* New York: Vintage Books, 1994.

Hurston, Zora Neale. *Their Eyes Were Watching God.* New York: J. B. Lippincott, 1937; rpt. New York: Perennial Library, 1990.

Hymans, Jacques Louis. *Léopold Sédar Senghor: An Intellectual Biography.* Edinburgh: Edinburgh University Press, 1971.

Ikonné, Chidi. "René Maran, 1887–1960: A Black Francophone Writer between Two Worlds." *Research in African Literatures* 5, no. 1 (Spring 1974): 5–22.

Jackson, Regine O. "The Failure of Categories: Haitians in the United Nations Organization in the Congo, 1960–64." *Journal of Haitian Studies* 20, no. 1 (August 2014): 34–64.

Joyce, Joyce A. "The Black Canon: Reconstructing Black American Criticism." *New Literary History* 18, no. 2 (Winter 1987): 335–44.

Kallé, Le Grand et l'African Jazz. *Succès des années 50/60*. Vol. I. Sonodisc CD 36560,1984.

Kanza. Thomas. *The Rise and Fall of Patrice Lumumba: Conflict in the Congo*. Cambridge: Schenkman, 1977.

Kennedy, Ellen Conroy, ed. *The Negritude Poets: An Anthology of Translations from the French*. New York: Thunder's Mouth Press, 1975.

Krog, Antjie. *Country of My Skull: Guilt, Sorrow and the Limits of Forgiveness in the New South Africa*. Johannesburg: Random House, 1998.

LaBelle, Patti. *I'm in Love Again*. Philadelphia International Records / CBS LPFZ38539, 1983.

La Fontaine, Jean Sybil. *City Politics: A Study of Leopoldville, 1962-63*. Cambridge: Cambridge University Press, 1970.

McKay, Nellie Y. "Remembering Anita Hill and Clarence Thomas: What Really Happened When One Black Woman Spoke Out." In *Race-ing Justice, En-gendering Power: Essays on Anita Hill, Clarence Thomas and the Construction of Social Reality*, edited by Toni Morrison, 269–89. New York: New Pantheon Books, 1992.

Mandela, Nelson. *Long Walk to Freedom: The Autobiography of Nelson Mandela*. London: Abacus, 1994.

Mandela, Winnie. *A Part of My Soul Went with Him*, edited by Anne Benjamin and adapted by Mary Benton. New York: Norton, 1984.

Maraire, J. Nozipo. *Zenzele: A Letter for My Daughter*. New York: Crown Publishers, 1996.

Martin, Lori Latrice, Biko Mandela Gray and Stephen C. Finley, "Endangered and Vulnerable: the Black Professoriate, Bullying, and the Limits of Academic Freedom," *Journal of Academic Freedom* 10 (2019). http://aaup.org/AF10/endangered-and-vulnerable-Black-professoriate-bulling-and-limits-academic-freedom#.XOpimMhKjlU.

Mbuyazi, Nondamiso. "Fear Was the Killer." *Daily News*, June 8, 2011. http://www.iol.co.za/dailynews/fear-was-the-killer-1.1190629.

Morrison, Toni. *The Bluest Eye*. New York: Pocket Books, 1972.

———. *Beloved*. New York: Vintage, 1987.

Mudimbe, Valentin Y., ed. *The Surreptitious Speech: Présence Africaine and the Politics of Otherness, 1947–1987*. Chicago: University of Chicago Press, 1992.

N'Dour, Youssou et le Super Étoile de Dakar. *Gaindé*. Éditions Africaine Vol. 14. SAPROM Productions, 1988.

No author. "Mourning March for Congo Ex-Premier." *The Sydney Morning Herald,* February 16, 1961. Accessed April 27, 2012. http://www.news.google.com/newspapers?nid= 1391&dot=19610216&id =E4BWAAAAIBAJ&sj.

———. "Black Studies Is an Unpopular Major." *The Journal of Blacks in Higher Education* 36 (Summer 2002): 14–15. https://www.jstor.org/stable/3133905.

———. "The Snail-Like Progress of Blacks into Faculty Ranks of Higher Education." *The Journal of Blacks in Higher Education*, 62 (2007): 24–25. Accessed July 27, 2013. http://www.jbhe.com/news_views black-faculty-progress.html.

———. "1965: John Harris: White Anti-Apartheid Martyr." *South African History Online*, April 1, 2020. Accessed March 2, 2013. http://www.sahistory.org.za/people/frederick-john-harris.

No author. "Senegal," *2016 CIA World Factbook*. Accessed January 10, 2019. http://www. allcountries.org/world_fact_book_2016/senegal/index.html.

Paravicini, Giulia. "Belgium Apologizes for Colonial-Era Abduction of Mixed-Race Children," *Reuters*, April 4, 2019. http://www.reuters.com/article/us-belgium-congo/belgium apologizes-for-colonial-era-abduction-of-mixed-race-children - idUSKCN1RG2NF.

Patel, Khadija. "South Africa: Remember the Black Consciousness Movementand the 1977 Murder of Steve Biko." *Pambazaka News*, September 17, 2011. Accessed May 12, 2013. http://www.revolutonaryfrontlines.worldpress.co/ 2011/09/17/south-africa-remembers=the-bl.

Patton, Stacey. "Black Studies: Swaggering into the Future," *The Chronicle of Higher Education,* April 12, 2012. http://www. chronicle.com/article/black-studies-swaggering-into-the-future.

P'Bitek, Okot. *Song of Lawino & Song of Ocol.* Oxford, England: Heinemann International, 1966.

Petry, Ann. "Like a Winding Sheet," In *Miss Muriel and Other Stories.* Boston: Houghton Mifflin, 1971. 198–210.

Rabbitt, Kara M. "The Geography of Identity in Suzanne Césaire's 'Le grand camouflage.'" *Research in African Literatures* 39, no. 3 (Fall 2008): 121–31.

Ramphele, Mamphele. *Conversations with My Sons and Daughters.* Johannesburg: Penguin Books, 2012.

Reed, Roy. "Alabama Police Use Gas and Clubs to Rout Negroes." *New York Times,* March 8, 1965, 1; 20.

Rojas, Fabio. *From Black Power to Black Studies: How a Radical Social Movement Became an Academic Discipline.* Baltimore: The John Hopkins University Press, 2007.

Rooks, Noliwe M. *White Money/Black Power: The Surprising History of African American Studies and the Crisis of Race and Higher Education.* Boston: Beacon Press, 2006.

Ross, Diana. *Diana Ross.* Motown LP M6-86151, 1976.

Ross, Eric S. *Cultures and Customs of Senegal.* Westport: Greenwood Press, 2008.

SABC Truth Commission Special Report, Nomonde Calata Case ECOO28/96, TRC Human Rights Violations Hearings Transcript, East London, Day 2, April 16, 1996. http://www.sabctrc.saha.org.za/documents/hrvtrans/east_london/55192.html.

Sadji, Abdoulaye. *Maïmouna.* Paris: Présence Africaine, 1953.

———. *Nini, la mulâtresse du Sénégal.* Paris: Présence Africaine, 1954.

Schmidt, Peter. "Oklahoma Scholarships Seek to Make Amends for 1921 Riot." *The Chronicle of Higher Education*, July 13, 2001, A22.

Scott, Ian. *Tumbled House: The Congo at Independence.* New York: Oxford University Press, 1969.

Selvon, Samuel. *The Lonely Londoners.* Harlow, England: Longman, 1956.

Sembène, Ousmane, dir. *Mandabi* (The Money Order*).* France / Senegal: CFFP, Filmic Domirev, 1968. 105 min.

Shapiro, Norman R., ed. *Negritude Poetry: Black Poetry from Africa and the Caribbean.* Bilingual Edition. New York: October House, 1970.

Sharpley-Whiting, T. Denean. *Négritude Women.* Minneapolis: University of Minnesota Press, 2002.

Smith, Barbara. "Racism and Women's Studies." *Frontiers: A Journal of Women's Studies* 5, no. 1 (Spring 1980): 48–4.

Somerville, Sean. "Whites Only: Sit-Ins Yield Civil-Rights Victory." *Daily Press,* January 16, 1989. http://www.dailypress.com/news/dp-xpm-19890116-1989-01-16-8901160049-story.html.

Sylvander, Carolyn Wedin. *Jessie Redmon Fauset, Black American Writer.* Troy: Whitston Publishing Company, 1981.

Teachout, Terry. *Pops: A Life of Louis Armstrong.* Boston and New York: Houghton, Mifflin Harcourt, 2009.

Timberg, Craig and David Halperin. *Tinderbox: How the West Sparked the AIDS Epidemic and How the World Can Finally Overcome It.* New York: The Penguin Press, 2012.

Tutu, Desmond Mpilo. *No Future without Forgiveness.* New York: Doubleday, 1999.

"Tutu and the TRC," BBC, Video. 7:05. http://www.youtube.com/watch?y=ujOL 8F52wv4. Posted on part of a blog: Wednesday December 23, 2009. http://www. mhambi.com/2009/12/truth-reconciliation-left-me-dazed-confused/.

"The Ubuntu Experience (Interview with Nelson Mandela)," Interview by Tim Modise, SABC, November 1, 2006, Video, 1:36. http://www.youtube.com/watch? v+HnKqpiqJC10.

"U.S. Congressman John Conyers Jr. Introduced Bill H.R. 40." Accessed February 10, 2013. http://www.conyers.house.gov/index.cfm/reparations.

Van den Boagaerde, Pierre and Chamalambos Tsangarides. "Ten Years after the CFA Franc Devaluation; Progress toward Regional Integration in the WAEMU." IMF Working Paper W/P/05/145, July 2005. http://www.ssrn.com/abstract=888014.

Vanthemsche, Guy. *Belgium and the Congo.* Translated by Alice Cameron and Stephen Windross. Revised by Kate Connelly. New York: Cambridge University Press, 2012.

Voyles, Karen. "Marking History: Sign Memorializes Those Who Died in Rosewood." *The Gainesville Sun,* May 5, 2004, B1-B2.

Walker, Alice. *The Color Purple.* New York: Harcourt Brace Jovanovich, 1982.

Watkins, Mel. "Sexism, Racism and Black Women Writers." *New York Times,* June 15, 1986. http://www.nytimes.com/1986/06/15/books/sexism-racism-and-black-women-writers.html.

Watson, Denise M. "Lunch Counter Sit-Ins: 50 Years Later," *The Virginian Pilot,* February15, 2010. http://www.pilotonline.com/life/vp-aat-lunch-counter-sitins-50 -years- later-20200209-ia6qhzmpmbei3cp3b65uvo5diq-story.html.

Index

About the Author

Brenda F. Berrian is professor emerita of Africana Studies at the University of Pittsburgh. She is the author of *Awakening Spaces: French Caribbean Popular Songs, Music and Culture* (2000) and essays about African, African American, and Caribbean writers and musicians in academic journals and edited books. She is currently working on a collection of interviews with French Caribbean musicians.

www.ingramcontent.com/pod-product-compliance
Lightning Source LLC
Chambersburg PA
CBHW050640280326
41932CB00015B/2729